LAUREN ELKIN

Flâneuse

Women Walk the City
in Paris, New York, Tokyo,
Venice and London

VINTAGE

1 3 5 7 9 10 8 6 4 2

Vintage
20 Vauxhall Bridge Road,
London SW1V 2SA

Vintage is part of the Penguin Random House group of companies
whose addresses can be found at global.penguinrandomhouse.com

Penguin
Random House
UK

Copyright © Lauren Elkin 2016

Lauren Elkin has asserted her right to be identified as
the author of this Work in accordance with the Copyright,
Designs and Patents Act 1988

First published by Vintage in 2017
First published by Chatto & Windus in 2016

penguin.co.uk/vintage

A CIP catalogue record for this book is
available from the British Library

ISBN 9780099593379

Printed and bound by Clays Ltd, St Ives Plc

Penguin Random House is committed to a sustainable future
for our business, our readers and our planet. This book is made
from Forest Stewardship Council® certified paper.

To Trivia

goddess of crossroads

'She is the wanderer, bum, émigré, refugee, deportee, rambler, strolling player. Sometimes she would like to be a settler, but curiosity, grief, and disaffection forbid it.'

– Deborah Levy, *Swallowing Geography*

CONTENTS

On a street in Paris, a woman pauses to light a cigarette. She holds up a match with one hand, its box and a glove in the other. Her tall figure aligns with the shadow of a lamp post, two forward slashes on the wall behind her as a photographer closes the shutter. She is fleeting; pausing; permanent.

There are clear instructions on the wall: *Défense d'Afficher et de faire aucun Dépôt le long de ce* – and the warning is interrupted by the frame. *Défense d'afficher*, the walls of Paris often protest. *No Advertisements,* a late-nineteenth-century ban intended to prevent the city from becoming a wasteland of billboards. Above the sign, some letters are stencilled – defiantly? Or were they there first? – announcing that *charcuterie* could once have been obtained there, or nearby. Below that, someone has drawn the crude outline of a face.

It is 1929. Women smoking in public has become more of an ordinary sight. But the photograph still retains an element of transgression. The day will end, the woman will move on, the photographer will move on, the sun itself will move on, and the lamp-shadow with it. But for us, this is all we can see of this place in the past: a woman, visible against the wall behind her, in a field of proscriptions and defiances, about to light up a cigarette. She stands out in her anonymous, immortal singularity.

I've always been struck by the black-and-white urban photography from this period, especially by women – Marianne Breslauer, who captured this image, or Laure Albin-Guillot, or Ilse Bing, or Germaine Krull, Walter Benjamin's friend, who liked to skulk around the arcades with him, and without him, photographing them, haunting them. These women came to the city (or perhaps they were born there, or came from other cities) to pass unnoticed, but also to be free to do what they liked, as they liked.

I have constructed other, similar images in my mind's eye, moments that lacked a photographer, recorded in diaries, or novels. There's one of George Sand, who dressed like a boy to walk through the streets, lost in the city, an 'atom' in the crowd. Or Jean Rhys, whose female characters walk past cafe terraces and cringe as the clientele follow her with their eyes, knowing she's an outsider. Breslauer's photograph, and the others I have in mind, set out the key problem at the heart of the urban experience: are we individuals, or are we part of the crowd? Do we want to stand out, or blend in? Is that even possible? How do we – no matter what our gender – want to be seen in public? Do we want to attract or escape the gaze? Be independent and invisible? Remarkable or unremarked-upon?

Défense d'afficher. Do not advertise. And yet there she is. *Elle s'affiche.* She shows herself. She shows up against the city.

FLÂNEUSE-ING

Where did I first come across that word, *flâneur*, so singular, so elegant and French with its arched *â* and its curling *eur*? I know it was when I was studying in Paris, back in the 1990s, but I don't think I found it in a book. I didn't do much required reading, that semester. I can't say for sure, which is to say I became a *flâneur* before I knew what one was, wandering the streets around my school, located as American universities in Paris must be, on the Left Bank.

From the French verb *flâner*, the *flâneur*, or 'one who wanders aimlessly', was born in the first half of the nineteenth century, in the glass-and-steel-covered *passages* of Paris. When Haussmann started slicing his bright boulevards through the dark uneven crusts of houses like knives through a city of cindered chèvre, the *flâneur* wandered those too, taking in the urban spectacle. A figure of masculine privilege and leisure, with time and money and no immediate responsibilities to claim his attention, the *flâneur* understands the city as few of its inhabitants do, for he has memorised it with his feet. Every corner, alleyway and stairway has the ability to plunge him into *rêverie*. What happened here? Who passed by here? What does this place mean? The *flâneur*, attuned to the chords that vibrate throughout his city, knows without knowing.

In my ignorance, I think I thought I invented *flânerie*. Coming from suburban America, where people drive from one place to another, walking for no particular reason was a bit of an eccentric thing to do. I could walk for hours in Paris and never 'get' anywhere, looking at the way the city was put together, glimpsing its unofficial history here and there, a bullet in the facade of an *hôtel particulier*, leftover stencilling way up on the side of a building for a flour company or a newspaper that no longer existed (which some inspired graffiti artist had used as an invitation to add his own work) or a row of cobblestones revealed by roadworks, several layers below the crust of the current city, slowly rising ever upward. I was on the lookout for residue, for texture, for accidents and encounters and unexpected openings. My most meaningful experience with the city was not through its literature, its food or its museums, not even through the soul-scarring affair I carried on in a garret near the Bourse, but through all that walking. Somewhere in the 6th arrondissement I realised I wanted to live in a city for the rest of my life, and specifically, in the city of Paris. It had something to do with the utter, total freedom unleashed from the act of putting one foot in front of the other.

I wore a groove into the Boulevard Montparnasse as I came and went between my flat on the avenue de Saxe and school on the rue de Chevreuse. I learned non-textbook French from the names of the restaurants in between: Les Zazous (named for a kind of jazzy 1940s hepcat in a plaid blazer and a quiff), Restaurant Sud-Ouest & Cie, which taught me the French equivalent of '& Co.', and from a bakery called Pomme de pain I learned the word for 'pine cone', *pomme de pin*, though I never learned why that was a pun worth making. I bought orange juice on the way to class every day at a pretzel shop called Duchesse Anne and wondered who she was and what was her relationship to pretzels. I pondered the distorted French conception of American geography that resulted in a TexMex restaurant called Indiana Café. I walked past all the great cafes lining the boulevard, La Rotonde, Le Sélect, Le Dôme and La Coupole, watering holes to generations of American writers in Paris, whose ghosts hunched under cafe awnings, unimpressed with the way the twentieth century had turned out. I crossed over the rue Vavin, with its eponymous cafe, where all the cool *lycéens* went when they got out of school, assertive cigarette smokers with sleeves too long for their arms, shod in Converse sneakers, boys with dark curls and girls with no make-up.

Soon, emboldened, I wandered off into the streets shooting out from the Jardin de Luxembourg, a few minutes' walk from school. I found myself up near the church of Saint-Sulpice, which was under renovation then, and, like the Tour Saint-Jacques, had been for decades. No one knew if or when the scaffolding around the towers would ever come down. I would sit at the Café de la Mairie on Place Saint-Sulpice and watch the world go by: the skinniest women I'd ever seen wearing linen clothing that would be frumpy in New York but in Paris seemed unreplicably chic, nuns in twos and threes, yuppie mothers who let their small boys wee on tree trunks. I wrote down everything I saw, not knowing yet that the French writer Georges Perec had also sat in that square, in that same cafe, during a week in 1974, and noted the same comings and goings – taxis, buses, people eating pastries, the way the wind was blowing – all in an attempt to get his readers to notice the unexpected beauty of the quotidian, what he called the *infraordinary*: what happens when nothing is happening. I didn't know, either, that *Nightwood*, which would become one of my favourite books, was set at that cafe and in the hotel upstairs. Paris was just beginning to contain – and to generate – all of my most significant intellectual and personal reference points. We had only just met.

As an English major I had wanted to go to London, but thanks to a technicality wound up in Paris instead. Within a month I was transfixed. The streets of Paris had a way of making me stop in my tracks, my heart suspended. They seemed saturated with presence, even if there was no one there but me. These were places where something could happen, or had happened, or both; a feeling I could never have had at home in New York, where life is inflected with the future tense. In Paris I would linger outside, imagining stories to go with streets. In those six months, the streets were transformed from places in between home and wherever I was going into a great passion. I drifted wherever they looked interesting, lured by the sight of a decaying wall, or colourful window boxes, or something intriguing down at the other end, which might be as pedestrian as a perpendicular street. Anything, any detail that suddenly loosened itself, would draw me towards it. Every turn I made was a reminder that the day was mine and I didn't have to be anywhere I didn't want to be. I had an astonishing immunity to responsibility, because I had no ambitions at all beyond doing only that which I found interesting.

I remember when I'd take the metro two stops because I didn't realise how close together everything was, how walkable Paris was. I had to walk around to understand where I was in space, how places related to each other. Some days I'd cover five miles or more, returning home with sore feet and a story or two for my room-mates. I saw things I'd never seen in New York. Beggars (Roma, I was told) who knelt rigidly in the street, heads bowed, holding signs asking for money, some with children, some with dogs; homeless people living in tents, under stairways, under arches. Every quaint Parisian nook had its corresponding misery. I turned off my New York apathy and gave what I could. Learning to see meant not being able to look away; to walk in the streets of Paris was to walk the thin line of fate that divided us from each other.

And then, somehow, by chance, I learned that all that walking around, feeling intensely, constantly moved to scribble what I saw and felt into the floppy notebooks I bought at the Saint-Michel bookstore Gibert Jeune – all that I did instinctively, others had done to such an extent that there was a word for it. I was a *flâneur*.

Or rather – a good student of French, I converted the masculine noun to a feminine one – a *flâneuse*.

+

Flâneuse [*flanne-euhze*], noun, from the French. Feminine form of *flâneur* [*flanne-euhr*], an idler, a dawdling observer, usually found in cities.

That is an imaginary definition. Most French dictionaries don't even include the word. The 1905 *Littré* does make an allowance for '*flâneur, -euse*'. *Qui flâne*. But the *Dictionnaire Vivant de la Langue Française* defines it, believe it or not, as a kind of lounge chair.

Is that some kind of joke? The only kind of curious idling a woman does is lying down?

This usage (slang of course) began around 1840 and peaked in the 1920s, but continues today: search for '*flâneuse*' on Google Images and the word brings up a drawing of George Sand, a picture of a young woman sitting on a Parisian bench and a few images of outdoor furniture.

+

Back in New York for my final year of university, I enrolled in a seminar called 'The Man of the Crowd, the Woman in the Street'. It was the second half of the title that interested me: I was hoping to build a genealogy, or a sisterhood, for this eccentric new hobby of mine. The notion of the *flâneur* as someone who has slipped the bounds of responsibility appealed to me. But I wanted to see where a woman might fit into the cityscape.

As I began researching my senior thesis on Zola's *Nana* and Dreiser's *Sister Carrie*, I was startled to find that scholars have mostly dismissed the idea of a female *flâneur*. 'There is no question of inventing the *flâneuse*,' wrote Janet Wolff in an oft-quoted essay on the subject; 'such a character was rendered impossible by the sexual divisions of the nineteenth century.'[1] The great feminist art historian Griselda Pollock agreed: 'There is no female equivalent of the quintessential masculine figure, the *flâneur*: there is not and could not be a female *flâneuse*.'[2] 'The urban observer [. . .] has been regarded as an exclusively male figure,' noted Deborah Parsons. 'The opportunities and activities of *flânerie* were predominantly the privileges of the man of means, and it was hence implicit that the "artist of modern life" was necessarily the bourgeois male.'[3] In Rebecca Solnit's *Wanderlust: A History of Walking*, she turns away from her 'peripatetic philosophers, *flâneurs*, or mountaineers' to ask 'why women were not out walking too'.[4]

This woman in the street, according to the critics, was most likely a streetwalker. So I did a bit more reading and came upon two problems with this idea of the *flâneuse* as prostitute. Firstly there were women on the street who weren't selling their bodies. And secondly there wasn't anything like the *flâneur*'s freedom in the street prowler's prowl; prostitutes didn't have free range over the city. Her movements were strictly controlled: by the mid-nineteenth century there were all sorts of laws dictating where and between which hours she could pick up men. Her clothing was strictly policed; she had to register with the city and visit the sanitary police at regular intervals. This was no kind of freedom.

Our most ready-to-hand sources for what the streetscape looked like in the nineteenth century are male, and they see the city in their own ways. We cannot take their testimony as objective truth; they noticed certain things, and made assumptions about them. Baudelaire's mysterious and alluring *passante*, immortalised in his poem 'To a (Female) Passer-by', is generally thought to have been a woman of the night, but for him she is not even a real woman, only his fantasy come to life:

> The deafening street roared around me
> Tall, slender, in heavy mourning, majestic in her grandeur
> A woman walked past me, her sumptuous hand
> Lifting and swinging her hem as she went.
>
> Swift and graceful, with legs like a statue's
> Twitching like a madman, I drank in
> Her eyes, a pallid sky where storms are born
> the sweetness that charms and the pleasure that kills.[5]

Baudelaire can barely gauge her: she is too fast (though somehow, at the same time, statuesque). He is disinclined to consider who she might actually be, where she might be coming from, where she might be going. For him she is the keeper of mystery, with the power to charm and to poison.

Of course the reason the *flâneuse* was discounted from histories of city walking had to do with the social conditions of women in the nineteenth century, when our ideas about the *flâneur* were codified. The earliest mention of a *flâneur* is in 1585, possibly borrowed from the Scandinavian noun *flana*, 'a person who wanders'. A person – not necessarily a male one. It doesn't really catch on until the nineteenth century, and this time it's gendered. In 1806, the *flâneur* took the form of 'M. Bonhomme', a man about town who comes from sufficient wealth to have the time to wander the city at will, hanging out in cafes, and watching the various inhabitants of the city at work and at play. He is interested in gossip and fashion, but not particularly in women. In an 1829 dictionary, a *flâneur* is a man 'who likes to do nothing', who relishes idleness. Balzac's *flâneur* took two main forms, that of the common *flâneur*, happy to aimlessly wander the streets, and the artist *flâneur*, who poured his experiences of the city into his work. This was the more miserable type of *flâneur*, as Balzac notes in his 1837 novel *César Birotteau*, 'just as frequently a desperate man as an idle one'.

Baudelaire's *flâneur* is an artist who seeks 'refuge in the crowd', modelled on his favourite painter, Constantin Guys, a man who ambled about town, who might have fallen into obscurity had Baudelaire not made him famous. Edgar Allen Poe's short story 'The Man in the Crowd' opens up other questions: is the *flâneur* the person who follows or is followed? Does he blend and elude, or step back and write what he sees? In French the words for 'I am' and 'I follow' are identical: *je suis*. 'Tell me who you follow and I'll tell you who you are,' wrote André Breton in *Nadja*. Even for the male *flâneur*, *flânerie* does not universally signify freedom and leisure; Flaubert's version of *flânerie* reflects his own feelings of social discomfiture.[6] In the early nineteenth century, the *flâneur* was compared to a policeman. In Québec, says a friend who's spent time there, a *flâneur* is a kind of con man.

Both surveyor and surveyed, the *flâneur* is a beguiling but empty vessel, a blank canvas onto which different eras have projected their own desires and anxieties. He appears when and how we want him to.[7] There are many contradictions built into the idea of the *flâneur*, though we may not realise it when we talk about him. We think we know what we mean, but we don't.

The same could be said of the *flâneuse*. Of course, what kinds of spaces women had access to, and which they were barred from, is an important question. In 1888 Amy Levy wrote, 'The female club-lounger, the *flâneuse* of St James Street, latch-key in pocket and eye-glasses on the nose, remains a creature of the imagination.'[8] Fair enough. But surely there have always been plenty of women in cities, and plenty of women writing about cities, chronicling their lives, telling stories, taking pictures, making films, engaging with the city in any way they can – including Levy herself. The joy of walking in the city belongs to men and women alike. To suggest that there couldn't be a female version of the *flâneur* is to limit the ways women have interacted with the city to the ways *men* have interacted with the city. We can talk about social mores and restrictions but we cannot rule out the fact that women were there; we must try to understand what walking in the city meant to them. Perhaps the answer is not to attempt to make a woman fit a masculine concept, but to redefine the concept itself.

If we tunnel back, we find there always was a *flâneuse* passing Baudelaire in the street.

+

If we read what women had to say for themselves in the nineteenth century, we do find that bourgeois women out in public ran all sorts of risks to their virtue and their reputations;

to go out in public alone was to risk disgrace.[9] Upper-class ladies displayed themselves in the Bois de Boulogne in their open carriages, or took chaperoned constitutionals in the park. (The woman in the closed carriage was a figure of some suspicion, as the famous carriage scene in *Madame Bovary* attests.) The distinct social stakes for an independent young woman of the late nineteenth century are made very clear in the eight volumes of the diaries of Marie Bashkirtseff (abridged and published in English under the incredible title *I Am the Most Interesting Book of All*), which recount her transformation from cosseted young Russian aristocrat to successful artist, showing her work at the Paris Salon a mere two and a half years after she started seriously studying painting, until her death from tuberculosis at the age of twenty-five. In January 1879 she wrote in her journal:

> I long for the freedom to go out alone: to go, to come, to sit on a bench in the Jardin des Tuileries, and especially to go to the Luxembourg, to look at the decorated store windows, to enter churches and museums, and to stroll in the old streets in the evenings. This is what I envy. Without this freedom one cannot become a great artist.[10]

Marie had relatively little to lose; she knew she was condemned to an early death — why not walk alone? But she nurtured a hope she would get well until the month before she died; and while she would have happily embarrassed her family, she had also internalised her culture's objection to a young woman of good family going out alone to such an extent that she would chastise herself for even wanting to, writing in her journal that even if she did defy social strictures, she 'would only be half free, because a woman who prowls is unwise'.

Though she trailed an entourage behind her, she *did* spend

days walking the slums of Paris with her notebook in hand, sketching everything she saw, research which would produce numerous paintings, including 1884's *A Meeting*, which now hangs in the Musée d'Orsay in Paris, and depicts a group of young street urchins gathered on a street corner. One of them holds a bird's nest, and shows it off to the others, who lean in with that boyish interest that tries to disguise itself as total indifference.

But she found a way to include herself in the streetscape. To the right of the group of boys, leading down another street, we can see in the background a young girl from behind, braid down her back, walking away, possibly on her own, though it's difficult to know for sure because the frame cuts off there; we can't even see her right arm. This, for me, is the most wonderful part of the painting: Marie's signature is placed below the young girl, in the bottom right-hand corner. I don't think it's overreaching to surmise that Marie has painted herself into the canvas, in the figure of the possibly solitary young girl on her way off, leaving the boys to it.

+

The argument against the *flâneuse* sometimes has to do with questions of visibility – 'It is crucial for the *flâneur* to be functionally invisible,' writes Luc Sante, defending his own gendering of the *flâneur* as male and not female.[11] This remark is at the same time unfair and cruelly accurate. We would love to be invisible the way a man is. We're not the ones who make ourselves visible, in the sense that Sante means, in terms of the stir a woman alone in public can create; it's the gaze of the *flâneur* that makes the woman who would join their ranks too visible to slip by unnoticed. But if we're so conspicuous, why have we been written out of the history of cities? It's up to us to paint ourselves back into the picture, in ways we can live with.

Though women of Marie Bashkirtseff's class were mainly identified with the home until late in the nineteenth century, women of the middle and lower classes did have many reasons to be in the street, going out to play or to work as shop girls, charity workers, maids, seamstresses, laundresses, or any number of other occupations. And these were not merely functional or professional outings; in his vivid picture of working-class women's lives in his study of Paris in the eighteenth century, David Garrioch shows that, in a way, the streets belonged to women. At the Parisian markets they ran most of the stalls, and even at home they would sit out in the street together, practising what two hundred years later Jane Jacobs would call 'eyes on the street': they 'kept an eye on what was going on and were often the first to intervene in quarrels, plunging in to separate men who were fighting. Their commentary on the dress and behavior of the passers-by was itself a form of social control.'[12] They knew more about what was going on in the neighbourhood than anyone.

By the late nineteenth century, women of all classes were enjoying the use of public space in cities like London, Paris and New York. The rise of the department store in the 1850s and 60s did much to normalise the appearance of women in public; by the 1870s some guidebooks to London were already beginning to feature 'places in London where ladies can conveniently lunch when in town for a day's shopping and unattended by a gentleman'.[13] James Tissot's series of the 1880s, *Fifteen Portraits of the Parisienne*, depicts women in the city doing all kinds of things, from sitting in the park (accompanied by Maman) to attending artists' lunches with their husbands (as stiff in their corsets as the caryatids in the background) and riding chariots dressed as Roman warriors at the Hippodrome, Statue of Liberty-style diadems on their heads. His 1885 canvas *The Shop*

Girl takes the viewer right into the painting; the eponymous shop girl, tall and thin, soberly dressed in black, holds the door open to us, in welcome or in respectful adieu. On the table is a dishevelled pile of silken fabric; a ribbon has fallen to the floor. The painting aligns women in public with the crass commercialism of the marketplace, but is also suggestive of loose mores and intimate disarray, of ribbons fallen to floors in other, more private, interiors.

The 1890s saw the arrival of the New Woman, riding her bicycle where she pleased, and the girls who gained their independence by working in shops and offices. As cinema and other leisure activities became popular in the early twentieth century, and taken with the large-scale entrance of women into the workforce during the First World War, women's presence in the streets was confirmed. But this was dependent on the emergence of safe semi-public spaces in which women could spend time alone and unharassed, like cafes and tea rooms, and the rise of those most intimate of public spaces, ladies' lavatories.[14] Also key to women's urban independence were respectable, affordable boarding houses for the unmarried; very often, it was difficult to find both of those qualities in the same establishment. As Jean Rhys's novels attest, many women skirted the boundaries of respectability in down-at-heel places whose morals rose in direct ratio to their level of seediness. The more louche the establishment, the more strict the *patronne*. Rhys's single women in the city are forever clashing with the landladies of their fleabag hotels.

+

The names a city bestows on its landmarks – especially its streets – are reflections of the values it holds, which change over time. In the effort to secularise (and, ostensibly, democratise) public space, cities in the modern era renamed streets that once honoured female saints, royal women, or mythical figures, replacing them with secular, democratic heroes – all men, intellectuals, scientists, revolutionaries.[15] But this fair-mindedness can also ignore those who lack the cultural or gendered capital to rise within a culture's ranks, and succeeds in identifying women with the outdated regime, associating them with 'the private, the traditional, and the anti-modern'.[16]

When they do appear – and it's not often, there are twice as many statues of dogs in Edinburgh as there are of women – women are decorative or idealized, cast in stone as allegories or slaves. The obelisk at the Place de la Concorde in Paris, which stands at the spot where the king was guillotined (and the queen, and Charlotte Corday and Danton and Olympe de Gouges and Robespierre and Desmoulins and thousands of others whom history has rendered nameless), is surrounded by statues of women representing the various French cities. The model for James Pradier's sculpture of Strasbourg was alternately said to be Victor Hugo's mistress, Juliette Drouet, or Gustave Flaubert's, Louise Colet.[17] Which is why I like to think of the statue as an allegory not only of Strasbourg but of all the mistresses of great writers and artists, who scribbled and painted and may never get out of their lovers' shadows, though they sit at the centre of Paris in broad daylight, abstracted into a city fought over by two nations.[18]

In 1916, Virginia Woolf reviewed E. V. Lucas's *London Revisited* for the *Times Literary Supplement*. In his account of London past and present, Lucas includes a catalogue of monuments in the city. But he omits one in particular, and Woolf asks: 'why is there no mention of [. . .] the woman with an urn which fronts the gates of the Foundling Hospital?'[19]

She kneels there still, with her pitcher, on a traffic island across from Coram's Fields, atop a modern-looking drinking fountain.[20] The sculptor is unknown. Dressed in some kind of toga or tunic, with curled hair in coils down her neck, she is sometimes called 'The Waterbearer' or the 'Woman of Samaria', after the woman who spoke with Jesus at a well, and recognised him as a prophet.

Walk through the streets of any big city, and if you're paying attention you'll notice another kind of woman standing around, immobilised. The French director Agnès Varda made a short film in the 1980s, *Les dites-cariatides* (*The So-Called Caryatids*), in which she and her camera wander around Paris looking for examples of the architectural oddity that is the caryatid, the stone women who serve as load-bearing columns, holding up the great buildings of the city. They're all over Paris, these caryatids. They come in sets of two or four and sometimes many more than that, depending on the building's ostentation. Sometimes they're male. These are called atlantes, named for Atlas, who holds up the world. The male caryatids, Varda observes, are shown with muscles bulging, while the females are all lithe and lissome, posing elegantly, effortlessly: if they find the building too much to bear, we'd never know it from looking at them.

But then, we never really look at them. Varda's film concludes with an enormous caryatid in the 3rd arrondissement, so large it takes up three storeys of a building on the busy rue Turbigo. She asks the people in the neighbourhood what they think of the stone woman. They haven't even noticed she was there. As the writer Robert Musil once pointed out, it is the nature of monuments to go unnoticed. 'Doubtless they have been erected to be seen,' he wrote, 'even to attract attention; yet at the same time something has impregnated them against attention.' Still, on some level we're aware of them. In her book *Monuments & Maidens*, Marina Warner surmises that if someone removed the statue of the Law (allegorically represented as female) from the Place du Palais-Bourbon, we would all somehow sense that something was missing, even if we didn't know what. We're more attuned to our environment than we realise.

+

The *flâneuse* is still fighting to be seen, even now, when, as we'd like to think, she more or less has the run of the city.

A more politically engaged descendant of Baudelairean *flânerie* reigns today, one that operates by *dérive,* or 'drift'. A mid-twentieth-century group of radical poets and artists calling themselves the Situationists invented 'psychogeography', in which strolling becomes drifting and detached observation becomes a critique of post-war urbanism. Urban explorers use the *dérive* to map the emotive force field of the city, and the way architecture and topography combine to create its 'psychogeographical contours'.[21] Robert Macfarlane, a masterful writer-walker of the countryside, offers this summary of the practice: 'Unfold a street map of London, place a glass, rim down, anywhere on the map, and draw round its edge. Pick up the map, go out into the city, and walk the circle, keeping as close as you can to the curve. Record the experience as you go, in whatever medium you favour: film, photograph, manuscript, tape. Catch the textual run-off of the streets; the graffiti, the branded litter, the snatches of conversation. Cut for sign. Log the data-stream. Be alert to the happenstance of metaphors, watch for visual rhymes, coincidences, analogies, family resemblances, the changing moods of the street.'[22] Psychogeography is a term that many of Macfarlane's contemporaries alternately embrace (sometimes ironically) or refuse; Will Self uses it to title a collection of his essays; Iain Sinclair is sceptical of the word, as it's been co-opted to become a 'very nasty sort of branding'; he prefers to think of it as 'deep topography', a term he got from Self's buddy Nick Papadimitriou (who talks of making a 'close study' of a set environment on certain walks).

Call them what you will; these late-century heirs to the Situationists also inherited Baudelaire's blinkered approach to the women on the pavement. Self has declared – not without some personal disappointment – psychogeography to be a man's work, confirming the walker in the city as a figure of masculine privilege.[23] Self has gone so far as to declare psychogeographers a 'fraternity': 'middle-aged men in Gore-Tex, armed with notebooks and camera, stamping out boots on suburban train platforms, politely requesting the operators of tea kiosks in mossy parks to fill our thermoses, querying the destinations of rural buses [...] prostates swell[ing] as we crunch over broken glass, behind the defunct brewery on the outskirts of town.'

Really, he doesn't sound very different from Louis Huart, defining the *flâneur* in 1841: 'Good legs, good ears, and good eyes [...] these are the principal physical advantages needed for any Frenchman to be worthy of the club of *flâneurs* as soon as we start one.'[24] The great writers of the city, the great psychogeographers, the ones that you read about in the *Observer* on weekends: they are all men, and at any given moment you'll also find them writing about each other's work, creating a reified canon of masculine writer-walkers.[25] As if a penis were a requisite walking appendage, like a cane.

A glance at the psychogeographical fanzine *Savage Messiah*, drawn by the graphic artist Laura Oldfield Ford, shows this isn't true; Ford walks all over London, verging from the 'inner city' out to the suburbs, and the sketches she creates out of what she sees reveal a capital surrounded by Ballardian suburbs, cubes of housing estates, disused, temporary structures, anchors in a sea of litter, refuse, anger. Even Woolf, Britain's most decorous modernist, the favourite target of literary men beefing up their virility by slagging her off, liked to tramp around the filthy places of London. One day in 1939 found her down near Southwark Bridge, where she 'saw a flight of steps down to the river – I climbed down – a rope at the bottom – Found the strand of the Thames, under the warehouses – strewn with stones, bits of wire . . . Very slippery; warehouse walls crusted, weedy, worn . . . Difficult walking. A rat haunted, riverine place, great chains, wooden pillars, green slime, bricks corroded, a button hook thrown up by the tide.'[26]

It would be nice, ideal even, if we didn't have to subdivide by gender – male walkers, female walkers, *flâneurs* and *flâneuses* – but these narratives of walking repeatedly leave out a woman's experience.[27] Sinclair admits that the work he admires in deep topography makes the walker into a very British figure, the naturalist.[28] This is not a way of interacting with the world that particularly interests me. I like the built environment, I like cities. Not their limits, not the places where they become not-cities. Cities themselves. The heart of them. Their manifold quarters, sectors, corners. And it's the centre of cities where women have been empowered, by plunging into the heart of them, and walking where they're not meant to. Walking where other people (men) walk without eliciting comment. That is the transgressive act. You don't need to crunch around in Gore-Tex to be subversive, if you're a woman. Just walk out your front door.

+

Nearly two decades after those first early experiments in *flâneuserie*, I still live and walk in Paris, after having walked in New York, Venice, Tokyo and London, all places I've lived in temporarily for work or love. It's a hard habit to shake. Why do I walk? I walk because I like it. I like the rhythm of it, my shadow always a little ahead of me on the pavement. I like being able to stop when I like, to lean against a building and make a note in my journal, or read an email, or send a text message, and for the world to stop while I do it. Walking, paradoxically, allows for the possibility of stillness.

Walking is mapping with your feet. It helps you piece a city together, connecting up neighbourhoods that might otherwise have remained discrete entities, different planets bound to each other, sustained yet remote. I like seeing how in fact they blend into one another, I like noticing the boundaries between them. Walking helps me feel at home. There's a small pleasure in seeing how well I've come to know the city through my wanderings on foot, crossing through different neighbourhoods of the city, some I used to know quite well, others I may not have seen in a while, like getting reacquainted with someone I once met at a party.

Sometimes I walk because I have things on my mind, and walking helps me sort them out. *Solvitur ambulando*, as they say.

I walk because it confers – or restores – a feeling of *placeness*. The geographer Yi-Fu Tuan says a space becomes a place when through movement we invest it with meaning, when we see it as something to be perceived, apprehended, experienced.[29]

I walk because, somehow, it's like reading. You're privy to these lives and conversations that have nothing to do with yours, but you can eavesdrop on them. Sometimes it's overcrowded; sometimes the voices are too loud. But there is always companionship. You are not alone. You walk in the city side by side with the living and the dead.

+

Once I began to look for the *flâneuse*, I spotted her everywhere. I caught her standing on street corners in New York and coming through doorways in Kyoto, sipping coffee at cafe tables in Paris, at the foot of a bridge in Venice, or riding the ferry in Hong Kong. She is going somewhere, or coming from somewhere; she is saturated with in-betweenness. She may be a writer, or she may be an artist, or she may be a secretary or an au pair. She may be unemployed. She may be unemployable. She may be a wife, or a mother, or she may be totally free. She may take the bus or the train when she's tired. But mostly, she goes on foot. She gets to know the city by wandering its streets, investigating its dark corners, peering behind facades, penetrating into secret courtyards. I found her using cities as performance spaces, or as hiding places; as places to seek fame and fortune or anonymity; as places to liberate herself from oppression or to help those who are oppressed; as places to declare her independence; as places to change the world or be changed by it.

I found many correspondences between them; these women all read from each other and learned from each other, and their readings branched outward and outward in a network so developed it resists cataloguing. The portraits I paint here attest that the *flâneuse* is not merely a female *flâneur*, but a figure to be reckoned with, and inspired by, all on her own.[30] She voyages out, and goes where she's not supposed to; she forces us to confront the ways in which words like *home* and *belonging* are used against women. She is a determined, resourceful individual keenly attuned to the creative potential of the city, and the liberating possibilities of a good walk.

The *flâneuse* does exist, whenever we have deviated from the paths laid out for us, lighting out for our own territories.

exit 53 Sunken Meadow north, exit SM3E, right at the Friendly's, left by Northgate

you really need a car

LONG ISLAND

NEW YORK

New York was my first city.

When I was growing up, my parents would occasionally drive the hour to Manhattan from Long Island, where we lived, to take my sister and me to the theatre, or to a museum. Back then, under Mayor Koch, some Long Islanders did not feel comfortable taking their children to New York. My parents were both from the Outer Boroughs – the Bronx and Queens – and they had purposefully raised us away from *the city*, in the quiet suburbs on the North Shore. They were part of a mass middle-class exodus. The suburbs better suited their dispositions, in any case: my mother dislikes the crowding of too-proximate neighbours; my father likes boats and boatyards. There are a lot of those on Long Island, and no people on the other sides of the walls and floor.

When we drove in to *the city*, my parents would become edgy and protective. Emerging from the Midtown Tunnel, the automatic locks on the car doors abruptly went *thunk*. 'Don't make eye contact,' my mother would warn as we walked in Times Square. It was the 1980s, and Giuliani's big sanitisation project was a decade off; Times Square was still gritty, full of strip clubs and junkies and religious fanatics with beards and bullhorns shouting *BURNING! YOU ARE ALL BUUUURNIIIIING!* But if you ask me, it is far more terrifying today, packed with tourists posing for pictures with young men dressed as Smurfs and Ninja Turtles.

When the time came to go to university, I was not permitted to apply to schools in *the city*. Off I went then to study musical theatre upstate, not far from the Canadian border, where the frigid cold blew in from Lake Ontario and we walked to class through two feet of snow. When my parents came to visit, they sat in on one of my acting classes and saw what their money was paying for: an activity in which we mimed the throwing, and catching, of invisible tennis balls. A year later, realising I was constitutionally unsuited to showbiz, I transferred to Columbia University to study English. My parents thanked their lucky stars and didn't say a word against its location, just south of Harlem. I've lived in cities ever since.

I felt at home in the crowds, amid the hum and the neon, with the grocery store downstairs open all night, and the Ethiopian restaurant on the corner doing great takeaway; it felt, the moment I stepped outside, like I was actually a part of the world, that I could contribute to it and take from it and we were all in it together. It's very hard to put words to this, but psychologically, in the city, I felt I could look after myself in a way I couldn't out in the suburbs.

Now when I go home to Long Island, I find the empty streets of my parents' neighbourhood terrifying. The very appearance of another human, walking on foot, seems out of place and menacing. I don't look out the windows after nightfall lest I see someone lurking in the back garden, staring in at me. If the doorbell rings while I'm home alone, I don't answer, but go and hide in windowless rooms: the bathroom, the pantry. I realise this is antisocial and nearly pathological behaviour. I blame the suburbs.

+

The suburban American dream was born on Long Island, the work of a man called William Levitt, who came home from fighting in the Second World War, bought up huge expanses of land on Long Island, and got to work building home after home for other returning veterans. The houses he built in Levittown were (are) of a striking uniformity, the same one-storey rectangle of pre-cut lumber on a concrete foundation with an unfinished attic repeated over and over, at equal spacings on quarter-of-an-acre plots. Cheap to build and cheap to buy, they sold at astonishing rates – in 1949, as many as 1,400 homes in a day. Anywhere from $7,990 (or $78,000 today) to $9,500 ($93,000) would get you a Levitt house – with a washing machine thrown in for free. During the first few years of their existence, Levittown houses had a clause in their contracts forbidding buyers to rent their homes to African Americans.

+

'The history of suburbia,' writes Rebecca Solnit, 'is the history of fragmentation.'[1] It is also the history of exclusion. Today most Americans live in suburbs (or the giant suburban conglomerates now referred to as 'exurbs'), having fled the congested, polluted industrial city. They were hoping to get a bit of green and some room to breathe, and to be able to raise their children somewhere, as the saying went, 'decent', but in so doing they abandoned the slum-ridden cities to the poor and disenfranchised, and guaranteed a rise in crime that merely confirmed for them their reasons for leaving. It is a story about breaking away from the collective in all its variety to dwell among similar people.

If suburbanites are buffered from encounters with the strange and different by their cars and their single-family houses, this is in part a result of zoning laws which divide towns up into single-use enclaves. Residential, commercial and industrial areas are kept strictly apart, which demands that you drive everywhere as your orbit between work, home, shopping and leisure becomes ever wider. Originally bedroom communities clustered around railway stations with easy access to the cities on which they depended, the suburbs in time became autonomous, spreading away from their town centres. This was mainly the fault of the automobile, which became the pre-eminent way of getting around in the second half of the twentieth century, causing an intricate system of motorways to loop and lace through the landscape, connecting each town to all the others, blurring them into a sprawling mass of units with no easy means of getting from one to the other on foot.

The attempt to accommodate automobile traffic caused the suburbs to look the way they do. In 1929, faced with the problem of how to thread this new kind of traffic through residential areas, a planner came up with a template that replaced the grid layout of the city with the curving streets of the suburb. Self-enclosed 'neighbourhood units' were set along these interior streets, and connected by arterial roads on which could be found all the commercial and industrial resources the towns needed. 'Neighbourhood' became a buzzword for an almost utopian way of life, in which neighbours could relate to each other and to their community in a more meaningful way, where children could walk to school and adults to work without being endangered by traffic. This is not how the suburbs turned out.

Getting around by car often means residents end up travelling far and wide to work and to play, which is not the way to build local solidarity. As home-based entertainments like radio and later television developed, families tended to relish their privacy, and the 'neighbourhood unit' was further undermined. And unfortunately, these discrete 'units' soon became an excuse for horrific instances of racial and class-based segregation. With no way of seeing how other people lived, the only access any of us had to the real world was through the television, which piped in visions of white suburban families not so different from our own.

The models the culture provided for us were car-bound ones. The television shows in the eighties and early nineties were about mostly white families in suburbs. *The Cosby Show* – a rare exception to this rule – took place in New York, but the set was no more of a real city block than the one on *Sesame Street*. Even *Full House*, set in urban San Francisco, showed the family driving their car (an aspirational red convertible) across the Golden Gate Bridge. Films were set in the suburbs, with occasional forays into the big bad city turning out to be great adventures (*Ferris Bueller's Day Off*, *Adventures in Babysitting*) that concluded with everyone safe and sound, back at home in their massive colonials.

In many suburban neighbourhoods, there are no sidewalks.

I worry about my parents when they drive places, and end my phone conversations with them not with *love you* but *drive safely*.[2] Everywhere they go, they go by car. They have good friends who live just up the block, maybe a five-minute walk, seven minutes at the most, but they take the car to go see them. This is hard to explain to people who don't live in suburbs: I wouldn't *want* them to walk. It would be all right in the daytime, but the street is full of hills and curves and not well-lit; drivers wouldn't expect there to be pedestrians on sidewalk-free streets. It's jarring to see someone out walking in the road if they don't have a dog with them and aren't wearing a tracksuit. It's especially unusual to see someone walking on the main arterial roads, where the shops are. If you don't own a car, you belong to a strange suburban underclass, a caste of untouchables visible only when you are out of place, walking along the side of a road everyone else is driving down.[3]

+

My parents were among the thirteen million people who left the city for the suburbs in the 1970s. The move meant that cities fell into disrepair, as the jobs followed the middle classes out to the suburbs. 'As far back as 1942, AT&T Bell Telephone Laboratories moved from Manhattan to a 213-acre campus in Murray Hill, New Jersey, which offered more space, quiet, and the same graceful curving roads and bucolic feel of burgeoning suburban divisions,' Leigh Gallagher explains in her book on the suburbs. 'But the '70s saw the beginning of an exodus of blue-chip companies from the cities that would continue for decades: IBM moved from New York City to Armonk, New York, GE to Fairfield, Connecticut, Motorola from Chicago to Schaumberg, Illinois. By 1981, half of office space was located outside central cities. By the end of the 1990s, that share would grow to two-thirds.'

And that is how my father built up his architectural practice, designing steel-and-glass headquarters for those companies on the off-roads of the Long Island Expressway. My father's hero is the German architect Mies van der Rohe, because his buildings are reasonable, symmetrical, clear, simple. In that spirit my father built some of the nicer-looking buildings on the Island, many of them industrial or commercial, their form and space and use all carefully balanced. He has done what he can not to blight the landscape – even won awards for some of his designs – but he is constrained by what his clients are willing to pay. One of the things he is most proud of is that aside from their aesthetic appeal, his buildings *work*. They don't leak, and they don't fall down. You'd be surprised how few buildings you can say that about.

I can't remember a time when I didn't think about buildings, about spaces and their meanings. I grew up measuring my height against rolled-up plans for buildings; the tools of my father's trade were my childhood toys: drafting tables, cut-out plastic triangles, compasses, coloured pencils. My father taught me to be sensitive to environment. Perhaps this is why I have never felt at ease on Long Island. I'm not from a town like Northport, Huntington or Port Jefferson, with quaint clapboard houses and historic main streets lined with haberdashers and fishermen's pubs. We lived two miles south of those places, but a small distance makes all the difference. Our town coagulates around Jericho Turnpike, a six-lane main drag featuring strip mall after strip mall, functional eyesores thrown up in the 1970s and 80s for no money at all, home to garages, car dealerships, gas stations (really anything to do with your car), along with tattoo parlours, long out-of-business Chinese restaurants, Haven Pools, Crazy Diamond, a place where you can buy a gun permit, the Dix Hills Diner, Puppies Puppies Puppies! Grooming 7 days a week. A drive east or west takes you past flat-roofed garages divided from a flat sky by telephone wires strung pole to pole; lone brick buildings surrounded by asphalt where SUVs and family sedans nose in and back out; faux chalet roofs, faux Tudor facades; the blue-topped IHOP; the red-topped Friendly's; cinder-block buildings whose sans serif font signs advertise FURNITURE, HAND-WASH, BILLIARD, RITE AID. I know exactly what the inside of that bank will be like: it will smell of carpet, there will be fluorescent lighting, Formica-plated desk furniture and swivel chairs.

+

+

It's not pretty, but it's home.

+

These buildings exist to house the small businesses inside them, but just barely, like bomb shelters. You get in, you do what you need to do, you get out. They are life-draining for the people who work in them, and a daily misery for the people who visit them, though they may not realise it. Marc Augé calls them 'non-places', and they are unfortunately the defining spaces of the late twentieth – and by all appearances, the twenty-first – century in America.

What we build not only reflects but determines who we are and who we'll be. 'A city is an attempt at a kind of collective immortality,' wrote Marshall Berman in an essay on urban ruin: 'we die, but we hope our city's forms and structures will live on'.[4] The opposite is true in the suburbs. They have no history and don't think about the future; very little there is built to last.[5] Posterity is irrelevant to a civilisation living in an ongoing, never-ending present, with as much care for the future or sense of the past as a child. In his classic 1961 study *The City in History*, Lewis Mumford describes the naivety of the suburbs, which sustain in their inhabitants a 'childish view of the world', a false impression of security, if not an outright political apathy.[6] Terrible things happen elsewhere, but never here, not now, not to us. It's the most natural parental instinct to want to give your children a better childhood than your own; but the generation of city dwellers who invented the suburbs blew past 'better' in their pursuit of an impossible social isolation. It is as if they were trying to give not only their children but *themselves* the childhood they never had. The suburbs present the world to their children as if padded in felt, as if life were something gradually accumulated through commercial transaction, store by store. Often American literature and films about the suburbs feature children and adults alike losing their innocence, surprised, unprepared, for how terrible life can be: *The Virgin Suicides*, *American Beauty*, *Revolutionary Road*, *Weeds* – all of these ask not only 'is that all there is?' but 'is there really that, too?'

I feel angry when I drive up Jericho, looking at these provisional structures. Don't we deserve better? Humans don't just thrive no matter where you put them. Environment matters. Environment is determinative, constitutive; it makes you who you are, it makes you do what you do. My father's best architecture teacher, Louis Kahn, used to tell his students to think like the beams, feel like the beams, what's pushing you in, what's pulling you down, and that's how you think through a building.

That's the way I think through the city.

+

It would have been nice, when I was growing up, to be able to walk somewhere. In our town there was no place to gather, no downtown, no town centre. When I was in high school we hung out at the Dunkin' Donuts in an industrial park, which mysteriously stayed open until around ten at night even though all the other local businesses were closed by then. There was nowhere to walk or bike to from my house except the shopping centre on the corner of Plymouth Boulevard and Jericho Turnpike, which Google Maps tells me is 1.6 miles away, a 31-minute walk. This sounds right. It was a bit far, but worth it if only to get *somewhere*. There was a video store (a place of as much freedom as the library, where I familiarised myself with the canon of eighties comedies like *Fletch*, *Airplane!*, *Beverly Hills Cop* and *Splash*) and some kind of massive five-and-dime store called Cheapo Charlie's or something to that effect, where I bought tons of candy – that powdered sugar stuff in multiple colours you ate with a hardened white sugar stick.

We felt cut off from *places*. In the very early mornings, shuffling into the kitchen to let the dog out into the backyard, in the cotton wool of dawn, I could hear the faint sound of a train crooning into Kings Park station, a couple of miles north of us. I loved that sound. That we could hear a train reminded me that we were located somewhere; it lent coordinates to our suburban limbo.[7] *There's a way out of here*, I thought. *I could take a train.*

+

The first time I was on my own in the city was my first year of university. I took a Greyhound bus down to visit a friend who was studying at NYU; she had class my first morning, so I was left to my own devices in Greenwich Village. Two hours to myself and I could go anywhere I wanted in the entire city! Did I want to visit Central Park? Or one of the museums? Or see what Times Square was like on my own? I'd never before felt really and truly independent. The city seemed so huge, every street its own option. I walked out onto 10th Street and stopped in my tracks. Which way was – anything? There was a church on the corner. Was that east? Or west? I had it in my head that I wanted to go west but how could I know which direction that was unless I started walking, and I didn't want to waste a minute of time, I wanted to *go* where I was *going*, even if I didn't know where that was yet. I ventured towards the church and hit Broadway. I ventured a little further and found Fourth Avenue. I didn't even know there *was* a Fourth Avenue. I retraced my steps and went round in circles trying to find the St Mark's diner my friend had taken me to the night before. I think I wound up spending the morning in the Barnes & Noble at Union Square.

Sophomore year I moved to New York, where I lived in a dorm on 121st and Amsterdam, and fell in love with the Upper West Side. Up and down the length of those avenues I went walking, Broadway, Amsterdam, Riverside, which turned into West End Avenue, down to 110th Street and across to Central Park, down Central Park West to the Museum of Natural History. I gaped at the gargantuan ornate apartment buildings, the wide boulevards, Zabar's, H&H Bagels, the Hungarian Pastry Shop with its sticky glazed croissants, the men selling books on folding tables on Broadway. To sit in a restaurant on Broadway with the world walking by and the cars and the taxis and the noise was like finally being let in to the centre of the universe, after peering in at it for so long.

I fantasised about my life after graduation. I would live in an *apartment*, and not a house. A musty book-filled one on

Riverside Drive, or West End Avenue, in the kind of building with an awning that extended out onto the sidewalk. I didn't much care about the doorman, but I wanted the awning. And I would have built-in bookshelves, and Turkish rugs, and my psychoanalyst friends would come over and we would drink lapsang souchong while talking about the books we were writing and the affairs we were pursuing. It was a fantasy cobbled together from Woody Allen films, a few visits to professors' homes, and someone's great-aunt's apartment.

Let loose in the city, I would walk down 116th Street, past the curved buildings, to Riverside Park and sit on a bench and feel so lucky, so lucky to be able to get up and go someplace like that whenever I wanted to. That was the definition of freedom. Not just the time, and not just the transit: being able to do that in an environment that felt created for people, not machines, shaped and sustained by some kind of belief in having nice places for people to be, together, in public.

There was something haunting the city then, the ghost of Dorothy Parker or Edith Wharton or someone I hadn't read yet. It lived in the buildings lopsided with age on Barrow Street, in the brownstones in Murray Hill coming up from the Midtown Tunnel. It was in those book-stuffed apartments on West End Avenue. It was in the square tiles in their beat-up bathrooms. I wanted to capture it in my writing; I wanted to *be* it. A woman who interviewed me to be her research assistant took me for a drink at the Algonquin and I thought: *This.* This is making it.

+

At Barnard I learned to think critically, and I turned this new power on the suburbs. I became suspicious of an entirely vehicle-based culture; a culture that does not walk is bad for women. It makes a kind of authoritarian sense; a woman who doesn't wonder – what it all adds up to, what her needs are, if they're being met – won't wander off from the family. The layout of the suburbs reinforces her boundaries: the neat grid, the nearby shopping centre, the endless loops of parkways, where the American adventure of the open road is tamed by the American dream. Think of all the rebellious suburban women killed off in literature, from *Madame Bovary* to *Revolutionary Road*. Dream big, end up dead. Thelma and Louise could never come home to the suburbs. I began to think of houses the way Marguerite Duras did: places 'specially meant for putting children and men in so as to restrict their waywardness and distract them from the longing for adventure and escape they've had since time began', but to 'children and men' I added 'and women'.[8]

As I became alert to the city, I became alert to women's history, literature, politics, as if it were impossible to learn about one without the other. I read everyone from Simone de Beauvoir to Susan Brownmiller. Once I became aware of that alternative history, it gave me something to move towards, and I began to seek out its clues, scattered throughout the world.

I wasn't naive enough to idealise the city as a place of equal access and possibility. Certainly Columbia University's complicated history with its neighbourhood testified to the contrary.[9] But it is in the practice of the city that we have the best chance of making a just world. Freedom of movement is an intrinsic part of that.

+

Let me walk. Let me go at my own pace. Let me feel life as it moves through me and around me. Give me drama. Give me unexpected curvilinear corners. Give me unsettling churches and beautiful storefronts and parks I can lie down in.

The city turns you on, gets you going, moving, thinking, wanting, engaging. The city is life itself.

line 10 at Duroc get off at Cluny-la-Sorbonne walk north up rue Boutebrie get lost in warren of medieval streets full of Turkish and Greek restaurants whose owners implore you to step inside with promises of plates broken against walls and all the doner meat you could dream of past the old Tunisian bakery out past the church and left onto the rue Saint-Jacques clogged with tourists and a right onto a small street just south of the park whose name nobody knows except the people who live on it, and those who work in the bookshop

PARIS

CAFES WHERE THEY

But what if it were heaven when she got there?
— Jean Rhys, 'In the Rue de l'Arrivée'

I was in Shakespeare and Company on the Left Bank of Paris when I saw her looking at me. This dark-eyed Modigliani woman with an elongated neck and dark almond holes for eyes, reclining in a passionate attitude on the cover of a paperback book called *After Leaving Mr Mackenzie*. She looked troubled, distraught, aroused, all at once. I picked it up, turned it over, and read the back cover:

JULIA MARTIN IS IN PARIS AND AT THE END OF HER ROPE.

The author was someone called Jean Rhys. It was the 'Rhys' part that first caught my interest. I had a brief love affair with all things Welsh as an early teenager after inhaling the historical fiction of Sharon Kay Penman, which was largely about Wales's loss of independence in the thirteenth century. As a teenager stuck in the suburbs, I think I sympathised with Wales.

There were a couple of other books by this Welsh person, which all seemed to be about Paris. There was one called *Quartet*:

> AFTER HER HUSBAND IS ARRESTED, MARYA ZELLI FINDS HERSELF ALONE
> AND PENNILESS IN PARIS.

And one with the Dickinsonian title *Good Morning, Midnight*:

> SASHA JENSEN HAS RETURNED TO PARIS, THE CITY OF BOTH HER HAPPIEST
> MOMENTS AND HER MOST DESPERATE.

The publishers couldn't have targeted their copy to their audience more effectively if they had held a focus group made up specifically of oversensitive American co-eds. These were just the words to resonate with a twenty-year-old who's beginning to suspect − nay, to *hope* − that life is going to be far more unhappy than she had previously supposed. I read everything I could get my hands on by and about Jean Rhys, whose taut, terse sentences were steeped in gorgeous sorrow yet skirted sentimentality. From her, I learned an aesthetics of pain that refused to self-romanticise. That's an important distinction, one that took me a while to understand, and one that's often overlooked by those who misread her. The novels made suffering feel purposeful, meaningful − if I have to live through this horrible thing at least I can write about it. But it's a slippery slope; before you know it you're putting yourself through horrible things just so you can write about it.

Rhys is smarter than that. We have to be, too, to read her right.

+

At twenty, I hadn't experienced anything like what Rhys's characters had been through: exile, poverty, abandonment, abortion, the death of a child, alcoholism, near-prostitution, or that scourge of Rhys's Paris novels, the onset of age. A twenty-year-old doesn't know what physical decline is; she can only imagine, as inconceivable as a moon-landing, the arrival of lines on her face, the deepening of grooves she didn't know she had, the loss of elasticity in her skin, the hair follicles that give up making pigment, the suddenly unreliable joints, the once-legible typeface that now seems impossibly small. I was lucky enough to have parents who supported me through college. Rhys's women have little to no family, no personal income, and often can't hold down a job. It's up to them to find a man to buy them a drink, give them a fiver, buy them some clothes, pay the rent.

And yet I felt jaded and cynical, used-up. 'Oh God I'm only twenty and I'll have to go on living and living,' Rhys wrote in the black exercise book she picked up one day in London that served as her journal. The final lines of her 1939 novel *Good Morning, Midnight* rang true to me: when, having lost the man she thinks she could have loved, Sasha allows a complete stranger – a neighbour who for most of the novel has been a menacing presence in the hallway – to enter her room and make love to her. She lies in bed, holding her arm over her eyes. Someone enters her bedroom. It might be René, the man who has just left. It might be the man who lives in the bedsit next door. She knows without looking which one it is. The very last lines of the book go like this:

He stands there, looking down at me. Not sure of himself, his mean eyes flickering. He doesn't say anything. Thank God, he doesn't say anything. I look straight into his eyes and despise another poor devil of a human being for the last time. For the last time . . . Then I put my arms around him and pull him down to the bed, saying 'Yes – yes – yes . . .'[1]

I hadn't yet read Joyce's *Ulysses*, so I didn't see that this was a grim response to that novel's infamous last lines, Molly Bloom's incantatory *yes I said yes I will Yes*. The earthy affirmation of Molly's monologue is mocked by Sasha's deadened acceptance of whatever life has in store for her. It's that first loss of love that does it, separates us into Sashas and Mollys. It's how you respond to that loss when nothing coheres any more, when you feel your life is spent, and you no longer care what happens to you or who you allow into your bed.

The women Rhys describes are similar enough that they used to be referred to in the singular, as the Rhys heroine. Definitely Sashas rather than Mollys; there is not a joyous one in the bunch. Life has beaten the joy out of them. But they are not all the same woman; and they are not quite fictionalised doubles of their author. They are, on the contrary, spectres of Rhys's worst nightmares of how her life could have been, based on the few autobiographical details they share. Anna in *Voyage in the Dark* has much in common with Rhys: a West Indian upbringing, a stint as a chorus girl, an affair with a wealthy older man; in the original manuscript she dies of a botched abortion. (Rhys's publishers made her change this.) *Quartet*'s Marya is a cipher, with no real backstory beyond occasional references to having lived in England where she had a brief stint as a chorus girl. She is an expatriate everywoman, with no country, no past, no future. The romantic mess she finds herself in, however, was inspired by Rhys's affair with the writer Ford Madox Ford. Julia, whose story picks up where Marya's leaves off, returns to London midway through *After Leaving Mr Mackenzie*, in the hopes that her family – poor but respectable – can give her some support. She is the first Rhys woman to have lost a child, like Rhys, unless you count Anna's abortion. Julia has a trans-European background – her child, Mackenzie recalls, died 'in

Central Europe, somewhere' – but she also has a mother, and a sister, and childhood memories in England. In short, she has a context. Sasha, in *Good Morning, Midnight*, has the fullest backstory and shares Rhys's biography more closely than Marya and Julia, except for the fact that by Sasha's age Rhys was married to Leslie Tilden Smith and living in London, returning to Paris to research her novels. She may have felt desperation during those years, but nothing like Sasha's.

They can seem maddeningly passive; dependent on men for money, they spend it on clothing the moment they get any. They have a self-destructive streak, and their author was at times comfortable, even thrilled, by self-abasement: Rhys writes of finding it 'humiliating and exciting' to think to herself: 'I belong to this man, I want to belong to him completely.'[2] Many of Rhys's readers recoil at a character like Sasha, who seems to abdicate responsibility for herself, and let what will happen, happen. I'm not sure it's passivity so much as a will not to be hurt by the things that happen to a single woman who gets attached too easily. But the alternative is not to get attached at all, and what is the point of a life without attachments?

Rhys relates in her unfinished autobiography, *Smile Please*, that she once told a Frenchman: '"I can abstract myself from my body." He looked so shocked that I asked if I was speaking bad French. He said "*Oh non, mais . . . c'est horrible*." And yet for so long that was what I did.' This willingness can make Rhys's women seem passive, static, stagnant, as if they're daring the world to do its worst. In *After Leaving Mr Mackenzie*, when Julia goes to London, she chooses her hotel by asking the taxi driver to take her somewhere. By *Good Morning, Midnight*, Sasha is taking excessive amounts of veronal 'so I could sleep fifteen hours out of the twenty-four'.[3] Marya, the protagonist of *Quartet*, is described as 'reckless, lazy, a vagabond by nature';[4] it seems as if she makes no choices for herself, but rather 'ends up', again and again. Even as she wants to run away from the Heidlers, Marya can't bring herself to leave. She is fully aware that it is something irrational which keeps her there: 'I don't like him or trust him. I love him.'

Paris, a city with a soundtrack in a minor key, is the ideal setting for this kind of self-relinquishing. There is a certain pain, related to love, and loss, that it amplifies until it almost feels good. And it was the ideal setting for my own first encounter with the addictive pleasure of despair.

+

Rhys's inability to operate by the same social guidelines as everyone else frequently brought her trouble, if not outright tragedy. Her first child died in infancy – of neglect, she believed. She was frequently brought up on charges of drunkenness and disorderly conduct. She did a stint in Holloway prison. She had an estranged daughter, Maryvonne, who spent time in a concentration camp during the Second World War. She suffered from alcoholism, cultural dislocation, alienation. Depressive rage. Bursts of creativity. All of this made it into her novels and short stories. But Rhys left so little primary material behind – she explicitly said she did not want to be the subject of a biography – that those who went ahead and wrote her life anyway resorted to calling on Rhys's fiction as if it provided an eyewitness account of her life, recreating Rhys as one of her characters.

Born Ella Gwendolen Rees Williams in 1890 in the West Indies, her father was Welsh (aha!) and her mother Scottish/Creole. Her plantation-owning family had lived in Dominica for three generations. Though her father was doting, her mother was emotionally distant, and neither kept a particularly close eye on their daughter, to such a point that at least one of their friends helped himself to her adolescent charms while no one was looking.

But on the whole, and in retrospect, Rhys was happy in Dominica. Everything was suspended there; it was as if nothing would ever come due. But there was no longer any future there for the Rhys clan; their fortune lost, they were slowly trickling home. After an early life spent dreaming among the wild colours and languid Caribbean foliage, Rhys was sent to school in England in 1906. When she first arrived, she was devastated by the grey drabness of it all. All 'brown' and 'dingy', it did not match the England of her fantasies, which she had imagined full of colour and light. It should have been a homecoming, but instead it was the most disheartening kind of reverse exile. She suffered through boarding school in Cambridge, where the other students ridiculed her sing-song Caribbean accent, calling her a 'coon'. She gave riveting performances in the school theatricals, and, thinking that her talents perhaps lay in the theatre, she persuaded her father to let her study at Tree's School in London, today the Royal Academy of Dramatic Art. But her accent kept her from fitting in there, too. Another girl might have worked to neutralise her speaking voice, but Rhys refused. She expected to be taken as she was. To be rejected on the basis of something as petty as her voice, she thought, was more of an indictment of the world than of her.

When her father died, the family ordered her home to Dominica, as they could no longer support her abroad. But she took matters into her own hands. Rather than return home, or languish, depressed, in London, she got herself moving, touring the north as a chorus girl in a production of *Our Miss Gibbs*. The provincial towns were as cold and wet as London, but they at least provided some adventure. She became aware of her charms, and how to use them to her advantage, eventually becoming involved with a wealthy man. Of course, it didn't work out. His name, most improbably, was Lancelot. This was the great love Rhys never recovered from, and for decades to come, she would turn to Lancelot when things looked bleak. She was too contrarian and too 'vague' (her word) to hold down a job; she came to rely on the kindness of friends and lovers. In search of stability, she married, often.

+

In 1919, Rhys drifted into Paris, the place that would make her into a writer. In fact, she walked there.

Having spent the war living on an allowance from Lancelot, volunteering at a canteen in Euston for soldiers on their way to France, in early 1918 she met a Dutch journalist called Jean Lenglet. He had a flat near hers in Bloomsbury; they had friends in common, and would spend evenings smoking and arguing at the Café Royal. He had joined the French Foreign Legion and worked in intelligence: he wouldn't tell Jean exactly what he did, but it called for him to travel covertly through Germany, the Netherlands, London and Paris. Jean waited for him when he went away. The Armistice gave them the reprieve they needed: by Christmas they were engaged, and on 30 April 1919 they were married in The Hague.

Rhys was delighted to escape England, but the stateless Lenglet was perhaps not the best horse to bet on. A passionate man who, like Rhys, leapt before he looked, Lenglet had lost his Dutch citizenship when, in the passionate early days of WWI, he volunteered for the French Foreign Legion without first getting Dutch approval, which was apparently an excommunicable offence in Holland. After the war, he longed to return to Paris with Rhys, who was pregnant. Unfortunately, passports had recently been made a requirement for international travel, and Lenglet no longer had one; by extension, neither did Rhys. He decided they would circumvent that tiny issue by taking the most direct route from Belgium into France: on foot. In her diary, Rhys remembers: '. . . here I was without money & without a passport & going to have a baby. Going without a passport to cross from Belgium to France. How? Just by walking over the frontier. By walking along the road between rows of poplar trees at night. A quiet night with a moon up. Walking along until you get past the sentry & finding yourself in Dunkirk in the early morning so tired so tired . . . And the fear . . . And there we were in France without passports or money & me going to have a baby.' That year, the powerful men of the world had gathered in Paris to negotiate the peace, and to carve up Europe, drawing new borders, and here was Rhys, walking there, right past the guards. It was a terrifying night-walk, but Rhys learned something about the reliable value of putting one foot in front of the other.

They arrived in Paris in the autumn of 1919. She fell in love with the city on the spot. The weather was fine: they sat at a cafe outside, eating spaghetti, the sun shining down on them. The sun she had missed so much in England – not hot like in Dominica, but sun nonetheless. No wonder she said it felt like getting out of prison: even outside on the streets of London, she felt as if she were cooped up inside. 'I've been very faithful and never really loved any other city,' she later wrote.

Although Paris and Dominica were nothing like each other, they were both totally unlike London, and they were both Paradise, to Jean Rhys. The boulevards of Paris couldn't have been more different from the rocky dirt byways of

Dominica. Haussmann shot them through like rays of light, creating the perfect atmosphere in which to wander and dream, or to see and be seen, depending on your inclinations. In Dominica it could take hours to travel a short distance. Rhys's editor, Diana Athill, wrote that she could only truly understand Rhys's 'foreignness' once she had visited her island. 'Except for the one between Roseau and Portsmouth, Dominica's narrow bumpy roads still inspire awe just by existing: so much forest to be cleared, so many ups and downs to be negotiated hairpin after hairpin after hairpin, so many tropical downpours to wash away what has just been achieved . . . and so little money and no earth-moving equipment! They are valiant little roads, and keeping them in repair is a heavy task.'[5] An attempt was made to build a road across the island, proudly named the Imperial Road, but it was never completed (thus go all empires). For Rhys, then, roads were freighted with meaning. Being able to walk anywhere she liked was empowering enough, but to do it in the beauty of Paris was a gift.

+

Paris in 1919 must have felt like the centre of the civilised world. From January to July, the world's great leaders gathered there for the Peace Conference – everyone from Woodrow Wilson, Lloyd George and Georges Clemenceau to T. E. Lawrence, Marie of Romania, and Ho Chi Minh. The Lenglets arrived after the signing of the Versailles Treaty and the inauguration of the League of Nations, and that energy lingered. Although economists like John Maynard Keynes warned that the treaty was inequitable and would prove disastrous in the long term, the world was so relieved that the war was finally over that the naysayers were drowned out. Paris was still fragile from the war; there was a giant hole where the Tuileries rose garden used to be; along the boulevards the trees had been cut down for firewood. The stained-glass windows in Notre-Dame were slowly being replaced (they had been removed and stored away), and there wasn't enough coal, milk or bread. But determined to move on, Paris kicked up its heels at the feeling of having a fresh start. Rhys felt the same way: Paris was a refuge. And she wasn't alone: immigrants flocked to Paris, fleeing the pogroms, revolutions and poverty sweeping across Eastern, Central and Southern Europe. The arts saw a simultaneous flourishing of avant-garde movements as well as a Return to Order (*rappel à l'ordre*) that turned to traditional art forms, initiated by Georges Braque's 1919 show at the gallery L'Effort Moderne. In retrospect, the avant-garde clearly won out. Picasso, Modigliani, Giorgio de Chirico, Marc Chagall, Kees van Dongen, Chaim Soutine, Chana Orloff, Constantin Brancusi, Tamara de Lempicka, Man Ray, Lee Miller, Tsuguharu Foujita, Robert Capa, André Kertész: all came to Paris from around the world, drawn by the formal experimentation taking place there and the cutting-edge modernity it represented. 1919 was a big year for literature in Paris: Marcel Proust won the Goncourt for the second volume of *In Search of Lost Time*; André Breton and Philippe Soupault founded the journal *Littérature* (soon to become the official organ of the nascent Surrealist movement), Sylvia Beach opened her bookshop Shakespeare and Company in the rue Dupuytren near Odéon; and Jean Rhys came to town.

Eighty years later, Paris seemed like the unacknowledged centre of the civilised world. I couldn't believe my good luck, landing in a city where you could buy cheap used paperbacks at bookstalls by the river, or a newspaper covered with dense print (news, not entertainment), and sit and read it in a cafe for hours, where the books on the front table in any bookstore (and there were hundreds of them, everywhere) would be emblazoned with names like Derrida, Foucault, Deleuze. Paris was a heady intellectual melange of ideas to process in extremely stylish settings. I liked La Coupole, on the Boulevard Montparnasse, for its art deco columns and mosaics, and the dish of trail mix they'd bring you with your Kir if you drank at the bar, or the Sélect Café across the street, which managed to be modern and traditional at the same time, and whose impeccably professional tuxedoed waitstaff were jolly and flirtatious.

And it wasn't just intellectual ideas I was trying to process, but personal ones, which, back then, I regarded as one and the same. Soon after I arrived in Paris, I met an American at a friend's party. We danced on tables in a sweaty, smoky bar in the 2nd arrondissement until four in the morning. He too was from Long Island; he too was studying abroad. He looked like a Jewish Patrick Dempsey. I was insecure, and amazed that someone so attractive would be interested in me. One of our first conversations was about my background. 'What kind of name is Elkin?' he asked. 'Russian,' I said. 'So you're Jewish.' 'Half,' I answered. But to a Conservative Jew there are no halves, you either is or you ain't. I wasn't 'Jewish enough' to be his girlfriend, so I became his non-girlfriend and hoped eventually he would come around.

I hadn't yet discovered how important it is to agree to terms. I thought together was together and it didn't matter what you called it. But the longer we were together, the more unsatisfying, insulting even, this arrangement began to feel. We slept together, we travelled together, but if I touched his face he'd push my hand away. He had clamped down: no love would get in, or out. He made not being Jewish – or not Jewish enough – feel like a class inequality, like he was some kind of swell, destined for a society marriage, and I was his youthful indiscretion.

Then I read *Voyage in the Dark*, based on Rhys's affair with Lancelot, about a chorus girl who becomes the mistress of a gentleman. He takes her out and shows her off in certain contexts but not in others, and eventually grows tired of her. Rhys's novels provided a means of understanding what was happening with Jewish Patrick Dempsey. I was his chorus girl! But breaking up with him was out of the question. He was in the ad hoc circle of friends that always stitches together among students abroad; he was at every party, every bar, he was brought up in every conversation. I wouldn't be able to avoid him. And anyway, I didn't want to give up. I was convinced that he would eventually love me back: this wasn't a Jean Rhys novel. I found out from his friend that I was the first person he'd ever slept with. That has to count for *something*, I flattered myself.

Oh, honey, don't flatter yourself, I can hear Rhys cackle.

+

In Rhys's life with Lenglet, fate was kind in some ways and cruel in others. The baby she carried died of pneumonia weeks after his birth. And their stay in Paris was not to last: a few months later Lenglet was dispatched to Vienna, and then Budapest, and then Brussels, where their second child was born. Billeted in these cities, Lenglet seemed able to keep them in relative luxury, but only at a price: they had to flee Lenglet's debtors and take refuge once again in Paris, where, after an attempt to seek temporary asylum in Amsterdam, Lenglet was arrested on charges of theft and imprisoned. With no money and no one to support her, Rhys sent her daughter to be looked after at a clinic in Brussels, and in 1924 moved in with a journalist friend called Pearl Adam.

Good move, Jean. It's all about who you know, especially in Paris in the twenties. Throwing herself on the kindness of friends in this way led to her big break as a writer. As Rhys tells the story, she went to Adam to try to get journalism work for Lenglet; Adam didn't care for his writing, but she asked Rhys if she had done any writing of her own. Rhys showed Adam some notebooks she had been keeping as a diary. Adam, impressed, put them together to create a manuscript she called *Suzy Tells*, in three parts, with each part named for a different man, and sent them off to Ford Madox Ford, then editor of the *transatlantic review*. He decided to mentor Rhys, and when her first story collection, *The Left Bank*, was published in 1927, he wrote the preface.

Rhys was not part of the expatriate scene in Paris. Though she writes about the bohemian 5th and 6th arrondissements, staying close to the river in Saint-Michel and Saint-Germain, she herself lived in the down-and-out 13th, a neighbourhood in the south of Paris that to this day has still not quite thrown off this air of shabbiness. In a 1964 letter to Diana Athill, she commented, 'The "Paris" all these people write about, Henry Miller, even Hemingway etc. was not "Paris" at all – it was "America in Paris" or "England in Paris." The real Paris had nothing to do with that lot – As soon as the tourists came the *real* Montparnos packed up and left.'[6] She met Hemingway and Gertrude Stein and Alice B. Toklas through Ford; the so-called 'Queen of Bohemia', Nina Hamnett, called her 'Ford's girl'.[7] But she avoided their company.

Ford was a large – Hemingway said 'walrus'-like – man and a powerful one, too. The renowned editor of the *transatlantic review* and *English Review,* which had published authors like D. H. Lawrence and Wyndham Lewis, and the author of *The*

Good Soldier (1915), Ford's opinion was well known and well respected in the literary world. Ford's personal life, however, raised a few eyebrows. In spite of his physical appearance he was quite the ladies' man, and his unconventional love life caused such a scandal he had to leave London and move abroad with his mistress, the Australian painter Stella Bowen, in the early 1920s. James Joyce would write of him:

> O Father O'Ford you've a masterful way with you
> Maid, wife and widow are wild to make hay with you.

Ford was another of these solid, protective types Rhys sought out over and over. He quite literally created Jean Rhys, by suggesting she change her name from Ella Lenglet. More profoundly, Ford helped her not only to become a writer but to see herself as one. She had a work ethic, spending hours locked in her room committing ink to paper, but he educated her literary judgement. He helped her understand when a story was getting too melodramatic, and he gave her writing exercises: if a sentence wasn't working, he suggested, try translating it into French, and if it still wouldn't do, chuck it out. Ford had, in his youth, lived with the older writer Joseph Conrad, working at all hours together, collaborating on three novels. When Rhys came to live with Ford and Stella Bowen, it was his turn to play the live-in mentor. But Rhys was no bearded middle-aged Polish sailor. For a man of Ford's appetites, a lovely young woman living in your spare room is difficult to resist, and the relationship inevitably went beyond mentoring.

Things ended badly, of course. Rhys would later find it difficult to take the full measure of Ford's impact on her, writing to Francis Wyndham, 'I don't *think* he influenced my writing, but he influenced me tremendously which is the same thing. [...] I'm afraid I can't write about it coherently so won't try.'⁸ But their affair proved to have nearly limitless literary potential, as each of the parties went on to write their own fictionalised account of it: Rhys wrote *Quartet* (first published in 1928 as *Postures*), Ford *When the Wicked Man* (1932), Bowen her autobiography, *Drawn From Life* (1941, in which she described Rhys as 'a really tragic person' who 'had written an unpublishable sordid novel'), and Lenglet a novel called *Barred* (1932).⁹ Though it defies credulity, Rhys herself translated *Barred* into English, edited it heavily, and fought hard to see it published, under the pseudonym Edward de Nève. Some suggest she completely rewrote it: it does read very much like her own novels.

+

In Paris in 1999, I had no Ford Madox Ford to learn from: instead I had Ernest Hemingway. Swaggering Hemingway, whose every period is a bullet hole, in whose work, as the critic Jacob Michael Leland has written, 'the Hemingway hero loses some version of his maleness to the first World War, and he replaces it with a tool – in Upper Michigan, a fishing rod or a pocketknife; in Africa, a hunting rifle'.¹⁰ The man who married sweet Hadley Richardson, then betrayed her with Pauline Pfeiffer, whom he then left for Martha Gellhorn, the first woman who was his equal as a writer and reporter, and whom he tried to outfox and out-scoop when she made him feel inadequate. (After their marriage dissolved, Gellhorn would walk out of the room if anyone tried to bring up her years with Papa.) I learned from this most unlikely of teachers, until I found Jean Rhys.

To say I found my copy of *A Moveable Feast* inspiring would be an understatement. Whereas today I would be too embarrassed to be seen in public in Paris holding a copy of it – when I taught *The Sun Also Rises* I refused to take it out of my bag on the métro – back in 1999 I was guileless, and sat happily reading away in a cafe near my flat, pausing to write in long draughts. From the first chapter, I knew this book wasn't like anything I'd read previously, as young Hemingway evokes the city I was coming to love, what makes a cafe good to work in, and tucks in to a *café au lait*, a rum St James, a dozen oysters and a half-carafe of white wine while writing a short story and looking at all the people in the cafe. For most of my teenage years I had been reading anything I could get my hands on, which basically meant whatever they had at the Smithtown branch of the Commack Public Library: from Madeleine L'Engle and Toni Morrison to Sylvia Plath and romance novels set in the Regency period (will the high-spirited Josephine marry the soldier or the rake?). Even books I came to at university, like Jeanette Winterson's *The Passion*, or E. M. Forster's *A Room With a View*, were all novels, and distant from my experience. But *A Moveable Feast* showed me a young American in Left Bank Paris, sitting in cafes and learning to be a writer. Hemingway wasn't much older than I was, although he had been through the First World War, and was married, not to mention a macho macho man, whereas I was a single, naive young university student from the suburbs, who had only ever seen a war mediated through television and photographs, pre-digested by the American news machine. But in spite of the biographical differences between us, I felt we had the same instincts. The happy intersection of the cafe, with all its stimulants, the work and the random people the city brought across my path, gave me the ideal context in which to write.

In the *papeterie* of the Galeries Lafayette I found these two smallish spiral notebooks, about the size of a paperback book,

filled with unlined pages of a nice stock, not too hefty, not too
light, one with a mint-green cover, the other vanilla, and
carried one then the other all over Paris with me, filling the
blank pages whenever I had a spare moment. I still carry a
notebook with me everywhere I go. I learned to do that from
Hemingway.

But I was put off by Hemingway's habit of approaching
the city and its inhabitants with a sense of mastery. Spying a
lovely young woman sitting near the door of the cafe,
Hemingway felt inspired to 'put her in the story' he was
writing about Michigan, but, he writes, 'she had placed
herself so she could watch the street and the entry and I
knew she was waiting for someone'. It's almost a non
sequitur – it seems as if Hemingway is going to explain why
he couldn't write her into the story, and instead he says she
was waiting for someone, as if to say she already belonged
to someone, somewhere else, and could therefore not be
'put' anywhere Hemingway wanted her. Unruffled, he finds
a way around her boyfriend, writing, famously, 'I've seen
you, beauty, and you belong to me now, whoever you are
waiting for and if I never see you again, I thought. You
belong to me and all Paris belongs to me and I belong to
this notebook and this pencil.'[11] I sat in my own cafe and
looked around me, but I didn't see any particularly lovely
girls, or lovely boys, and if I had it's doubtful I would have
felt they belonged to me. It's hard today for me not to bristle
at Hemingway's association of seeing with power – women,
Paris, everything he surveys 'belongs' to him and his pencil.
What I felt, on the other hand, was not a sense of possession,
but one of belonging.

+

Rhys also became a writer by accident, after buying some notebooks. At loose ends in London after her love affair with Lancelot failed, she had moved into a depressing, bare bedsit in a neighbourhood appropriately named World's End. 'I must get some flowers or a plant or something,' she recalls thinking, so she went out to look for some.[12]

I passed a stationer's shop where quill pens were displayed in the window, a lot of them, red, blue, green, yellow. Some of them would be all right in a glass, to cheer up my table. I went into the shop and bought about a dozen. Then I noticed some black exercise books on the counter. They were not at all like exercise books are now. They were twice the thickness, the stiff black covers were shiny, the spine and the edges were red, and the pages were ruled. I bought several of those, I didn't know why, just because I liked the look of them. I got a box of J nibs, the sort I liked, an ordinary pen-holder, a bottle of ink and a cheap ink-stand. Now that old table won't look so bare, I thought.

This crucial step towards writing came from wandering, from a need to cheer up an ugly table, to make a room her own. These notebooks were the ones Rhys would show to Pearl Adam.

The time Rhys spent with Ford helped her claim herself as a writer. In order to become a writer, Rhys had to 'give up her dream of being a happy woman. And it was Ford himself who made her give that up, finally and forever . . . Like Mackenzie with Julia, he had "destroyed some necessary illusions about herself".'[13] This seems a heavy-handed reading of the affair, one that subscribes to the notion that people – especially women – must suffer for their art. Rhys's women are not artists, as she herself unquestionably was; if anything, this is why they suffer: they don't have anything to sustain them. And just because Rhys was unhappy when things went south with Ford does not mean that she remained unhappy ever after; she married two more men, and one must suppose there was some joy in those relationships. Let us remember that she was not an innocent young woman who was taken advantage of by a more worldly older man; by the time Ford came along she was already a thirty-year-old wife and mother. Ford was a turning point in her life; just as for Julia in *After Leaving Mr Mackenzie* there was a before and an after Mackenzie, for Rhys there was a before and an after Ford. He was not some harbinger of the innate misery of the writer's life. Rather, he was the catalyst that led to the realisation that she was irretrievably different from other people, and would never be able to get along as they did. This, I think, was the source of much of whatever unhappiness there was in her life, that drove her to drink as she did.

Rhys saw the world with what Virginia Woolf called a 'difference of view'. It's there in her female characters: they can't dress right or talk right or give the right answers to questions; they give too much information or not enough or the wrong kind. The city is a place where we can finally be ourselves, but even in Paris, there's still no escaping other people's judgement. Some of us live 'outside the machine', as Rhys put it in a story about a young Englishwoman suffering from depression in a French clinic, where she's awaiting some unspecified surgery.[14] She sees the nurses and other patients as being 'like parts of a machine', which gives them 'a strength, a certainty', that she lacks, and that she is convinced they will find out she lacks. The machine is always right, and it has the power to dispose of broken parts: '"Useless, this one," they would say.' In Rhys's 1969 story 'I Spy a Stranger', set in wartime England, Laura herself has become part of the machine, which even as it assimilates her aims to destroy her: '[There was a] mechanical quality about everything and everybody which I found frightening. When I bought a ticket for the Tube, got on a bus, went into a shop, I felt like a cog in a machine in contact with others, not like one human being associated with other human beings. The feeling that I had been drawn into a mechanism which intended to destroy me became an obsession.'[15]

The men Rhys's women get involved with are very much 'inside the machine'; and so must they be, as providers of money and protection. In *After Leaving Mr Mackenzie*, the title character stands for an English moral code. Mr Mackenzie is described as someone who had once had rather romantic ambitions. 'Once, in his youth,' Rhys writes, 'he had published a small book of poems'; but then he discovered that those 'who allow themselves to be blown about by the winds of emotion and impulse are always unhappy people'.[16] He consequently 'adopted a certain mental attitude, a certain code of morals and manners, from which he seldom departed'. This is the code he attempts to hold Julia to. 'My darling child,' Heidler, the Ford character in *Quartet*, says calmly, 'your whole point of view and your whole attitude to life is impossible and wrong and you've got to change it for everybody's sake.'[17] She must learn to keep up appearances. As Heidler rags on, Marya thinks to herself: 'He looks exactly like a picture of Queen Victoria.'

Rhys is a much funnier writer than she is generally given credit for being.

The code, the machine, the game. *Your whole point of view and your whole attitude to life is impossible and wrong.* Rhys's woman can't play the game; she rejects its inhuman and arbitrary rules, rules which are stacked against her. Why can't she seem to get on? everyone around her wonders. Surely she's not really trying. 'Get on or get out,' Anna thinks in *Voyage in the Dark*.[18] I felt the same way; but while Rhys's women can't find an escape anywhere from the social forces that keep them down, and repeatedly make the worst of the limited choices available to them, I saw Paris as an escape from a place where I had wanted to fit in, but didn't. Maybe that's why I took up with this boy from Long Island: he was exactly the kind of guy who never would have gone for me back home. Dating him, no matter how humiliating, was a way of showing – who? – that I could, in fact, *get on*, if I really wanted to. But on some level, I understood that I was kidding myself.

+

I went walking with Rhys in the streets of Montparnasse. I walked up and down the boulevard, between home and school; I dined at its restaurants, sat in La Coupole, where for five francs you could get a big pot of coffee and an equally big pot of steamed milk, and stay at your table for hours and hours. Sometimes I went to Le Sélect and played with their enormous lazy cat. On rare occasions I switched to La Rotonde, just for a change. Cafes where Rhys's women would drop in for an aperitif, a second aperitif, a third aperitif, until some nice man would stand them some dinner. I didn't know how to get a man to pay for my dinners – this is not a skill you pick up at Barnard. Instead I sat for hours scribbling into those notebooks, worrying for pages over what was happening in my life. I suspected that all my wondering about this boy, analysing his every word, was a way of avoiding the truth. We were doomed; he was a dick. But, I had decided, I *loved* him. I would fight on.

Like Rhys, Ford was an enthusiastic city walker. In fact, he went so far as to credit a walk in London with having cured him of a nervous breakdown in 1904. In his autobiography, he recounts having been told by a certain Doctor Tebb that, given his strung-out mental condition, he would surely be dead in a month. Where another person might go home and try to get some rest, Ford headed straight for Piccadilly Circus, and walked around there for an hour and a half, muttering, 'Damn that brute. I will not be dead in a month.' As he fought the traffic round Piccadilly, his physical ills disappeared: by walking in this extremely unpleasant part of London, he more or less *shocked* himself well.[19]

This improvised walking cure inspired Ford to write about the city. The book he produced in 1905, *The Soul of London*, would launch his career. Ever Conrad's student, Ford invokes the language of the sailor to express London's unknowability. 'One may sail easily round England, or circumnavigate the globe. But not even the most enthusiastic geographer . . . ever memorised a map of London. Certainly no one ever walks round it. For England it is a small island, the world is infinitesimal amongst the planets. But London is illimitable.' To comprehend it, Ford writes, calls for a very particular combination of skills: 'an impressionability and an impersonality, a single-mindedness to see, and a power of arranging his illustrations cold-bloodedly, an unemotional mind and a great sympathy, a life-long engrossment in his "subject", and an immense knowledge, for purposes of comparison, of other cities. He must have an avidity and a sobriety of intellect, an untirable physique and a delicately tempered mind.' He must be, in other words, a *flâneur*.

Ford said it was crucial for the novelist to be able to 'pass unobserved in the crowd if he himself is to observe'. The very first thing the novelist must learn, he wrote, 'is self-effacement – the first and that always'. This aligns the novelist with the *flâneur*, who is at once a man of the crowd and an observer of it.[20] This is impossible for a woman like Rhys, or the women she invents. How to walk past a cafe terrace unnoticed, when the chairs face the street, the better to allow patrons to scrutinise the world as it goes by? While the *flâneur* – and the male novelist – has the freedom to pass unobserved in the crowd, Rhys's characters move through the city, painfully aware that they are mocked. They try, desperately, to be invisible. They may spend all their money on clothing – the astrakhan coat as protective camouflage – but they are inevitably caught out, accosted by men who are disappointed to find they aren't as beautiful close up as they appeared to be from afar. They try for self-effacement, but this is impossible. They avoid meeting people they know; they steel themselves against the smirks and glares they expect to receive. '*Pourquoi êtes-vous si triste?*' strange men in the street ask Marya and Sasha, and the question echoes through each novel like a marble dropped into a pipe. Sasha stares at herself in the mirror, downstairs in a cafe bathroom. 'What do I want to cry about?'

Rhys and Ford had different ideas about the best way to write Paris. In Ford's preface to *The Left Bank* he laments Rhys's refusal to include physical descriptions of the city in her stories. Not even some of its 'topography'? he asked. Not only did she say no, he recalled, but she went and cut the few descriptive words that had somehow crept in. She refused to romanticise Paris for him. 'Her business was with passion, hardship, emotions: the locality in which these things are endured is immaterial,' he observed.[21]

Reading these stories and novels, it's hard to agree. They're saturated with Paris, though perhaps not in such a way that might delight the armchair traveller, as Ford would have liked. Rhys takes some of the more familiar aspects of Left Bank Paris – the Boulevard Saint-Michel, the Boulevard Montparnasse; the Seine, a *quai*, a cafe, a shop – and transforms them as she filters them through the emotional life of her protagonists. In *Quartet*, when Marya's husband has been arrested, the trees on the Boulevard Clichy stretch 'ridiculously frail and naked arms to a sky without stars', as if the city and Marya were one, bereft and exposed; as if the shock had transformed Marya into a dryad, or the dryad into the city.[22] Later, walking down the rue Saint-Jacques, which she renames 'the street of homeless cats', she identifies with the felines she sees there, 'prowling, thin vagabonds, furtive, aloof, but strangely proud'.[23] Instead of making the city an object, Marya turns it into a fantastical mirror. Then, too, walking can be a form of self-avoidance: she spends the next 'foggy' day 'in endless, aimless walking, for it seemed to her that if she moved quickly enough she would escape the fear that hunted her'.[24] When she has decided it's no use worrying about things, the 'endless labyrinth of Parisian streets' fill her with a 'strange excitement'.[25]

Sasha's Montparnasse has a very personal topography, comprised of 'cafes where they like me and cafes where they don't, streets that are friendly and streets that aren't, rooms where I might be happy, rooms where I shall never be'.[26] All the novels are set mainly in cafes, hotels and the city streets their heroines walk after humiliating encounters in these cafes and hotels. A bit of *lèche-vitrine* – window-shopping – gives them something to aim for: a new hat, a new dress, a new coat, and all will be well. The city streets may blend together, or continue interminably, or remind her of London, but they contain untold surprises. Hope, in a Rhys novel, is never knowing what's around the next corner. Marya catches at bits and scraps – the 'drone of a concertina', as a man tries to play 'Yes! We Have No Bananas'. His mangling of the song gives Marya 'the same feeling of melancholy pleasure as she had when walking along the shadowed side of one of those narrow streets full of shabby parfumeries, second-hand bookstalls, cheap hat-shops, bars frequented by gaily-painted ladies and loud-voiced men, midwives' premises . . .'[27]

Rhys's heroines prefer the bits of Paris that stick out, rough and untameable, to those which are sanded-down, well-travelled. Against her husband's wishes, Marya goes *flâneuse*-ing past the limits of respectable Montparnasse and out into the interstitial parts where the 14th meets the 15th, turning down side streets and discovering places like the restaurant 'full of men in caps who bawled intimacies at each other; a gramophone played without ceasing; a beautiful white dog under the counter, which everybody called Zaza and threw bones to, barked madly'.[28] Even on the beaten path Marya finds the places that really aren't *comme il faut*. The Café Zanzi-Bar, for instance, on the much-travelled Boulevard Montparnasse which is 'not one of those popular places swarming with the shingled and long-legged and their partners, who all wear picturesque collars and an incredibly contemptuous expression. No, it is small, half-empty, cheapish. Coffee costs five centimes less than in the Rotonde, for instance.' In Rhys's story 'The Blue Bird', her protagonist goes to the popular cafe Le Dôme. It is a hot day, and everyone sits outside on the terrace ('There were the usual number of young gentlemen with high voices, carefully shabby trousers, jerseys, caressing gestures, undulating hips, and the usual number of the stony broke sitting haughtily behind cafés-crème'). The woman and her companion, however, sit inside, away from the crowd.[29]

Among the odd and the idiosyncratic is where Rhys's women feel at home. In one of Julia's walks she is fascinated by a shop window 'exhibiting casts of deformed feet, stuffed dogs and foxes, or photographs of the moon'.[30] She spends a long time standing in front of a shop in the rue de Seine, whose window features a picture 'representing a male figure encircled by what appeared to be a huge mauve corkscrew. At the end of the picture was written "*La vie est un spiral, flottant dans l'espace, que les hommes grimpent et redescendent très, très sérieusement*". Life is a spiral, floating in space, that men climb up and down very, very seriously.[31] Women like Julia stand outside, watching them do it. But outside can be a very soothing place to be. Wandering the streets, looking in shop windows, going nowhere in particular, Julia feels 'serene and peaceful'. 'Her limbs moved smoothly; the damp, soft air was pleasant against her face. She felt complete in herself, detached, independent of the rest of humanity.'[32] It is the tragedy of Rhys's novels, and the lives of the women they describe, that they are denied the right to stand quietly alone outside: the machine doesn't work that way.

+

Rhys was a Left Bank girl, like I used to be. We only crossed the river for business or love. Or attempts at love. I spent many nights with him in his small room in the 2nd arrondissement, near the Bourse. On his street, the rue du Quatre Septembre, right next to his building, there was a cafe called Le Saint-Laurent. That my name glowed in neon right next to where he lived I took to be a good – well, a good sign. The nights all run together now, and announce themselves as one night, the first and the last. He is wearing a red long-sleeved polo and the apartment is too warm. A cat named Myrtille belonging to his flatmate (a girl whose name, unlike the cat's, I've forgotten) stalks by. The kettle has boiled; a tea bag is in the mug: *thé à la menthe*. A jar of solid honey stands beside it. The memory of that first night, when I made the choice to stay, is distilled like the dried leaves in the bag, any time I make mint tea on a winter's night in Paris. A little hot water and it all comes back, a room six storeys above a courtyard daubed with steel-grey cobblestones looking out over a clatter of rooftops and chimneys, the night sky shot through with bleach. I could hear Björk in my head as I looked out over the rooftops into the courtyard, Björk imagining the sound of her body *slamming against those rocks*. The mouth of the window welled open so wide that the rooftops and cobblestones seemed more real, more crisp, than the unreality of what was happening inside the bedroom. But the cold reality of the cobblestones kept me in place, kept me from twirling out.

Rhys didn't commit suicide, she didn't even try. She thought it was sentimental, and cowardly. But she inched close to the edge, drugging herself with luminal, as I did with alcohol, and we both lay in bed, inert, the day after. We rolled ourselves closer to the edge to prove we could keep from going over, to savour how it might feel there. There was no perspective to be gained from our great heights; the higher we went, the closer in we got. The French have an expression for it: *la joie du malheur*. The Modigliani cover is just the right choice for this book, which includes a passage in which Julia feels both entranced and judged by the painting. The things that are the most fascinating can be the most hurtful.

Lying in the narrow bed in the early morning as the birds began to sing, him on his side facing the wall, me pressed against his back, my thoughts wandered. What am I doing here, in this grey morning, with this person who doesn't want me, but doesn't want me to go?

I listened to Björk a lot in those days, especially that song, with its wish to feel protected. That was all I wanted when I was twenty: to feel safe again, once I had learned what it felt like to feel unsafe. I was letting this machine person drive over me: I had to learn to push back, to get up, to back away from the window.

+

I was reminded of all of this well over a decade later, when I was now the professor in the study-abroad programme, teaching *Good Morning, Midnight* in a class on Paris in literature. The students identified with Sasha's plight, just as I once did, on the basis of their own unhappiness, native to the twenty-year-old who has not yet learned to ask for what she wants, or may hardly know it herself. Twenty-year-olds – the kind who wander the streets of Paris looking for meaning – are hungry for experience, but they haven't yet learned self-protection. They run headlong into despair, just to know how it feels, maybe to find out how strong they are.

A week later, I ran into the school psychologist. 'You're the culprit!' she said. 'You're the one who taught Jean Rhys last week.' 'Yes,' I said warily. 'Why?' 'I had four of your students come to see me, totally shattered by that book!' A couple of those students came to my office hours. One was the most dynamic person in the class, a flamboyant Gallatin major who had so identified with the book that he waved it in the air and declared: 'I am Jean Rhys!' He was having a tough time romantically, and was worried that there was nothing he could do to be happy again. It felt, he said, both lonely and fascinating to be so devastated so far from home. Another came to me in tears. Her boyfriend had cheated on her. He made her feel unattractive and uninteresting.

Twenty years old is like forty, that way. The person we're losing always feels like the last person who'll want us. We're always staring off the edge of the cliff, even before the lined face and the grey hair. It's just that when we're twenty, we can't imagine how much more desperate things can get.

I'll never meet anyone else who'll love me like he did, my student said. *Thank God for that*, I tried not to answer.

Northern line to Tottenham Court Road Station, up Tottenham Court Road, past the Carphone Warehouse, past Boots, past the massive Pret (you could be anywhere in London, anywhere in Britain), right on Bedford Avenue, anyone's guess from there

LONDON

BLOOMSBURY

*Also London itself perpetually attracts, stimulates, gives me a play
& a story & a poem, without any trouble, save that of moving my
legs through the streets.*

—Virginia Woolf, *Diary*, 31 May 1928

I'm standing on Bloomsbury Street, but on Google Maps it's
called Bedford Square.

Inspecting the yellow London streets criss-crossing the
small square screen of my BlackBerry, I click 'search map'. I
type 'Bloomsbury Street'. The search box suggests alternatives.
Did you mean Bloomsbury Way? Or Bloomsbury Square? it
asks. It wants to be helpful. It isn't. The blue dot blinks on a
corner that is, from all evidence, not the one I'm on. I can't
narrow the distance between where I am and where I need
to be because I'm not where the map thinks I am. But what
if I'm not where I think I am? Where am I? It's a smartphone-
prompted existential crisis. Where has Oxford Street gone?
Where has north gone? As I make turn after turn, the map on
the phone and the streets before me diverge in a proliferation
of nearly identical names: Bedford Square, Bedford Avenue,
Bedford Court Mansions. This is why I'm now standing on

Bloomsbury Bedford Street Square Way, in a hyper-aware
state of confusion. The slightest clue seems meaningful, but
what it means, there's no way of knowing. I think of a famous
1922 talk Virginia Woolf gave to her friends in their Memoir
Club, in which she asks, 'where does Bloomsbury end? What
is Bloomsbury? Does it for instance include Bedford Square?'[1]
As far as I can tell, all of Bloomsbury is contained within
Bedford Square, from which there is no escaping.

This is a neighbourhood I thought I knew. I've walked down
Tottenham Court Road many, many times. But today I've
encountered an unexpected amount of construction, and I'm
thrown. They are building something very deep in the bowels
of the city, and up here, on its skin, all the usual features are
deformed. I may well have taken a left into downtown Beijing.

I need to get to a conference in Senate House. I walk a
little further in the direction I understand to be correct.
Nothing familiar. I ask a construction worker if he knows
Malet Street. I assume, since he's reshaping the territory, he
must have a sense of the map. 'Malet?' he asks. I spell it. He
doesn't know. 'What is the name of the street we're on?' I ask.
He doesn't know. I gesture towards the end of the road, where
some kind of green area is visible. 'That over there, is that
Russell Square?' 'Why everyone ask me where is Russell?' he
replies. I thank him and leave him to his work.

The conference begins in ten minutes, and I have to make a
good impression. I'm a recently minted PhD, about to go on the
job market, a daunting prospect in this economy, and I don't
want to be the girl who comes in late on the first day. I cannot
cause a disruption. Please let me just slip in. Why didn't I leave
extra time? Or bring my *A–Z*? *Why do I always get so fucking lost?*

On a whim or a hunch, I turn left, and find myself directly
in front of Senate House.

+

Funny to be lost in Bloomsbury, when at one time I knew it better than any other place in London. I had never been there until 2004, the summer before I moved to Paris. I was in town for a conference on Virginia Woolf commemorating the hundredth anniversary of her move to Bloomsbury from Kensington, where she was raised. After their father's death, Woolf and her siblings left their family home at 22 Hyde Park Gate, and started a new life in what was, at the time, an unusual choice of neighbourhood. Woolf continued to live in Bloomsbury (with a ten-year exception when her husband made her live in the suburbs) until just before her death; it was a district that sustained her and inspired her and kept her pen in ink. I stayed in Gower Street, a row of terraced houses turned into hotels, with shared bathrooms on the landings in between floors – the kind of gently worn British establishment with sinks in the rooms, and a kettle. There, I could imagine myself an emancipated single young woman living in a 1920s bedsit, maybe working in a travel agency, like Emmeline in Elizabeth Bowen's *To the North*.

It was June (life, London, this moment in June) and London couldn't have been more different from my first visit, one rainy, wet January in 1999, which gave me the worst case of bronchitis I'd ever swallowed. It was Bloomsbury that corrected the terrible first impressions of London I had retained from that trip, when I was exposed to the wretched tourist itinerary of Trafalgar Square, Piccadilly Circus and Madame Tussaud's. I remember taking the Eurostar back to Paris in disgust. Why does anyone *bother* with London? I wrote in my journal. But that June of 2004 was the first time London had lifted her skirts and showed a shapely bit of ankle. Oh, I thought, I think I get it now. I picked up a few battered orange Penguin Classics for a pound at a used bookstore; I was handed my first Pimm's Cup outside at a pub, sitting at a picnic table. I bought an array of readyfood at Pret and sat down to eat it in a patch of sun on the grass in Russell Square, looking at the other people doing the same, who with my outsider's eyes I took to be Londoners, enjoying their city, but who may well also have been Americans on their second visit to London discovering its charms at the same rate as I was.

I wanted to see London as Woolf had seen it, and set to tracking down her various addresses. I strolled in Tavistock Square, where she lived from 1924 to 1939. In the park in the centre, I walked past a bronze bust of Woolf I did not like; I found out later it had been placed there by the very group who had organised the conference I was attending. The bronze was pockmarked, gnarled, her skin coarse and scaly as if she had lived to a hundred instead of fifty-nine. I tried to picture her with soft flesh, soft hair, instead of hard bronze, wrought into some expressionist idea of a great writer, and wondered what kind of shoes she was wearing. (Busts never have shoes.) This was the Bloomsbury square Woolf lived in the longest; this was where most of the novels were written. I walked round and round but couldn't find her building. I remembered the address was number 52, and knew that the house had been bombed in the war, but hadn't realised the site is now occupied by the Tavistock Hotel, a modern brick-and-glass building, institutional, vaguely medical-looking. As I stood contemplating the even, textureless brick, a million moments of Woolf's life flooded in, as if I were living them all at once, a compression of time through study and recall: Woolf walking around the outside of the square, one day in the mid-1920s, thinking up the *To the Lighthouse* in, as she later wrote, 'a great involuntary rush'.[2] Finding a flat in Bedford Row (or Place? or Square?) which was only to be let furnished, whereas the Woolfs already had furnishings, and which because of its unavailability came to seem to her the finest flat in all London.[3] Walking in Oxford Street in 1930, observing people fighting, struggling, '[k]nocking each other off the pavement. Old bareheaded men; a motor car accident; &tc,' then noting 'To walk alone in London is the greatest rest'.⁴ Woolf reviewing E. V. Lucas for the *TLS* and realising, 'Personally, we should be willing to read one volume about every street in the city, and should still ask for more.'⁵ Writing in her diary in 1925, 'I like this London life in early summer – the street sauntering & square haunting.'⁶ That moment in *The Years* when Peggy remembers the bombings of 1918 and thinks to herself, 'On every placard on every street corner was Death; or worse – tyranny; brutality; torture; the fall of civilization; the end of freedom. We here, she thought, are only sheltering under a leaf, which will be destroyed.' And then Woolf walking in Tavistock Square in 1940, looking at the bombed-out shell of their house: 'Basement all rubble. Only relics an old basket chair (bought in Fitzroy Square days) & Penmans board To Let. Otherwise bricks & wood splinters. One glass door in the next door house hanging. I cd just see a piece of my studio wall standing: otherwise rubble where I wrote so many books. Open air where we sat so many nights, gave so many parties.'⁷

Throughout 1940 and 1941, she and Leonard mainly lived in Sussex, but she came to town as often as she could, and would go walking, taking in the damage. It 'raked my heart', she wrote to Ethyl Smyth, to see 'the passion of my life, that is the City of London' reduced to rubble.⁸ It seemed, she wrote, 'like a dead city'. She grew sentimental, asking Ethel, 'Have you that feeling for certain alleys and little courts, between Chancery Lane and the City?'⁹ Then, in February 1941, she complained in her diary that she had not gone walking in 'ever so long', and, not incidentally, in the same entry, worried 'shall I ever write again one of those sentences that gives me intense pleasure?'¹⁰ A month later, she walked into the River Ouse with rocks in her pockets.¹¹

+

The following summer I was in my apartment in Paris when the square was bombed again. Wrote Ian McEwan, in the *Guardian*, 'It is unlikely that London will claim to have been transformed in an instant, to have lost its innocence in the course of a morning. [. . .] It has survived many attacks in the past.'[12] The reference, of course, was to my own city, New York, which had never been attacked before 2001. London, on the other hand, had seen battles. This was one more. Londoners were still unsettled, McEwan noted; they wanted to know: is it safe to ride the Tube, the bus? And the state would step in to assure that security. But, he wondered, 'how much power must we grant Leviathan, how much freedom will we be asked to trade for our security?'

It's a trade many of us are unwilling to make.

For months afterward there were tanks on the streets of Manhattan, and to this day, squadrons of men with machine guns roam the train stations. Today, there are eight armed guards standing outside my building in Paris, protecting the Jewish school next door, after the attacks on *Charlie Hebdo* and the Hyper Cacher.

And it becomes part of what life is.[13]

+

Since that summer, I've visited Bloomsbury with great regularity, to sit in the parks, to visit the British Museum, or the London Review Bookshop, or Persephone Books, to meet friends for Szechuan after a long day at the British Library. Which is why it was so odd to lose my way so utterly. Back in my room after the conference, squinting at my *A–Z*, I tried to map the Bedfords, so as not to repeat my mistake the next morning. It turns out everything around there is part of the

Bedford Estate, owned by the Russell family, the Dukes of Bedford. All the squares round there belong to them – Bedford Square, Bloomsbury Square, Gordon Square, Russell Square, Tavistock Square, Torrington Square and Woburn Square. Every square is secretly Bedford Square. And every square has its requisite blue plaques indicating the former residence of various members of the Bloomsbury Group. The one at Gordon Square reads:

Their informal society, which also included Roger Fry, John Maynard Keynes and E. M. Forster, was instrumental to the freedom Woolf discovered in that part of town, particularly after one night when Lytton Strachey broke the ice maintained over several years' cordiality by gesturing at a white stain on Vanessa's dress and asking, 'Semen?' Once she got over her shock, Woolf wrote, 'There was now nothing that one could not say, nothing that one could not do, at 46 Gordon Square.'[14] 'They lived in squares, painted in circles, and loved in triangles,' Dorothy Parker reportedly said. But before they were the Bloomsbury Group, they were a disparate assortment of educated and artistically inclined people who had their own ideas about things.

Though once genteel and bourgeois, Bloomsbury had declined in the early twentieth century, and you were more likely to find a young clerk living there than a respectable society lady. It was decidedly *not* the kind of place that young ladies like the Misses Stephen would move to, if they could help it. A deeply historical, literary neighbourhood, it surely would have appealed to Woolf on those grounds, and it did to me as well. The British Museum was built on the site of Montague House, which was once home to some famous frescoes and furniture, making it a place that has for many years housed things that are valuable to one regime or another. Russell Square was famously home to the Sedleys and Osbornes in Thackeray's *Vanity Fair* (Thackeray was related to Woolf by marriage; Leslie Stephen's first wife was the novelist's daughter). According to Augustus J. C. Hare, author of the 1879 volume *Walks in London*, which Woolf received on her fourteenth birthday from her half-brother George, the name is a corruption of 'Blemundsbury', which was the thirteenth-century manor of 'De Blemontes, Blemunds, or Blemonts'.[15] Everything in that neighbourhood 'commemorates the glories of that great ducal family'. Howland Street and Streatham Street, for instance, 'record the marriage of the second duke with the daughter of John Howland of Streatham in 1696. Gower Street and Keppel Street, built 1778–86, commemorate his son, who was made Lord-Lieutenant of Ireland in 1756.' Gordon and Torrington Squares indicate other marriages the family made. And not far from where I stood, totally lost near Bedford Square, number 6 had been home to a certain Lord Eldon from 1809 to 1815, in whose home, Hare recounts, the Prince Regent 'wrung from him the appointment to the vacant post of Master in Chancery for his friend Jekyll the wit'.[16]

The move to Bloomsbury was thanks, in part, to Vanessa; she packed up the old house, found them the new one, and organised the move across town, all while Virginia was in the countryside recuperating from her latest breakdown and suicide attempt. 'It was thus that 46 Gordon Square came into existence,' Woolf writes, as if Vanessa had done no less than construct the building herself, brick by brick. In a pair of essays delivered to the Memoir Club, an informal gathering in which Bloomsbury types would give autobiographical accounts of themselves, Virginia twice contrasted the Kensington house with her home in Gordon Square. It seemed she could not speak of the one without mentioning the other. In 'Old Bloomsbury' Woolf writes that the 'shadow' of 22 Hyde Park Gate lay across Bloomsbury; '46 Gordon Square could never have meant what it did had not 22 Hyde Park Gate preceded it', and, no doubt, the 'gloom' of 22 Hyde Park Gate was darkened in Woolf's mind by the free-spirited life she led afterward.[17] Bloomsbury seemed 'the most beautiful, the most exciting, the most romantic place in the world'.[18] Hyde Park Gate had a muffled, protected air around it, but in Bloomsbury she heard the 'roar' of traffic, and encountered all God's creation on the streets: 'Odd characters, sinister, strange, prowled and slunk past our windows.'[19]

As the neighbourhood had fallen out of favour Bloomsbury had become more affordable, attracting the shabbily genteel, if not the desperately poor; full of bedsits, it was home to many single young working women.[20] Jean Rhys lived in Torrington Square in 1917, in a cheap boarding house where there were 'hairs in the soup', that was 'draughty, dirty, and disreputable', but nevertheless 'comfortable, warm, *fun*'.[21] The local newspapers were full of advertisements of rooms to let, specifically for young women, and there were many boarding houses that were subsidised to help them out, 'often run by philanthropic organizations, where women could live communally with a private bedsitting room but shared dining and living areas'.[22] Thomas Burke, a popular writer of the time, claimed it was home to 'nests of the sorrier sort of bordel'.[23] It was also a hotbed for political reformers, with strong ties to the suffrage movement. The suffragettes began to march just as Woolf moved to Bloomsbury, and many organisations were headquartered there, including the Women's Social and Political Union in Russell Square, and the National Union of Women's Suffrage Societies, in Gower Street. In 1919, in her novel *Night and Day*, Woolf would house her feminist activist Mary Datchet in a Bloomsbury bedsit. 'One might argue,' writes Barbara Green, 'that Virginia Woolf was emboldened to streetwalk, because the suffragette marched first.'[24]

It's hard to imagine today what it meant for the Stephen siblings to move there; in our own time we're so used to people of means chasing down bargains in shabby parts of town. As they were house-hunting, Woolf noted in her diary that her brother-in-law warned that the neighbourhood was so 'bad' that 'we should never get anybody to come and see us, or to dine'.[25] But for Woolf it was a different ecosystem; the brackish waters and 'Oriental gloom' of her Victorian family's neighbourhood could be exchanged for the fresh, clean, Georgian terraced lines of Bloomsbury squares. In Bloomsbury, Woolf threw off the mantle of her family, of her mother, the Angel in the House, and her father, the Eminent Victorian. She wrote an early story, 'Phyllis and Rosamond', about a pair of young ladies clearly modelled on Virginia and Vanessa who visit their artistic doppelgängers, the Tristram sisters, in Bloomsbury, where the very architecture makes them realise they are condemned to a life lived behind 'stucco fronts' in the 'irreproachable rows of Belgravia and South Kensington'. Phyllis longs to trade those rows for Bloomsbury's 'great tranquil squares', where 'There was room, and freedom, and in the roar and splendour of the Strand she read the live realities of the world from which her stucco and her pillars protected her so completely'.[26]

In the fictionalised view of Kensington she offers in 'Phyllis and Rosamond', life was 'trained to grow in an ugly pattern to match the staid ugliness of its fellows'.[27] In Bloomsbury, they could remake the pattern themselves – and did, as the Omega Workshops would demonstrate, when the Bloomsberries founded them nearly a decade later, producing furniture, textiles and pottery in modern, Post-Impressionist-influenced designs. As the Stephen siblings set up home, Woolf recalled all the ways in which they decided their life would be different, rebellious, original. They were 'full of experiments and reforms', Woolf recalled to the Memoir Club. 'We were going to do without table napkins, we were to have [large supplies of] Bromo instead; we were going to paint; to write; to have coffee after dinner instead of tea at nine o'clock. Everything was going to be new; everything was going to be different. Everything was on trial.' (I imagine Bromo as some kind of Edwardian kitchen roll, which I find implausible but amusing.) Little Ginny discovered the joy of rearranging her bedroom, and she wrote in her diary that she turned it round and round until it was to her 'liking'.[28]

And so, to the Memoir Club, years later, she asked, 'where does Bloomsbury end? What is Bloomsbury?' For Woolf, Bloomsbury was not only a geographical neighbourhood but an abstract entity, an idea about creativity and bohemianism and an idea about freedom. Where did it end, where did it begin? What can be made of so much freedom: is it more than simply not using cloth napkins?

In the winter of 1905, tracing Bloomsbury's geographical outline, she gave that freedom a form.

+

When she was much older, she would create her heroine Mrs Dalloway (who 'dallies along the way', Rachel Bowlby points out), who is perhaps the greatest *flâneuse* of twentieth-century literature.[29] These are the very first words Mrs Dalloway speaks in the novel: "'I love walking in London," said Mrs Dalloway. "Really, it's better than walking in the country."' For Woolf to be able to walk in the city by herself was a hitherto unimaginable kind of freedom, and while the move helped her become a professional writer, it was her walks that gave her something to write about. The streets gave her everything she needed. As she walked through the city, she would rewrite scenes in her mind; the life she saw around her seemed 'an immense opaque block of material to be conveyed by me into its equivalent of language'.[30] Wondering about the people she saw pushed her forward in her literary project – how to represent 'life itself' on the page. And to do this, she turned again and again to the city that was the 'passion of [her] life'. The noise of the streets was a kind of language, she thought, one she would stop occasionally and listen to, and try to capture.[31] In *The Waves*, this becomes: 'I begin to long for some little language such as lovers use, broken words, inarticulate words, like the shuffling of feet on the pavement.'[32] The jangle and shuffle of London is the heartbeat of life itself.

In her diaries, novels, essays and letters alike, Woolf engages with the city, noticing, especially, women in the street. She admits this in *A Room of One's Own*:

All these infinitely obscure lives remain to be recorded,

I said, addressing Mary Carmichael as if she were present; and went on in thought through the streets of London feeling in imagination the pressure of dumbness, the accumulation of unrecorded life, whether from the women at the street corners with their arms akimbo, and the rings embedded in their fat swollen fingers, talking with a gesticulation like the swing of Shakespeare's words; or from the violet-sellers and match-sellers and old crones stationed under doorways; or from drifting girls whose faces, like waves in sun and cloud, signal the coming of men and women and the flickering lights of shop windows. All that you will have to explore, I said to Mary Carmichael, holding your torch firm in your hand.[33]

Woolf mined the streets for drama, filling her books with the people she observed, walking, shopping, working, pausing. Especially the women: in a character sketch of a woman she sat across from on a train, she famously declared that 'all novels begin with an old lady in the corner opposite'.[34] Of a girl in a shop, she noted: 'I would as soon have her true history as the hundred and fiftieth life of Napoleon or seventieth study of Keats and his use of Miltonic inversion which old Professor Z and his life are now indicting.'[35]

One of her first activities was to 'prowl [. . .] round book shops in the Charing X road, all the afternoon & saw many things, which, were my purse obliging, I would get. Paston Letters, Rabelais, & James Thomson. If I am taken on by the Times I shall think myself justified –, & I use my books.' She could 'wander about the dusky streets in Holborn & Bloomsbury for hours', she wrote over a decade later. 'The things one sees – & guesses at – the tumult & riot & busyness of it all – Crowded streets are the only places, too, that ever make me what-in-the-case of another-one-might-call think.'[36] Woolf began to walk everywhere, often taking Vanessa's dog, who initially seemed homesick as well. On foot and on paw, they both eventually came around. 'I think the variety of street smells make up almost for the Gardens,' she notes on 26 January, and she might be talking about herself or the dog.[37] Gurth the dog begins to follow his new partner in explorations around the house, and sits by her knee as she writes, hoping she'll take him out.

Soon she was very social, and went jaunting around town and beyond. She settled into habits, like taking a daily 'dash' before or after lunch, and what she called by late March her 'weekly concert'. It's endearing to see a young Virginia Woolf setting up this new life, with its customs and traditions, as if she will always have a weekly concert. This is independence-building. 'I like looking at things,' she admits in her diary on 22 February, and what she sees on Tottenham Court Road is far more interesting 'than the same space of Kensington High Street', with its furniture shops, and the bookshops in Oxford Street.[38] That first time I was in Bloomsbury – it was all a haze – I remember finding my way into a million used-book shops all up and down this one street which I was convinced was Tottenham Court Road, but on more recent visits turned out to be Charing Cross Road – not in Bloomsbury at all. I had unknowingly crossed over the Oxford Street border into Soho. These are the kinds of borders you're not aware of when you're a stranger to a place.

She didn't only travel around the city on foot; one of her favourite activities was to ride the bus to Hampstead, sometimes with Vanessa, always on the top deck. It takes an hour, in 1905, and is, in her words, a 'really good expedition', a bit of the country right there in London.[39] 7 May brings 'A holiday morning expedition to Hampstead, which, like the Cockney I am, still manages to delight me – There is something fantastic – I mean phantom like – about this little vision of country in the heart of London.'⁴⁰ Her earlier journals, from before her father's death, record other trips which excited her, like the time they went to Hampton Court and she tried to picture the ghosts. 'They were no cockney trippers making the whole place hideous with their noise & Cockney faces; no, these Ladies are part of the palace.' But as she makes these expeditions on her own, or with her sister, two independent women around town, we see Woolf grow into herself. This was adult life; this was independence, pushing the city to its very limits, to see what it includes, being inspired, finding the cockney in the Kensington girl. I try to picture the Misses Stephen on the bus, side by side in those little seats on top, looking out. Did they read? Did they talk? What did they talk about? Did they ever annoy each other? Were they ever silent, resentful? Did they giggle or did they laugh respectably?

Thoby died of typhus in 1906. Vanessa married in 1908. Things change and we have to change with them. If there's one thing Woolf's work teaches us, it's that.

Time passes.

+

There is a sense of the city you can't plot on a map, or a phone. It is an intense, embodied relationship to its atmosphere, and Woolf gives it to Clarissa Dalloway: 'For having lived in Westminster – how many years now? over twenty –, one feels even in the midst of the traffic, or waking at night, Clarissa was positive, a particular hush, or solemnity; an indescribable pause; a suspense (but that might be her heart, affected, they said, by influenza) before Big Ben strikes. There! Out it boomed. First a warning, musical; then the hour, irrevocable. The leaden circles dissolved in the air. Such fools we are, she thought, crossing Victoria Street. For Heaven only knows why one loves it so.'[41] That pause, before the bell rings, that charged awareness of its inevitability, indicates the bounds placed around each of our lives, which help make them meaningful, though we are doomed to extinction. As we progress through the city, there comes a point when we are no longer just reacting: we are interacting, created anew by this ongoing encounter. Woolf reminds us that there is something physically absorbing that keys us into the throb of the city, transformed by the quality of the light, of the air, of the road. One day, I skinned my knuckle on Southwark Bridge trying to cross the street. Why were my arms flailing? I don't know. But flail your arms in a city, and you will come in contact with it, or, equally likely, with its inhabitants. We flail. We hit up against its limitations, against our own limitations. The city surrounds us, and seeps in. Are we touching it or is it touching us?

A point of contact, yielding that nebulous affective content we refer to, in shorthand, as 'feelings'. All the most interesting ones are hard to put words to; we diminish their mystery as we hang official terms on them, like christening a byway with official nomenclature; we try to find words that won't deflate them. This, anyway, was the task Woolf set herself as a writer.

The city, she wrote in her diary in 1928, was forever 'attract[ing], stimulat[ing]' her, giving her 'a play & a story & a poem'.[42] In *Mrs Dalloway* Woolf turns this into a song of the city, sung in a language she could not understand by a woman who would haunt her novels and diaries. Peter Walsh, walking by Regent's Park Tube Station, passes a blind old woman begging for money, 'with one hand exposed for coppers', singing:

A sound interrupted him; a frail, quivering song, a voice bubbling up without direction, vigour, beginning or end,

running weakly and shrilly and with an absence of all
human meaning into

    ee um fah so

    foo swee too eem oo—

the voice of no age or sex, the voice of an ancient spring
spouting from the earth.[43]

The description of this woman echoes one Woolf made in her
diary twenty years earlier; soon after moving to Bloomsbury,
she noticed an old woman on Oxford Street, whom she
describes in almost exactly the same terms.[44] She appears in
the diary again on 8 June 1920; in this longer passage she stops
to reflect on why she finds the woman so striking.

> An old beggar woman, blind, sat against a stone wall in
> Kingsway holding a brown mongrel in her arms & sang
> aloud. There was a recklessness about her; much in the
> spirit of London. Defiant – almost gay, clasping her dog as
> if for warmth. How many Junes has she sat there, in the
> heart of London? How came she to be there, what scenes
> she can go through, I can't imagine. O damn it all, I say,
> why cant I know all that too? Perhaps it was the song at
> night that seemed strange; she was singing shrilly, but for
> her own amusement, not begging. Then the fire engines
> came by – shrill too; with their helmets pale yellow in the
> moonlight. Sometimes every thing gets into the same
> mood; how to define this one I don't know – [45]

Is it possible it's the same woman, in Kingsway, in Oxford
Street, singing her incomprehensible song? Or perhaps her
ghost? The woman, with her song, blends in, however
discordantly, with the song of the city, with that feeling the city
gives her that Woolf can't describe:

Nowadays I'm often overcome by London; even think of the dead who have walked in the city . . . The view of the grey white spires from Hungerford Bridge brings it to me: & yet I can't say what 'it' is.

Shape-shifting, sense-shifting, this unsayable thing wreathes around and through the city walker, binding her in a pact whose terms she doesn't understand. For Woolf, it will be a lifetime's work trying to articulate it, trying to find a form to fit an always unknowable feeling.

+

Woolf thought deeply about the relationship between women and the city. In 1927, she wrote her great essay on *flâneuse*-ing, which she called 'street haunting'. Two words, no hyphen. In search of a pencil, her narrator crosses London on foot, noticing. Her urban observer is 'a central oyster of perceptiveness'; not a miner nor a diver nor anything with a brain, even – just 'an enormous eye', carried downstream by the city. Woolf was very much aware of the ways that women's experience of the city was different from a man's, and the essay is informed by the great anonymity which Woolf believes is possible (even for a woman) during a ramble through London. Sailing out into a winter evening, surrounded by the 'champagne brightness of the air and the sociability of the streets', the observer feels blessed with the 'irresponsibility which darkness and lamplight bestow'. In the street we are no longer 'quite ourselves' – instead we become 'functions of the urban landscape'. Whereas once we were the objects of the gaze, as street haunters we become observing entities, de-sexed, un-gendered. We cloak ourselves in anonymity, and become as incomprehensible to the city as it often is to us.

(Think, for instance, what a chaos a map of pedestrians would look like.)

But just as important as what she sees is what the walk does to her sense of self. Within our houses, Woolf writes, we are surrounded by the objects that make us who we are: things we have chosen and arranged, which 'express' and 'enforce' our identities. But the moment we leave that setting, that 'shell-like covering which our souls have excreted to house themselves', we 'shed the self our friends know us by and become part of that vast republican army of anonymous trampers'.[46]

This androgyny is one of the values Woolf prizes most in *A Room of One's Own*, which recognises that, for some women, writing is a way of stepping out of bounds. 'What idea it had been that had sent me so audaciously trespassing I could not now remember,' Virginia Woolf writes, describing a trip to 'Oxbridge' when she walked on the grass and was shooed off by a beadle: only (male) faculty and students could walk upon the grass, or enter the library alone. *A Room of One's Own* is not purely about the need for a closed-off private quiet space. It is also about the boundaries women bump up against in the world outside the room; it is about intellectual trespassing, daring to ask questions about women and fiction and women and history that have not been addressed before. What if Shakespeare had a sister, Woolf asks, a girl who was as brilliant a writer as he? She would not have been educated, like him; she would not have been allowed to go where she pleased, like him. She would have been betrothed to some perhaps unwanted husband. So Woolf imagines Judith Shakespeare sneaking off to London in the middle of the night. She wants to act, but is laughed at by the stage managers. 'He bellowed something about poodles dancing and women acting – no woman, he said, could possibly be an actress. He hinted – you can imagine what. She could get no training in her craft.'

Finally she becomes pregnant and kills herself, and 'lies buried at some cross-roads where the omnibuses now stop outside the Elephant and Castle'.[47]

Reading this I realise how far I've come from the day in June 2004 when I stood in Tavistock Square and wondered which house was Woolf's. Then, I couldn't have pointed to Elephant & Castle on the map. Now, I have an intimate knowledge of and great fondness for south-east London, which includes an awareness of the absolute awfulness of Elephant & Castle as it is today; in Woolf's day there were the omnibuses; now it is a decaying late-capitalist dump where they are tearing down the decrepit public housing to make room for shiny new luxury flats, the public be damned. Perhaps one day soon the Elephant's chequered past will be a bit of trivia known mainly to psychogeographers, but for now it is a blight. Let its *laideur* stand for the ugliness of a society that lends no hand to the marginalised.

And so an Elizabethan woman could not have written the works of Shakespeare, because she simply would not have had the education or the leisure to create. But, Woolf asks, if she had, what would a woman's epic or a woman's poetic tragedy in five acts look like? '[T]hese are difficult questions which lie in the twilight of the future,' she writes. 'I must leave them, if only because they stimulate me to wander from my subject into trackless forests where I shall be lost.' For the sake of her argument – for the sake of convincing those who are determined not to be persuaded – Woolf recognises that she must stick to the clear open path of fact and reason, and not pursue hypotheticals. For Woolf, getting lost in thought is filled with creative potential, and her reference to the 'trackless forest' of specious reasoning is an ironic invocation of the mythical feminine as dark and irrational, the castrating darkness of the feminine a place from which travellers may not emerge. The mysteries and dark places of 'Mother Earth' are a common rhetorical figure in cultural commentary on who we are and how we got here: think of Marcel Duchamp's painting *Étant donnés*, which echoes Courbet's *The Origin of the World* and Darwin's tangled-bank hypothesis in his *Origin of Species*. All of us originate in the dark wilds of the female body, are born into the light, where we must remain if our arguments are to be taken seriously.

Our culture needs the unfathomable to exist; it provides refuge from logic and scrutiny, and we have been content to project it onto women, who struggle to find their way in a world that for centuries denied them full citizenship, and today denies them the right to be different from men. Louisa Gradgrind spends much of *Hard Times* staring into the fireplace; her brother finally asks her what she sees in it. "'You seem to find more to look at in it that ever I could find,' said Tom. "Another of the advantages, I suppose, of being a girl.'"[48] But if we find more to look at in the fire, we also have much to lose by pursuing what we see there. We may keep the home fire burning, or we may burn the house down; we may stay home, burning inwardly, or we may take off in a conflagration of self-assertion. We watch the fires of destruction, of desire, and of ambition, and wonder what we can risk, and what we might gain.

+

Even years after the move, Woolf was thinking about where she had grown up, and the way that Victorian world tried to constrain women to the interior. In her 1937 novel *The Years*, Woolf invented a family much like her own, the Pargiters. The novel begins in their sitting room in 1880, while the Angel in the

House – the Victorian matriarch – lies dying in the bedroom upstairs. *The Years* began life as a novel-essay, *The Pargiters*, which was intended to alternate chapters with essays reflecting on those chapters, as if addressed in a talk to an imaginary live audience. But eventually, Woolf's tone as an essayist proved impossible to reconcile with her aesthetic as a novelist, and she would excise the essayistic material in order to concentrate her energies on writing about the lives of these family members, mainly the women, as they age. Each chapter advances forward eleven years, then sixteen years, before the clock begins to slow down, and we visit 1907, 1910, 1911, 1913, 1914, and so on, finally ending in the present day, that is, the mid-1930s. This gambol through the decades allows Woolf to pause and briefly analyse sexual relations in each period, from the conquering, paternalistic male sexuality of Abel Pargiter, the family's patriarch, to the independent woman living in a 'dirty … sordid … low-down street', from the gay man who goes by so many names no one knows what he's really called, to young Peggy, who has entered the professions and become a doctor, and who listens to a young man stammer "'I, I, I'" and predicts that the moment she speaks, he will walk away: 'He can't be "you".'[49]

In the essay material, Woolf is sometimes more sociologically explicit; young Edward Pargiter, for instance, had from a young age been allowed to walk around London on his own, and had picked up a certain kind of 'knowledge' on the streets, which was complemented by what he heard from the other boys at school.[50] Analysing the different ways that men and women are allowed to use space was part of her feminist agenda. 'Eleanor and Milly and Delia could not possibly go for a walk alone – save in the streets round about Abercorn Terrace, and then only between the hours of eight-thirty and sunset.' Woolf says explicitly that 'For any of them to walk in the West End even by day was out of the question. Bond Street was as impassable, save with their mother, as any swamp alive with crocodiles. The Burlington Arcade was nothing but a fever-stricken den as far as they were concerned.'[51]

And yet the Pargiter women love to walk in the city; the excitement of the Strand gives Eleanor the feeling of 'expand[ing]'.[52] Through Eleanor, we see that charity work is one of the only ways for a middle-class woman to get out of the house on her own, walking in the poorer districts of the city. Though it isn't for enjoyment or distraction, but a Victorian gesture of care for those less fortunate, this does not lessen the sense of freedom women like Eleanor derived from it.

Then there is the youngest Pargiter sibling, Rose, who also wants to go out walking by herself. When she does, she cannot make sense of what she learns on the street; there is no school for her, where she could figure out, like her brother Edward, what's what. One evening, she sneaks out to the toy store to buy ducks and swans for her bathtub. She tiptoes into the front garden, like a tiny cat out for his first prowl, and when she reaches the corner she straightens up and casts herself in a heroic guise, imagining she is on a secret mission to a 'besieged garrison'. '"I am Pargiter of Pargiter's House," she said, flourishing her hand, "riding to the rescue!"'[53] As she nears the shop, that is, the garrison, a terrifying man leers in her face. She holds up her fingers to form a gun: '"The enemy!" Rose cried to herself. "The enemy! Bang!" she cried, pulling the trigger of her pistol and looking him full in the face as she passed him. It was a horrid face; white, peeled, pock-marked.' He thrusts out his arm and almost catches her. When she passes him again, on her way home, he begins to undress, and makes a 'mewing' noise.[54] Lying in bed that night, Rose can't sleep; her sisters can't understand why, and neither can she make sense of the fear and guilt that keep her awake. She can only say she saw 'a robber'. But what she has been robbed of is impossible to tell. She will grow up to be a suffragette, and refuse male domination in all its forms, whether it be over the public sphere of politics or the public space of the city.

The Years presses forward into Woolf's present day weaving and reweaving its cast of many, as the family proliferates in some places, and dies off in others. But the streets don't change. The car may have replaced the hansom, the Tube become a common means of transport rather than a novelty, we may cover them in and reroute them and build them elsewhere, but the streets can still be the site for a declaration of freedom, or, in Rose's case, resistance to forces that would curb that freedom. Though the novel is the history of a family through one long generation, it also charts the changing of attitudes and mores in British culture in general.

Like 'Street Haunting', it imagines a freedom for women on the streets of the city to come and go as they please, on foot. In the novel's final scene, the family comes together at a party given by Delia, who has long since left London with her Irish husband. They stay up into the wee hours of the morning talking, reuniting, and, Eleanor, now in her seventies, realises: "'all the tubes have stopped, and all the omnibuses," she said, turning round. "How are we going to get home?"

"We can walk," said Rose. "Walking won't do us any harm."'⁵⁵

+

The city that gave Woolf so many novels, stories, poems, so much literary and personal freedom – I have been looking for it since that June day in Bloomsbury in 2004. Staying there for regular periods since 2012, I have gained a real affection for the city, exploring its nooks and corners on foot, especially the leafy north, where a kind editor put me up for a while in her house in Primrose Hill, and the leafy south-east, where a kind architect rented me a room in her house in Brockley. I have walked everywhere, and come to know Peckham High Street and Highgate, Bethnal Green and Green Park, Holland Park and Honor Oak, the Isle of Dogs and Dulwich, Clerkenwell and Camberwell, Greenwich and Gravesend. But my London is a twenty-first-century city, one Woolf probably wouldn't recognise.

The London she loved: there are fewer and fewer people who remember it any more, leaving those of us who read her diaries and letters and books to reconstruct it for ourselves. We have to rebuild a world from the rustle of paper.

Or we could put on our shoes and go out the door.

*walk north-east on rue du Départ, bear right around Place du 18
Juin 1940, cross the boulevard, north on rue de Rennes, past the
Fnac, Naf Naf, H&M, right at St Placide and north-east on rue
de Vaugirard, past the Institut Catholique where I taught once,
keep an eye out for that lovely bookseller in an old butcher's shop,
past the Jardin de Luxembourg, follow the curve of it, then really
you have your pick of smallish streets, just move north-east,
north-east, till you emerge onto the Boulevard Saint-Michel and
follow it till you hit the river*

PARIS

CHILDREN OF THE REVOLUTION

For these roads are not straight, but have several revolutions.

— Josephus

Whenever I come across roadworks in Paris, I always stop to look at what they've dug up. I peer over the corrugated green and silver barriers down into the cross section of layers of street accumulated over the centuries. I look for the cobblestones further down, nestled under swathes of pavement laid after the upheaval of 1968. Traditionally, when there's been an uprising, Parisians have dislodged the cobblestones and thrown them at the authorities – the Republican army, the riot police, whomever – so in certain neighbourhoods a protective layer of asphalt was smoothed over the stones. I get a thrill in seeing them revealed again, the kind you get from seeing something you shouldn't, what's usually covered up, or hidden away, like when I walk past a *porte cochère* I've never seen open, and catch sight of the expansive courtyard stretching back behind it, or the muddy expanse of a worksite where a building used to be, or even, on elevated métro lines like the 6 or the 2, glimpse someone in their flat who doesn't know, or doesn't care, that they've been seen.

In Paris, when the city workers dig into the streets, it's as if they give passers-by access to long-finished, long-covered-over revolutions. How deep would they have to dig to reach the paving stones they replaced after 1848, after 1830? I wonder who walked those stones, planning the revolt to come. What drives a person to dig their fingers into the crust of Paris as if it were nothing but sand, prying loose the stone from its setting, perhaps with the aid of a chisel and a spade. *Sous les pavés la plage* ('Under the paving stones, the beach'), they graffitied on the walls of the city, sometimes the very ones on which was already printed *Défense d'afficher* ('It is forbidden to post'). *Défense de ne pas afficher* ('It is forbidden not to post'), someone wrote on the wall at Sciences-Po in 1968.

What do we see of a revolution after it's gone? A better world, perhaps. Some changes in the structure of society. But not always – sometimes there's no change at all. 'People must hope so much when they tear streets up and fight at barricades,' muses the young woman at the centre of Elizabeth Bowen's 1935 novel *The House in Paris*. 'But, whoever wins, the streets are laid again and the trams start running again.'[1] Karen longs for a total, irreversible upheaval, but the world into which she is born – upper class, Regent's Park, Georgian-terraced London – resists all attempts at change. She is talking more about private revolutions, the overthrow of family and custom, the kind she attempts in the novel's central transgression, and later pretends never happened.

Looking over their city, Parisians tend to write more about what's disappeared than what's still visible. 'Old Paris is no more (a city changes more quickly, alas, than the human heart),' wrote Baudelaire.[2] 'Alas! Old Paris is disappearing with terrifying rapidity,' sighed Balzac.[3] Louis Aragon, the surrealist poet, composed an elegy to the Passage de l'Opéra, built in 1822 but scheduled to be demolished in 1925 to make room for the

Boulevard Haussmann. Composed of the Thermometer Gallery, the Barometer Gallery and the Clock Gallery, all technologies for charting ambiance, it was the perfect surrealist territory. Guy Debord, in his autobiography *Panegyric*, lamented: 'To see the banks of the Seine will see our grief: nothing is found there now save the bustling columns of an anthill of motorised slaves.'[4] When Baudelaire sighs *alas, the form of a city changes faster than the human heart*, in a way he's talking about a rate of change the human heart can't measure, forces of change that go beyond individual capacity. Traces of the past city are, somehow, traces of the selves we might once have been.

Here and there we find them, and we fetishise them. A bit of faded, stencilled signage on the side of a building; the disused railroad track known as the Petite Ceinture, which can be glimpsed in places like the Parc Montsouris and Ménilmontant; a plaque on the ground near my old apartment informing anyone who notices it that the Bièvre flows under their feet, having been covered over for reasons of public sanitation in 1912. We peer at photographs by Atget and Marville, trying to imagine that those people we see in their aprons and flat caps leaning against doorposts in streets we don't recognise aren't characters from a Zola novel, but real people who lived and breathed, and stood still long enough to be captured on film. Unlike many of their fellow Parisians in these photographic cityscapes, who were moving too quickly for the slow-seeing lens to notice them.

Slow down: it's the only way to guarantee your immortality.

+

I am always looking for ghosts on the boulevards. So many people have passed through Paris; did they leave any residue? Some parts of town seem still to be inhabited by older souls who won't leave – up towards the Portes Saint-Denis and Saint-Martin I think I can feel them, crowds of people in bowler hats and long skirts, I can sense them pressing past me along with the people I recognise from my own time, bare-headed and in short skirts. Other places seem totally empty, *tabula rasa*, like the brand-new city-within-a-city near the library in the 13th, which looks a bit like Anytown, USA, with its wide sidewalks and pristine new buildings all in glass and steel. It's hard to believe anything else was ever there, or anyone else, that it isn't a bit of earth brought about by real-estate developers to be inhabited by render ghosts.

Most of the meaningful moments of my life have taken place here, since I moved here for good, on the cusp of adulthood. Bliss has unravelled, joy coalesced out of nothing; my life has pulsed in its streets alongside so many others. Key spots on my emotional map of Paris glow hot for a time, and then the heat and light subside; I can walk past that fountain near the Comédie Française, for example, and not remember that I once kissed someone there, or walk right by the flat I shared with an ex and not think about him. Which doesn't mean those places have lost their charge; it takes something unexpected to strike a match and set the air on fire. An unexpected face. A song. Someone's cologne.

But these signals come in on my own personal frequency; they wouldn't mean much to anyone else. We all have our own signals we're listening for, or trying not to hear.

+

'Places remember events,' James Joyce noted in the margins of *Ulysses*.[5] I want to see the evidence. Some inscription of what's gone before, beyond what I can read in a book. I want to read the city *like* a book. War embedded in the surfaces of building facades. Bullet marks. Plaques telling us who died where. Sacré-Coeur perches like a neo-Byzantine wedding cake atop the Mont des Martyrs, an architectural apology to God for the bloodshed of the Commune. I learned about the Commune when I was a university student in Paris, and couldn't believe it. Ten thousand people dead in the streets of Paris only 130 years before? It seemed shockingly barbaric. Why had I never heard of it? Why did no one talk about it? Plaques mark the spots from the schools from which Jewish children were deported or where *résistants* were gunned down in the forties, sometimes accented by a metal vase containing some long-wilted carnations. At least once a week I walk past the pavement plaque in the rue Monsieur-le-Prince dedicated to Malik Oussedine, the student who was beaten to death by the police during a student protest in 1986. He wasn't even one of the protesters. The Seine swallowed a hundred Algerians in 1961; they were heaved in by police commanded by the Nazi collaborator Maurice Papon for demonstrating in favour of the National Liberation Front, which was carrying out bombings in France in the name of Algerian independence; that was his excuse. In 1961 someone graffitied onto the walls of the bridge *Ici on noie des Algeriens* ('Here we drown Algerians'). Today, there's a memorial on the Pont Saint-Michel. But the water bears no trace of them.

+

Paris has always had a 'taste for tumult', as Théophile Lavallée noted in 1845, with its 'hurried, seething, tumultuous' population, but today it presents a serene face to the world, in spite of all this revolting and murdering.[6] To take a stroll through the lower levels of the Gare du Nord, or to watch the cop show *Spiral*, is to quickly locate the discord simmering in today's city.

And yet on some streets you could forget all that, places so beautiful it's as if no conflict has ever touched them.

Was this spot on the earth beautiful always? Did the Romans notice the light?

Yet the beauty of Paris is very much man-made, crafted out of speculation and conflict. In the late seventeenth century, Louis XIV asked his chief minister Jean-Baptiste Colbert to decide what would be the best stone to build with. They were looking for a new quarry, as the one they had been using directly under the city was having the predictable structural consequences. (Those quarries were shored up by Charles-Axel Guillaumot and became a useful spot for depositing all the bones from the Cimetière des Innocents when it was destroyed in the late eighteenth century.)[7] Colbert reported back that a commission had found a quarry in the Oise region, conveniently accessible by boat, which produced stones to match those used to build Notre-Dame. The bricks for Parisian builds have come from the Saint-Maximin limestone quarries ever since.[8] Did they know they were building houses that would absorb and reflect the light? And who drew the rooftops, with their sloping slate, and their chimney pots, their slices of masonry standing up from the curve of the rooftops like the finish of a ballerina's *port de bras*, the lilt and lift of their fingers Surrealist vessels for exhaling smoke?

Some of these buildings came into being through Haussmann's determined plan to modernise Paris, tearing down entire neighbourhoods and displacing thousands of residents in order to make way for the boulevards we recognise today as so quintessentially Parisian.[9] They represent at the same time a stunning feat of urban planning and a breathtaking disregard for the lives of everyday people. I'm in awe of the great beauty of the boulevards but wary of their size, devised as they were to facilitate the movement of troops and goods through the city to more easily quash any rebellions that might spring up (vivid was the memory of 1848, with its perfection of barricade warfare) while also increasing the amount of merchandise that could be sold through the newly built *grands magasins*, like the Bon Marché, fictionalised by Zola in his 1883 novel *The Ladies' Paradise*. An American friend who lives in London begrudges Paris its loveliness, preserved, she argues only somewhat facetiously, at the expense of collaborating with the Nazis. Give me the honest ugliness of post-war London any day, she says, and she's not wrong.

Then, too, London, like Paris, filled its coffers and built its wonders off the ravages of Empire.

Today, the policy of *façadisme* in Paris means the uniformity of the Haussmannian (and pre-Haussmannian) buildings is preserved even if the building behind it is not, a controversial practice that gives way to what I think is an interesting compromise, creating a hybridity of structure and use within a traditional Parisian aesthetic, but I understand the *anti-façadistes*, who hold that this reduces buildings to little more than adorable stage sets. I'm not sure retaining the facade works in every city, in every instance, and even in Paris it can be done badly, but in principle I don't mind it. An entire culture is distilled in that top layer, and without it Paris wouldn't be Paris. In the 4th arrondissement the policy has been applied to such an extreme that there is a delightful free-standing doorway on the rue Beautrellis, all that remains of a seventeenth-century *hôtel particulier*. Behind it, unconnected to the old doorway, stands a cement building from the 1960s. 'That's France for you,' an ex groused once, as we walked past it. 'A doorway to nowhere.'

When I look for the marks of time in the Paris streets, the scars of revolution and upheaval, I'm looking for evidence that Parisians fought back against what was imposed on them, that they weren't all trying to keep their lives as undisturbed as possible. Between 1789 and 1871 these people saw a bloody uprising every twenty years or so. I'm trying to understand how they could rise up, how a collection of everydays can overturn a king, and remake a world.

+

Where I come from, you don't just move abroad. No one I knew had ever done such a thing, except for my Italian family, but they were fleeing Mussolini. I was not escaping a fascist regime, so why pry myself loose from the place I was born, from my family, my friends, my city, my language? It's only a six-hour flight, but for many years when I flew to Paris from JFK, it felt like I was jumping off a cliff at the edge of the world. I would arrive in Paris in a depressed stupor that would linger for days with the jet lag. What am I doing here? What is it that keeps me here? The effect of having travelled too far, too quickly, left me feeling physically bereft, as if I had swallowed the distance between myself and the people I loved, and it split open my insides. It got me interested in logistics, but also in distances, in families that stretched across them. I kept thinking about George Sand, of all people, who in 1831 left her no-good husband and beloved children at Nohant, her estate in central France, to go and become a writer in Paris. In her day it took ten hours to travel from Nohant to Paris. That was a different kind of distance. There was no jet lag, but there were no telephones. She couldn't call her children to wish them goodnight. She was in the same country, completely cut off from them. Many women of her class were separated from their children, having sent them off as babies to the wet nurse, and when they were a little older, to school. But for the mother to leave her home – this was a scandal.

Revolution. The word implies movement, back to where one began, like a turn around an axis, like celestial bodies in the sky. In French, that which is *révolu* is completed, over. But speaking historically, temporally, it is impossible to come back to where we started. Even if a revolution is perceived to have failed, and not to have changed anything, like the events of 1832, I prefer the more unusual meaning of 'a turn or a twist, a bend or a winding'. The *OED* refers us to William Whiston's 1737 translation of Josephus: 'For these roads are not straight, but have several revolutions.'

I think of George Sand as this kind of revolution: a turn in the road.

+

We think we know the story: the cross-dressing, the cigars, the lovers, the many, many novels. Yet although her mythology is engraved on our cultural consciousness, we don't talk very much about her work. That's partly because it's not readily available in English – but partly because when her novels have been translated, readers have found them sentimental and disappointing; there is much weeping and fainting. We are light years away from the stream of black liquid running out of the dead Emma Bovary's mouth as she rots on a table, though Flaubert's masterpiece was published at the peak of Sand's career. Unlike Balzac and Flaubert, who were her friends and contemporaries, and who strove to render men and women on the page as they were, warts and all, Sand was trying to paint a picture of what people *could* be: emancipated from all social chains, including those of family, marriage, the Church and society. Her novels have that Romantic predilection for exotic locales, like Italy (she was very inspired by Madame de Staël's 1807 novel *Corinne, ou l'Italie*) and Reunion Island, and take place on some other plane of possibility, instead of the world we actually live in. Where one of her heroines, Indiana, is ready to throw her honour aside for love, another, Consuelo, tries to maintain her chastity and honour above all else, including love. In both novels, there is much weeping and fainting. They're not exactly what we expect from the trouser-wearing, cigar-smoking bohemian image we have of Sand.

Sand wrote passionately in favour of equality between men and women, but was not exactly a feminist. Indiana's greatest hope is that 'a day will come when everything in my life will be changed, when I shall do good to others, when someone will love me, when I shall give my whole heart to the man who gives me his; meanwhile, I will suffer in silence and keep my love as a reward for the man who will set me free'.[10] Yet because this is a character who has left her husband and run off with another man, this vision of marital equality is very daring for 1832. Asked by feminist groups of her day to join their cause, she retorted that she worked for the rights of all, not just of women.

In spite of these limitations, Sand's attempt to reconcile everyday life with her great ideals, and her refusal to live her life the way she was expected to, were inspiring in her own day – Alexander Herzen called her the 'incarnation of the revolutionary idea' and her novels would influence an entire generation of Russian radicals (the spread of her ideas in Russia would come to be known as *Zhorshzandism*) – and ought to inspire us today as well. But in our lunge for Sand the bohemian, we've missed the more interesting version of her: Sand the everyday radical. Especially in her autobiographical writings, Sand shows us that in the interstices of history are women eking out daily revolutions, and the emancipatory role of the city. Sand's problem was she could not quite imagine what a liberated woman looked like.

+

It's hard to place George Sand: she refused to be placed. Born Amandine Lucile Aurore Dupin in 1804, and known as Aurore, her father, Maurice Dupin, was an officer in Napoleon's army. Her mother, Sophie-Victoire Delaborde, was a dancer in one of the 'humblest theatres in Paris'. Born into the niche between democratic idealism and royalist luxury, Sand herself was politically contradictory. On one side her grandfathers were the King of Poland and the Maréchal de Saxe. On the other, a Parisian bird seller. In George Sand, wrote John Sturrock in the *London Review of Books*, 'the Ancien Régime was crossed, give or take a bar sinister, with the Paris proletariat'.[11] She took the part of the worker, of the common man, and woman, and though she lived a comfortable life in Paris and Nohant, it was mainly by the efforts of her own inexhaustible pen. Always moving between the country and the city, she longed for one in the other and the other in the one. Pragmatic and rational, she made an enemy of excess, yet she had more lovers and produced many more novels, long, long novels, the length of a nineteenth-century night, than anyone has been able to understand since. ('How the devil did George Sand do it?' wondered Colette in her memoirs.)[12]

Her life was punctuated by revolutions. She was born the year Napoleon crowned himself Emperor, putting an imperial end to the endless factioning and in-fighting that had prevailed since the Revolution fifteen years before, and turning the bloodletting on the rest of Europe. In his *Confession of a Child of the Century*, Alfred de Musset, Sand's lover, would write of their generation, 'Conceived in the intervals between battles, raised in schools to the beat of drums, thousands of boys exchanged grim looks as they flexed their puny muscles. From time to time blood-splattered fathers would appear, hold them up against chestfuls of golden metals, then put them down again and get back on their horses.'[13] Great Caesar commanded the youth of France to his side, and soon it fell. Yet, for its children, 'Something in that word liberty made their hearts beat with the memory of a terrible past and the hope of a glorious future.' The 'sons of the Empire and grandsons of the Revolution' gave themselves over to debauchery, 'plung[ing] into the dissipation of wine and courtesans': the 'malady of the age'. As for Sand, she got to work trying to cure it. 'You produce desolation,' she would later write to Flaubert, 'and I produce consolation.'

+

This was the nineteenth century in France: forever healing from one bloodshed only to inflict another, in the hope it would truly, this time, birth a more just world. It never arrived, though France is not done waiting for it.

+

In 1830, stuck in a loveless marriage out in the sticks, Aurore Dudevant's life was unbearable. All her illusions about love, marriage and respect were eradicated by her disappointing match; her marriage was not a beautiful union of souls, but cohabitation with someone she didn't have much in common with after all, besides a love of riding. She would rail against the 'marriage of reason' – and marriage itself – for the rest of her life. Her husband Casimir wasn't much to brag about in the bedroom, and wasn't shy about giving her a good slap. She had an idealised (that is, unconsummated) affair with Aurelien de Sèze, and an 'unidealised' one with Stéphane de Grandsagne, whom some think fathered her second child. Casimir messed around with the chambermaid, but no one took much note. It was Aurore people gossiped about. Aurore felt humiliated and unfulfilled. Her brother told her to hang in there; he tended to take her husband's side. There were the children; she had to stay for their sake. But the situation was untenable. Any exit plan was going to have to include them at some point.

That dry hot summer, rumours of revolution in the city sparked rebellion at Nohant as well. Her blood heated up, as she told her friend Jules Boucoiran. 'I feel within me an energy I didn't think I had. The soul develops with these events.'[14] Boucoiran, who was staying in Paris, sent her letters describing what was happening. Charles X (the second Bourbon king since the restoration of the monarchy in 1814) had grown ever more unpopular; he favoured the Church and the nobility, which violated the constitution of 1814, and he introduced certain measures to censor the press, which the Chamber of Deputies violently protested. In March of 1830 they passed a vote of 'no confidence' against the king and his key ministers.

The ambiance was tense; the people were just waiting for Charles to make a misstep so they could rise up against him. Charles gave them the excuse they needed on 25 July, when he signed the ordinances suspending the freedom of the press, dissolving the newly formed parliament before it could even meet, and barring the middle class from voting or running for office. On the 26th through the 28th, the people took to the barricades, in what became known as the *Trois Glorieuses*, or 'Three Glorious Days'. But however impassioned Sand felt by the people's cause, she was pragmatic by nature, and worried they had only 'mistaken words for ideas', leaving 'plenty of room for a *future* return to absolutism'.[15] That return came rather more quickly than anticipated: the revolution only succeeding in replacing one king with another, as Louis-Philippe of the House of Orléans ascended to the throne after Charles X abdicated.

Riding almost every day to nearby La Châtre to hear the news from Paris, Aurore encountered a young man called Jules Sandeau, who was visiting his father in La Châtre for the summer holidays. He was only nineteen to her twenty-six. They fell in love, and had a passionate affair, with promises to reunite quickly when he went back to Paris at the end of the summer leaving Aurore behind with her husband and children.

Things came to a head when, one day, looking for something in her husband's desk, she came across a sealed packet of letters, addressed to her and marked 'Only open after my death'. Though he was alive and well, Aurore opened the letters (wouldn't you?), and found them filled with vitriol. That's when she decided to leave. 'I want an allowance,' she announced to Casimir. 'I am going to Paris forever, my children will stay at Nohant.'

She was bluffing; it was a negotiating tactic. What she wanted – and what she eventually got – was to take her daughter with her, to spend half the year in Paris in three-month increments, and to receive an allowance of 3,000 francs a year. In early 1831, she went to live in her brother's apartment in Paris, at 31 rue de Seine. Within a short time she moved in with Jules, where they lived in a tiny garret with a view over the Pont Neuf. Later they moved to 25 Quai Saint-Michel, in a three-room flat with a view over Notre-Dame. When Sand describes this time in her autobiography, she leaves out her bedmate completely.

In her version, she came to Paris, penniless, with the intention of becoming a writer. She recounts how she lived in a fifth-floor walk-up ('I have never been able to climb stairs, but I had to, and often with my big daughter in my arms') and had no servant, only a faithful female porter, who served as a kind of cleaning woman for fifteen francs a month. The owner of the nineteenth-century equivalent of a greasy spoon brought Sand her meals for two francs a day. 'I myself scrubbed and ironed the linen underwear.' (Whatever would she make of our twenty-first-century lives, doing our own laundry and making our own meals? Would she be appalled, or envious?)

For so many young men and women over the centuries a move to the city from the country has been an opportunity for self-reinvention. The great French novelists of the nineteenth century have all chronicled this story, from Stendhal's *Le Rouge et le Noir* (1830) and Balzac's *Illusions Perdues* (1843) to Flaubert's *Education Sentimentale* (1869) and Zola's *L'Oeuvre* (1886). Sand saw that as a woman she wouldn't have the freedom to become an artist that Julien Sorel, Lucien de Rubempré, Frédéric Moreau or Claude Lantier possessed the moment they set foot in the city. She had to do something about all those skirts, those dainty shoes, her general appearance of vulnerability. In her autobiography, she writes:

So I had made for myself a *rédingote-guérite* in heavy grey cloth, pants and vest to match. With a grey hat and large woollen cravat, I was a perfect first-year student. I can't express the pleasure my boots gave me: I would gladly have slept with them on, as my brother did in his young age, when he got his first pair. With those little iron-shod heels, I was solid on the pavement. I flew from one end of Paris to the other. It seemed to me that I could go round the world. And then, my clothes feared nothing. I ran out in every kind of weather, I came home at every sort of hour, I sat in the pit at the theatre. No one paid attention to me, and no one guessed at my disguise . . . No one knew me, no one looked at me, no one found fault with me; I was an atom lost in that immense crowd.[16]

Her fine lady's clothing just wasn't designed for the kind of knocking around town she got up to with her coterie of artistically inclined young men from the Berry.

> Literary and political events, the excitement of the theatres and the museums, the clubs and the streets – they saw everything, they went everywhere. My legs were as strong as theirs, and so were my good little Berrichon feet, which had learned to walk on bad roads, balancing on thick wooden clogs. But on the pavements of Paris I was like a boat on ice. Delicate footwear cracked in two days; overshoes made me clumsy; I wasn't used to lifting my skirts. I was muddy, tired, runny-nosed, and I saw my shoes and clothing – not to mention the little velvet hats – splattered in the gutters, falling into ruin with frightening rapidity.[17]

Aurore had already cross-dressed in the country, mainly to ride horseback; that was something of a local tradition for young women in the Berry. But in Paris she took it a step further, trying – successfully – to pass for a man, or at least for a boy. In trousers and boots she could 'fly' from one end of the city to the other, in spite of the weather, the hour and the setting, blending with the crowd, like a true *flâneur*. How ironic that a trick to blend in would cause Sand to stand out. Cross-dressing turned Aurore Dudevant into George Sand, and she would remain conspicuous for the rest of her life.

I like this portrait of Sand so much better than the swaggering defiant cross-dresser with her cigar and her lover; I like the decision coming from pure frustration instead of lofty idealism. I can see her tossing her little velvet hat on the floor and stamping on it, growling and swearing. Another inspiration came from her mother, who had also lived in Paris on a tiny budget as a young woman. She confided that to save money Sand's father used to dress her like a boy: 'Our cost of living was reduced by half.'[18]

You can just see the wheels turning in Sand's head. Walking is a constant theme in her autobiography; in fact it ends on the word *marcher*, to walk, as in marching forward on the path of 'charity towards all'. Being able to walk on her own, true to her own spirit, was the basic declaration of independence, for Sand. Her beloved and very chic grandmother never walked anywhere, Sand recalls, except on days of mourning. '*Ma fille, vous marchez comme une paysanne,*' her grandmother once told her – 'you walk like a peasant'.[19] A jab at Sand's mother, the bird seller's daughter.

So Sand learned to walk like a lady. Then she learned to walk like a man.

Her heroines would adopt similar measures: Consuelo dresses like a boy for protection as she and Joseph Haydn walk, two vagabonds with faces younger than their years, from Bohemia to Vienna. The title character in *Gabriel*, a play, is born a woman but raised a man, until at seventeen years old s/he discovers the truth. 'I do not feel that my soul has a sex,' Gabriel declares.[20] Dressing like a man allows Sand's characters access to other experiences of life, other mindsets, or to point out inequalities between the sexes. Writing from a male perspective, as Sand often did, was another kind of cross-dressing, and allowed her to glimpse a different way of living.

+

Sand's trouser-wearing was in its way an act of revolution; at the very least, it was illegal. In the year 1800, a law had been passed forbidding women to wear them in public. This law is still in effect today, though of course ignored; but even in 1969, an attempt to overturn it failed. When the law was still actively defended, a woman who wanted to change out of her skirts had to apply for a cross-dressing permit. To obtain one, she would have to demonstrate, using medical records, that she had some kind of hideous deformity which made it unsightly for her to appear in skirts. And then once obtained, the permit still did not license be-trousered women to appear at balls, at the theatre or at public meetings.[21] A culture struggling to redefine itself against the blood-soaked Place de la Revolution fixated on the female body as a tool for instilling certain values in the heart of the new Republic.

An untold number of women fought in the French Revolution in drag, fighting alongside their husbands, lovers and brothers, dressed, like them, as male soldiers. But even in skirts, women have had a subversive power in French history, and that power has doubled when they've been on foot. The Revolution, for instance, truly kicked off when a mob of women marched on Versailles. The storming of the Bastille was more symbolic than anything else; only seven prisoners had been freed, including a couple of forgers and 'madmen'. But the Women's March on Versailles in October of 1789 persuaded the king and his family to return with the crowd to Paris, where they were imprisoned in the Tuileries Palace. The women had raided the armoury, taking all the weapons they could carry, and as they brandished them at the Palace gates, I'm sure they were terrifying.

Women had long been associated with armies, following them from camp to camp, working as washerwomen, servants and nurses, as canteen-keepers, as wives and mistresses, and, at the bottom of the food chain, earning no one's respect, as prostitutes, providing physical comfort to the soldiers. Those who did fight did so with guns, and cannon, on foot and on horseback; they wanted to display valour, and prove their worth on equal terms to their menfolk. They did not want to stay at home, defending the hearth and maintaining the distinction that allocated men to the public sphere and women to the private.

French women saw the Revolution as a chance to build the kind of world they wanted, and to demand their own political rights within it.

They were welcomed, in the beginning. Some were even awarded the Légion d'honneur. But as time went on, for whatever reason – perhaps because of the sexual promiscuity of women associated with armies – they were accused of committing fraud. The fates of Olympe de Gouges, author of the *Declaration of the Rights of Woman and the Female Citizen* (1791), and Madame Roland are a reminder of what the Jacobins did to women who overstepped the mark.

+

In 1831, years before she would militate for human rights, all Sand wanted was to be independent. The city played an important role in this. More immediate was the question of survival. To make money, as she wrote to Boucoiran, she had 'launched herself on the tumultuous seas of literature' writing for *Le Figaro*, which was back then an opposition newspaper, and quite a small outfit with very few subscribers. Nevertheless, they paid well enough for Aurore to make a modest living, and the pieces she wrote for them in which she was quite critical of the government quickly won her fame. With Jules she wrote for *La Revue de Paris*, and co-authored a novel entitled *Rose et Blanche* under the pen name 'J. Sand'. It was a great success, and their editor wanted more. But Aurore wanted to strike out on her own. She left their partnership (though not Jules himself until 1833), and took their pen name for her own. For a first name she opted for Georges, a common name in her native province of Berry, anglicising it, perhaps in homage to the English nuns who had taught her as a girl at her convent school. In changing her name, Sand made a 'new marriage' between 'the young apprentice poet that I was and the muse who consoled me for my efforts', asking 'What is a name in our revolutioned and revolutionary world?'[22] It was a name she forged for herself, not one that belonged to her husband or father, or even her collaborator.

Once launched, Sand became famous almost overnight. Her first novel, *Indiana*, was published in 1832, and the reviews were stunning. At least, Sand was stunned – by the great gasp of celebrity they brought with them, and by their vehemence in either praising or denouncing the political agenda the novel contained. She protested – perhaps disingenuously – that she had had no agenda other than to tell a story that would be true to its subject. More than one reader was convinced it had been written by a man, while another thought it evinced a 'spirited voluptuousness' that suggested it had been written by both a woman *and* a man: 'that a young man's hand must have tightened the strong, vulgar tissues, and that a woman's hand embroidered onto it silk and gold flowers'.[23]

The novel's premise bears a resemblance to Sand's own situation, before she set out for Paris. Indiana is a 'young Creole', born on the Île Bourbon (what is now Réunion Island), and raised outside of French society, a fact which is frequently offered to explain her extremely naive behaviour: in line with contemporary Romantic ideals, Indiana is presented as more innocent because of her far-flung upbringing. She is unhappily married to a colonel, who is some years older than her, and lives unhappily with him outside Paris, where she is loved in silence by Ralph, a sort of cousin, also from Réunion, who raised her when she was abandoned as a child. When she meets Raymon she is therefore in an ideal situation to fall madly in love with him, risking her reputation (a bit like a Romantic-era Jean Rhys character) and making perilous journeys across the sea from France to Réunion to be with him. Of course he proves faithless (she later learns he has had an affair with her lady's maid Noun, who drowns herself when he forsakes her for Indiana), and he marries someone else. Indiana has a breakdown that coincides with the July Revolution and ends up wandering the streets of Paris, her hair shorn off, her identity papers gone. From there on it's a strange narrative in which Ralph saves Indiana from drowning herself in the Seine only to confess his love and engage her in a suicide pact to throw themselves from a cliff in Réunion. The epilogue finds them alive and well and living in a hut in some kind of mystical commune à deux.

Readers saw in the novel a condemnation of marriage. Sand demurred, explaining in subsequent forewords that she had no intention of unseating society. 'Some people chose to see in the book a deliberate argument against marriage,' she wrote in her 1852 preface. 'I was not so ambitious, and I was surprised to the last degree at all the fine things that the critics found to say concerning my subversive purposes.'[24] This was perhaps protesting too much: the word *joug*, or yoke, appears some twenty times in the text.

It wasn't marriage itself, though, that Sand took aim at, but the received notions of morality held by her society at large. The ending of the novel demonstrates what Sand had in mind: a balance, an equilibrium, like Indiana and Ralph perched precariously in their hut on the side of a volcano. Sand was trying to articulate a truer, purer code of ethics than that prescribed by her times. Key to this was the notion of free will, and she fought for women and men to freely exert it in their own lives. 'We are born with instincts in our blood that would govern us with a terrible fatefulness if not for the free will which is accorded to each of us by divine justice,' she wrote.[25] Even her pastoral novels (*romans champêtres*) of the Berry, *François le Champi* and *La Petite Fadette*, which both seem like edifying, preceptive novels, are case studies of a kind, in which Sand could explore her ideas about living in harmony with others and with her conscience.

+

Entire movements of history are born of daily revolutions. 1830 saw the workers and students band together on the barricades to overthrow tyranny. What they got was more absolutist government, just from a different family. In 1832, the year after Sand moved to Paris, the students took to the barricades again, trying to whip up support to try to topple the monarchy for good. They were unsuccessful, and Sand witnessed the tragic denouement from her flat overlooking the Place Saint-Michel.[26]

She and her daughter were alone in Paris. The cholera epidemic was at its worst, and they were afraid to leave the city – it was said to be more dangerous than staying – and in any case, if they were carrying the infection, Sand didn't want to bring it to Nohant. In the middle of this tense moment, the conflict got underway in the narrow streets around the Saint-Merry church in the centre of Paris, on the Right Bank: the barricades went up in the rue Saint-Martin near the corner of the rue Aubry-le-Boucher and the rue Maubuée, which ran through what is now the Place Beaubourg and the Centre Pompidou. The rebels held off assaults from the National Guard from the south and from the north. The leader of the Saint-Merry resistance unit, Charles Jeanne, recounted in a letter to his sister: 'we let them get within pistol reach without returning the fire they showered on us, and then all at once we welcomed them with [gunfire and] cries of *Vive la république!* and they stopped short, unsure what to do next. They hesitated long and hard and then a new round of fire went off from the barricades and the open windows and totally cleared out their ranks. They were, then, no longer a disciplined military corps but a swarm of Cossacks in total disarray.'[27]

It is the condition of the historian to be constantly picturing the past, thrilled and obsessed by it, without for one moment wanting to be a part of it. Walking in the city, looking for visible clues to its history, I can't say I regret not having actually been a nineteenth-century Frenchwoman. It isn't nostalgia I feel, or longing for anything more 'authentic'. It would have been terrifying to live through Sand's century. It is unsettling enough to walk past soldiers in fatigues holding machine guns, as all of us in Paris have done since the Charlie Hebdo attacks. The past feels as distant as another planet, even when I'm standing on its terrain. What I feel is a desire for something to align, some connection to complete, that would make their world dissolve into ours.

Sand and her daughter were playing not far away, in the Jardin de Luxembourg, when Sand realised that a line of troops was on the move from each side of the park. They left, trying to get home by the side streets, avoiding the 'mobs of curious on-lookers who, after having been cordoned off and interrogated, were rushing about and crushing each other in a sudden panic'. Sand understood they would be safest if they were inside and rushed her daughter along 'without stopping to see what was happening, having never yet seen street warfare, and having no idea what I was about to see: the blood lust that takes hold of the soldier and which makes him, seized as he is by fear of surprise, the deadliest enemy you could encounter in battle'.[28] She muses over how unsurprising this is, given that, in the history of urban violence, most people have had no idea what is happening very close by, and attack out of fear that they will be attacked. The rumour of violence spreads 'through a million delirious fictions'.

Where once Sand found the freedom she craved in the street, she now found that freedom taken away by the zeal of the mob, but even though she retreated to her tiny flat above the Place Saint-Michel, she was not fully separate from the spectacle of insurrection. Outside, the streets were taken over by angry Parisians and terrified, bloodthirsty soldiers, but the horrors of street warfare threatened to penetrate Sand's home. She threw a mattress against the window to block stray bullets from entering, and comforted her daughter, who was sick with fear. 'I told her the people outside were bat-hunting, as she had seen her father and uncle do at Nohant, and managed to calm her and put her to bed in the midst of the gunfire.' She spent part of the night, she writes, on the balcony, trying to make out in the shadows what was happening below. (Paris was not yet the City of Light; gas lamps were only very slowly being installed in the streets in the early 1830s.)

This is one of the most exciting passages in the autobiography. I want to be appalled, I want to side with Sand. I'm there with her, terrified in her garret, but I'm here in my own as well, titillated and sheepish. It's incredible to read her account, to reflect on how little she knew – as she says – about what was going on just around the corner from her. As difficult as it is to conceive of events happening on the other side of the world, it's just as hard to comprehend what is happening in your backyard. Or even in front of your own eyes, as I struggled to do on 11 September 2001, watching from one mile uptown as the World Trade Center towers collapsed. Sand's account of the fighting is quite different; she doesn't see any of it, for one thing, and her culture had no conception of the total image saturation of our own. But she did grasp that in times of violence, spectacle replaces reality.

During the night, seventeen rebels took over the barricade on the Hôtel-dieu Bridge. During the night, the National Guard launched a surprise attack. 'Fifteen of these unfortunates,' wrote Louis Blanc, 'were cut into pieces and thrown into the Seine. Two were caught in the nearby streets and had their throats slit.'[29] Sand herself did not witness this 'awful scene, which took place hidden in the folds of the night', but she reported hearing 'the furious clamouring and the formidable roaring, then a deathly silence settled over the sleeping city, depleted from the fear'.

In the morning, the streets were silent. The bridges were guarded, as well as the entrances to nearby streets, and traffic did not circulate. 'The quais,' she noted, 'stretching long and empty in the bright sunlight took on the aspect of a dead city, as if the cholera had borne away its very last inhabitant.' The only movement was from the swallows skimming the surface of the water, 'with such anxious rapidity, as if this unusual calm had frightened them'. There was no sound, except for the 'bitter cry' of the birds circling around the towers of Notre-Dame. The captive populace of Paris went to their windows and onto the rooftops to see if they could catch a glimpse of what was taking place. And then the 'sinister' noise began again:

the firing squads carrying out their justice. Sitting on the balcony, and taking care to keep Solange occupied in her bedroom to keep her from looking outside, I could count every assault and retort. And then the cannon thundered.

Seeing the bridge congested with litters returning from the fighting, leaving behind a trail of blood, I thought the insurrection was still going strong. But its strikes were weakening . . . Soon silence returned, and the people came down from their roofs onto the street. The house porters, expressive caricatures of fearful home-owners, cried: *It's over!* And the conquerors, who had done nothing but watch, surged forth a tumult. The king walked on the quais. The bourgeoisie from city and country fraternised on every corner of the street. The troops were dignified and serious. They had believed, for a moment, that a second July Revolution was at hand.

The memory of that night would stay with Sand for the rest of her life. For several days, she wrote, the Quai Saint-Michel was stained with blood. For two weeks she could barely eat, and for a long time afterward, she could not eat meat, after seeing the streets run red with blood, the 'hideous masonry' of cadavers piled up in front of windows, and after breathing the 'fetid' odour of butchery which had risen, 'acrid and hot, to awaken me, the 6th and 7th of June, in the middle of the late exhales of spring'.

What was it all for? The bloodshed of June 1832 provoked no change in regime: its expression of desperation went unheeded. The monarchy went on with its business. Disgusted with the city, Sand retreated to Nohant and wrote *Valentine*, about a young aristocratic woman in love with a penniless farmer, and a return to Sand's major themes during that period: the restrictions of marriage for women, and the ways in which education would broaden their horizons and enable them to make better choices for themselves.

The blood has long been scrubbed from the Place Saint-Michel; any trace of it has disappeared beneath new layers of pavement. And I wonder: how many of those kids who congregate there on a Friday night, gabbing on their cell phones, cruising each other, flirting or failing while groups of teen boys break-dance and Pakistani men throw neon LED toys high, high up in the air, that never seem to come down, how many of them know what happened where they're standing, that once upon a time, 180 years ago, young men fell there, as they stood up to a monarch, and that George Sand looked down on them from her balcony, trying to make out their sacrifice in the shadows.

the quickest would be to walk across the river to Châtelet and take the line 1 to Gare de Lyon but the nicer way is to walk along the quay for half an hour, stopping to browse in the bookstalls along the way, then to cross the river, it's not far, then to get the night train, though these days you can catch a flight from Orly which you can also reach from Châtelet

VENICE

OBEDIENCE

I see myself at the labyrinth's gate, ready to get lost in this city and this story. Submissive.

— Sophie Calle, *Suite Vénitienne*

For a couple of years, instead of writing my PhD thesis, I wrote a novel about Venice.

I was reading Ian McEwan's *The Comfort of Strangers*, set in a noir, uncanny, unnamed city of canals and subterfuge, and it loosened something in my mind, or maybe it planted something, I'm not sure. Reading McEwan I felt compelled by something I didn't understand to write a story about love, and loss, and being lost, and to set it in Venice. Now I look back and think that unconscious thing had recognised Venice as a shadowy double for Paris, and chosen it as a way to talk about trying to make a life for myself in a place where I knew no one and where I had no real reason to be. Moving by myself to a new country seemed as absurd as building a home on the sea. As the novel began to take shape, I called it *Floating Cities*.

Some novelists — Jeanette Winterson, for example — have written about Venice without visiting the city, and manage to conjure it up through sheer force of imagination. But I need to see things for myself. I didn't want to invent Venice, I wanted to capture something of how it was in reality, not only in our cultural imaginary. In writing about it, I wanted to restore *placeness* to Venice.

I had visited Venice several times as a tourist, and done some basic reconnaissance, but it wasn't enough; I didn't feel I could write about life there with any authority. I decided to spend a month there, studying Italian at the Istituto Veneziana and taking notes on daily life in the city. This required learning as much as I could in advance, and anticipating what I might want to know that I wouldn't be able to find out unless I were there. Also, I was still working out the plot, and I hoped Venice would guide me, that in its streets the story would find its way.

The main character was a student, like me, but in art history, specialising in the early Renaissance. I'd always wanted to be an art historian, and this was my chance, sort of. I named her Catherine, after my Italian great-grandmother, and after the patron saint of unmarried girls, teachers and scholars. Her research would be on the history of the book. But she would be teaching a basic art-history course to students abroad, so I needed to know how to talk about palazzo facades, the mosaics of San Marco, the paintings in the Accademia. I wanted to learn the things that I had learned in Paris which I knew marked the difference between someone who has lived there, and someone who has only passed through. And because the book had a hidden synagogue at the heart of it, I had to find a place to put one, in a city with no basements.

I was high on my project, but trepidatious. As a graduate student in English, writing a novel wasn't exactly kosher. It's understood, at least in America, that in the course of completing a PhD, a process which may take up to eight years, sometimes longer, you will invariably work on other projects. But inventing a fictional PhD for a fictional character and spending all your time researching it instead of your own isn't the best way to build your CV.

But as any researcher knows, you have to follow the thread where it leads you.

+

I arrive on a Saturday on the 9.40 from Orly, and it's noon by the time the bus from the airport drops us at Piazzale Roma. I catch a vaporetto sloshing southward and lean out one side, opening my face to the city. A myriad references slide out of the water. The sun sparks off the canal, which curves with more hauteur than I remember; the palazzi are splendidly garish in their decay, like Quentin Crisp in Sally Potter's *Orlando*, but with Turkish windows. Stately strings play in my mind. Now I can tell late Gothic from early Renaissance, and recognise the round bas-relief sculptures shaped like dinner plates on the brick walls as *paterae*; I recall details of buildings from Ruskin's sketches in *The Stones of Venice*. My library is transformed into a living city: so much of what I read about has its corollary before me. I think of Mary McCarthy's wry notes on tourism in *Venice Observed*. 'One accepts the fact,' she writes, 'that what one is about to feel or say has not only been said before by Goethe or de Musset but is on the tip of the tongue of the tourist from Iowa who is alighting in the Piazzetta with his wife in her furpiece and jeweled pin.' Ever dutiful, I have brought along a little orange Claire Fontaine notebook and labelled it 'Venice, June 2007', which I will use to catch the things that weren't in those books, and put them in my own. Because yes, I believe it is possible, *pace* Mary McCarthy, to say something different about Venice. No one has seen it as I have; as my heroine has. We do not share a world view with Goethe or with the lady in furs from Iowa.

After getting off at San Stae, I have a few hours' wait before

Laura, the woman I'm staying with, will meet me; she is coming in that afternoon from Turin, where she has been tending to her sick father. I walk around Santa Croce, looking first for a place to have lunch, then for a place to have coffee, then for a place, just a place, to sit and pass the time. Someplace, preferably, where it is not too hot.

I try to enjoy the freedom of having nothing to do and nowhere to be, but I am encumbered by my suitcase. It is on wheels, but it is still heavy, and there are many bridges to cross, the Venetian kind with at least seven stone steps on each side. Instead of lifting the bag up and down the bridges, I resolve the problem in what I am later told is true Venetian style: I drag it up and then I drag it down. This is not a perfect solution. The crowd of tourists is thick, and I try not to trip anyone with my bag, but there are a few people who aren't looking down, and, well. I finally make my way back to the vaporetto stop at San Stae having caused minimal damage to the city, its inhabitants and its visitors, sit down on the steps of Sant'Eustacio, and wait for four o'clock, the breeze from the Grand Canal drying the sweat on my scalp.

+

I'm a tourist but I like to think I'm the good kind. I'm here to observe the city, instead of buying bits and pieces of it. As a 'good tourist' I hope the city will open itself up to me, if only a little. I hope to find places to be in, to eat in and drink in, that will feel unique and worthwhile. I hope the food will taste good, and the drinks.

I make mistakes. I try to avoid it, I hunt for something better, but I end up having lunch in a tourist trap under the Accademia Bridge. It's called a 'snack bar'. In the desert of Dorsoduro I have collapsed here, condemned to eat the sand. I'm so hungry I don't even care. The menu outside promises a pizza Margherita for seven euros. It arrives and the crust is so stale it's impossible to cut without making the entire table shake. The waiters eye me suspiciously. Am I bad for business?

The location does provide a good view on the tourists at rest. Some have as many as three camera bags around their legs or strapped around their waists, like weapons. It's such a cliché to call tourists an 'army', but like most clichés, it's true. They come in an organised group, wear a uniform (the same shorts and sneakers, or the same baseball cap reading 'Mt Laurel Soccer in ITALY!!!'), advance at the same pace, and are spurred on by someone shouting orders and toting an umbrella-bayonet.

I have no army. I am a poor scribe, foreign to these parts. I have no buffer and I mean no harm. But I am no different. I have come to take what I can from this place, and I am willing to pay what I must to do so.

Sometimes I get lucky. In a cafe on the Campo Santa Margherita the waitress is brusque but friendly: *"tenzione, ragazzi! Un altro martini bianco?'* Bright blue judo pants, red T-shirt and updo, with a bottle of Windex hooked onto her bumbag. She gives me potato chips with my Spritz.

I'm in the southern part of the city, because I've set my novel here. I didn't want my synagogue to be located in the Jewish ghetto; it had to be somewhere surprising. Somewhere no one would look for it. I liked the sound of Dorsoduro, and the meaning – hard back. The only part of Venice built on anything resembling terra firma. It's where the university is, so it makes sense for Catherine. I scan the buildings on the square, and think about housing her in one of them.

I am getting drunk.

I have to get to work. I have to pay attention. It is 6.15 p.m. The bells never stop around here, they ring every fifteen minutes for fifteen minutes. People move chairs around, and tables, drain drinks and read newspapers. Kiss on both cheeks, inhale their cigarettes, gesture heights and sizes, give directions, shake their knees under tables and explain things, exclaim 'ahh!' when they understand. The style seems to be flowing garments and interesting jewellery. A bearded man's newspaper is open to a story whose headline begins 'Quando Tintoretto' and I can't make out the rest. From where I am sitting I can see two pizzerias and a 'biostore' called Planet Earth. Dogs bark, babies cry, a radio is playing nearby. More bells. The ground is made of paving stones, not cobblestones as I would have thought; they're each about a foot long and six inches wide. Grey and full of pockmarks, filled with little puddles that seem to have seeped through the stones. It has not recently rained, but it looks like a giant flooded pizzeria. I make a note of it all.

+

One night Laura takes me to meet some people for drinks at Bancogiro, a bar and restaurant on the quay near Rialto, and we stand outside in the late-evening light and drink bright orange Spritzes. 'That's Toni Negri over there,' one of her friends says, this being the sort of place where Marxist philosophers come to mingle. The following night I strike out on my own, and find an outdoor pizzeria called Il Refolo. They pull out a table for me; I am the only person dining alone. I read *The Wings of the Dove* for company. A large party seated to my left is full of people speaking English and Italian, and I smile at them, feeling less lonely by proximity. Then, a deeply tanned man wearing glasses with blue plastic frames pulls up in a gondola and steps out into the patio of the restaurant, prompting a round of applause from the table beside me. It is Peter Weller. 'You only turn sixty once!' RoboCop says as he takes his seat at the head of the table.

+

Another day, Laura and I visit the Biennale. Laura's friend Ricardo is working in the French pavilion, and he has said he could get us in for free if we get there before two, when his shift ends. Hung-over and overheated, somehow we make it there on time, and are let into the Sophie Calle exhibit, *Prenez soin de vous*.

A cacophony of video, photography and documents under glass is laid out over something like four rooms. In each one, a different woman talks, sings, whispers, chants, dances, jumps, and clowns fragments of sentences, bits and pieces of what seem to be the same text: 'I wanted to tell you this in person but couldn't so here it is.' 'I thought it would be enough that your love ...' 'You told me you didn't want to be "number 4" ... but you continued to see B and R.' They all end with the sign-off *Prenez soin de vous* – Take care of yourself.

The text turns out to be a break-up email – an email! the bastard – Calle received from her boyfriend, identified only as X. Written in flowery, nay, haughty French (do lovers really still call each other *vous*?), the letter reads as recriminatory, alienating and cowardly. Its author, I learn later, was the writer Grégoire Bouillier, who had already made Calle a character in his novel *The Mystery Guest*. Calle, then, seems to have felt free to use him in one of her own works. The women who have responded include a sexologist, who writes her interpretation on a prescription pad, the singer Feist, the actress Arielle Dombasle, a Kabuki doll, an Italian actress chopping onions, a literature student who provides textual analysis, and a parrot who tears the letter to bits with its beak and squawks 'Take care of yourself!'

Calle often uses her life as a springboard to her art. I first heard of her when I read Paul Auster's novel *Leviathan*, which features an artist called Maria who is based on Calle. Maria sets herself certain thematic constraints which require her to organise her days or weeks by colour or letter; some weeks, Auster writes, Maria set herself a 'chromatic diet', eating only foods that were a certain colour, while others were alphabet-themed, 'spent under the spell of *b*, or *c*, or *w*'.[1] Delighted, Calle responded by playing out these games in real life, photographing and eating modified versions of Maria's chromatic diet, adopting her own letter days. The cover of her book *Double Game*, a collection of her projects, depicts Calle enacting Maria Turner's *b* day, dressed as a blonde 1960s pin-up girl, perched on a bed, looking coyly into the camera, surrounded by a menagerie of animals, over the caption 'B for Beauty and the Bestiary, for Bat, Bantam, Boar, Bull, for Bug, Badger, Bray, Bellow, Bleat, Bark, for Beastly Birdbrain, for BB'.[2]

These projects were collected in a book called, in French, *De l'obéissance*: On Obedience. I liked the subtle irony of the title, as if Calle were not only making a game of her fictional double, but lightly ribbing Auster with her subservience. We know it's an act; Calle is in control of how she wants to appear. And yet the title activates the paradox of Calle's work, in which she sets up a scenario in which she, or her collaborators, must obey a set of rules in order for the work (and the game) to begin; once the rules are established, Calle no longer has total control over the work that results.

Obedience, and disobedience, are central motifs in Calle's life as well as her art. In 1970, Calle dropped out of Nanterre University, where one of her professors was the philosopher Jean Baudrillard, who would theorise that contemporary life is a simulacrum of itself. Two years earlier, in Nanterre – located in a working-class suburb west of Paris – the 'events' of May 1968 had broken out, in a controversy over co-ed sleeping arrangements in the dormitories. In order to allow Calle to graduate, although she hadn't completed all of her coursework, Baudrillard allegedly submitted another student's paper in place of Calle's. After that, Calle went off travelling for seven years: the Cévennes, in the south of France, then to Crete, then

– after showing up at a travel agency with all the money she had, asking where such a sum could get her – she found herself in Mexico, then the US, then finally in Canada, where she worked in a circus. All of these travels, she has said in interviews, were to flee someone or join someone.

Back in Paris, Calle moved in with her father. He liked to hang out at the Closerie des Lilas, with a bunch of young people who, she says, were always perfectly coiffed and laughed too loudly. He tried to get Calle to come with him, but the people there made her feel like the little match girl.[3] She had no job, no friends of her own; she didn't know what to do with herself. She felt lost. This is why she began following people: to have something to do.

+

When you're young, when you have so many choices, how can you decide among them? Each one is a narrowing. You want someone to tell you where to go, what to do. Please take from me this responsibility for my own life, that I didn't ask for and don't know what to do with. *Put me somewhere.* I once followed a man – we'll call him X, like Calle – all the way to Tokyo, just to avoid choosing not to.

+

One day Calle followed a woman down the rue Froidevaux 'because her hairdo astonished me'. Two men she followed took the rue Claudel, then the rue de l'Odéon, walking in the middle of the street. But even following people around seemed to require something beyond her capabilities. 'I lack perseverance,' she wrote in her journal. 'I start following someone but the pursuit fatigues me or escapes me . . .' 2.25 p.m.: she's back at the Jardin de Luxembourg. 'The day is bad and I feel a bit glum. I decide to make do with a pigeon.'[4] She can't slip easily into the passive role of follower. One evening at a gallery opening, Calle encounters a man she had been following earlier that day, someone she had lost sight of. The coincidence seems like a sign. When he mentions he is travelling to Venice the next day, she decides to follow him there, too. It's a more active choice. A more interesting choice anyway, in its total boundary-thrashing weirdness.

It's her first time in Venice, and it's the trip, and the project, that will launch her career, and make possible her return, almost thirty years later, this time as an International Art Superstar. It seems fated that she would be so tied to the city; her surname, after all, is the Venetian word for street.

+

The tense slips to the present. Calle arrives on Monday 11 February 1980.[5] She has packed a notebook, and her entries provide most of the text of the project. She records what happens like a gonzo journalist, or like a private investigator, every day a set of notes. Henri B., she calls him. He is a photographer, so she decides to photograph him, everywhere he goes in Venice. In her suitcase (which is not on wheels) she has packed a blonde wig, several hats and veils, sunglasses, gloves – everything she'll need to disguise herself. She has also brought along her Leica camera, and a Squintar lens, which is constructed with a set of mirrors so you can photograph people without pointing the camera directly at them. Calle is too shy to photograph people head-on in the street; she only feels comfortable shooting sideways.

Oh, and it happens to be Carnevale, that traditional time of masked debauchery and anonymous encounters, before the self-denial of Lent.

+

For centuries, civic power in Venice was maintained through a system of surveillance. People find this fascinating; Donna Leon has made a whole career out of it, writing mystery novels about a present-day Venetian police commissioner. The Council of Ten had their *bocche di leone* installed so that Venetians could anonymously inform on their fellow citizens (there was not, at that time, an efficient police system). Then, too, these were the accepted conduits by which the average citizen could get in touch with his government. Because of the nature of Venice's government – a republic and not a monarchy – decisions were taken by up to 250 senators, each of whom had his own entourage. In such a fragmented setting, power became a game of amassing the most information. Secrets were traded. Your barber might be a spy. Or your gondolier. Information about the way the republic was run was carefully guarded, unless a senator slipped up; your apothecary could know more about what was being discussed in the government than you did. Writers thrived: the Venetian version of a journalist was called a *novellisti*, and they would exchange information with other *novellisti* in different sectors of the city, spinning the stories that would pass for news.

Calle's first stop in the city, after her hotel, is the Questura, the main police station. She has been told that they keep the hotel registration forms on file. But the clerk will not tell her where her 'friend' is staying; it's 'against policy'. He recommends she ask at the train station. *'Why don't I have the audacity to bribe him?'* she wonders.[6] At the train station they refer her to the Questura. It's the administrative equivalent of walking in circles.

+

The man is hard to track down. She half remembers him mentioning a *pensione* called the San Bernardino, but there is no hotel in Venice by that name. She calls all the hotels with saints' names, but no one has an Henri B. staying there. At 2 p.m. on Friday 15 February she sits down with a list of all the hotels in Venice, organised by class, and begins calling each of them: Bauer Grunwald, Cipriani, Gritti, Carlton Executive, Europa & Brittania, Gabrielli, Londra, Luna, Metropole, Monaco & Grand Canal, Park Hotel, into Serenissima, Spagna, Stella-Alpina, San Maurizio, and so forth. There are 181 of them, an entire world of hotels inspired by countries and cities and constellations and saints and Venetian families. At 6.45 p.m. she calls the Casa de Stefani and is informed that Henri B. has gone out for the day.

'*I see myself at the labyrinth's gate,*' she writes in her journal, '*ready to get lost in this city and this story. Submissive.*'[7]

The labyrinth is one of the city's power metaphors: we need a word for the way it twists out of our reach just as we think we've understood it, for the way it seems to have an agency all its own, the way it thwarts us, confuses us, loses it, the way it takes all our savvy to find ways to defeat it. Theseus goes into the labyrinth to fight the Minotaur, leaving a trail of thread given him by his love, Ariadne, to find his way back to her. But a labyrinth is actually an arrangement of paths that lead you, in time, to their centre. You can't get lost in them; they are comprised of only one winding corridor. It slows you down, that's all. A maze, on the other hand, is a structure built to confuse, that gives you the feeling you might never arrive. A maze gives you choices: this way or that? And if this, what of that? Where the Minotaur was kept would have had to have been a maze.

Why do we persist in making this mistake? Why do we want the city to be something we have to struggle with, or against?

We want to make choices, and have some agency in getting lost, and getting found. We want to challenge the city, and decipher it, and flourish within its parameters.

And if we should have to confront the Minotaur, we want to be able to get back out again.

+

Calle worries that she's wasting time, and becomes impatient. '*I must stop pondering possible outcomes, wondering where this story is leading me. I will follow it to the end.*'[8]

+

I feel guilty chasing imaginary synagogues in Venice. I try to budget my time strictly: attend Italian class in the morning, walk around Venice in the afternoon, do my homework in the evening and read Virginia Woolf at night. In a tight schedule, there's no room for surprises, and there's no time to get lost.[9]

But Venice is not a city you approach with an itinerary: you are certain to get lost, and to be late almost before you've set out. Even those blessed with a superior sense of direction are not spared; as you walk through the city the streets rearrange themselves dexterously, like a dealer shuffling cards. If you see a shop or restaurant you'd like to try, do it then and there because the chances of finding it again are slim. There are some places in Venice that, like Brigadoon, only emerge from the mist once in a hundred years. Unless you're having one of those days where you can't get off the same trajectory, back and forth along the same bridges, until you're sick to death of seeing that shop and you can't remember why you ever wanted to stop there and all you want is to see a different shop. That happens too.

Some years ago they posted yellow signs here and there pointing to the Piazza San Marco, to Rialto, to the Accademia Bridge, to the train station. Some mischievous Venetians have 'helped' in their own way, tagging unmarked corners and archways 'Per Rialto!', but obey them at your own risk: you're more likely to wind up at the other end of town.

Those yellow signs turn what is actually a maze into a labyrinth. To and from, to and from, Rialto, San Marco, Accademia. Time slows down as we weave the same path, over the same bridges, again and again. This path is so well trodden, we think. I want to get off of it. We want to disobey.

+

One day, en route to an appointment to interview someone for the novel up in Cannaregio, the site of the old Jewish ghetto, I lose my way. With time slipping away and the hot sun beating down, I turn from *calle* to *calle*, can't recall if I've seen that Internet cafe or that fruit seller five minutes or five days before. I refuse to retrace my steps, believing with the naivety of someone from a grid city like New York or a wheel city like Paris that if I just keep going I'll right the wrong turn and make it to my destination eventually. Maybe it is to avoid the boredom of coming back the way I'd come. Or a prideful inability to admit topographical defeat.

Then I turn into a long, narrow street that I have a good feeling about. Yes, I tell myself, this is the way, it must surely run north-north-west and then I should come out on that street near that bridge and then I'll be nearly there . . . I follow along for a few solid minutes, until the road abruptly ends in water. No way forward without a boat or a wetsuit.

It feels like it Means Something: like for every bit of progress I make in one area of my life, I have to waste time retracing my steps in another, to catch up and reorient myself, and forge forward again. Nothing goes in a straight line. There is much doubling back.

Ignore the signs. Put down the map. You're going to hit dead ends. But don't worry: you won't end up in the water.

You don't want to be too dutiful, in Venice.

+

Once Calle has found her man, his itinerary becomes hers; his Venice becomes her Venice. She takes note of all the streets they walk down (for he is with his wife, who wears a flowered shawl on her head), the shop windows they stop and look in, the photographs he takes. Calle imitates him, taking pictures where he does, stopping where he stops, and as she traces his path in her notebook she inscribes herself all over the city, and over his trajectory; what he thinks are choices, what are indeed choices, have her secret imprint on them: 'calle de Camai, calle del Chiovere, campo San Rocco, calle Larga'.[10] When she loses track of the couple, she goes to the old Jewish cemetery on the Lido. One of the things she knows about him is that he loves cemeteries. It is where he should have gone, she writes. '*I have high expectations of him.*'[11]

The labyrinth of the city is built to foster desire. Everything we want, disappearing around the next corner, always a few steps ahead. Although at the beginning Calle's curiosity is born of coincidence, Henri B. becomes an obsession. She has to remind herself that she has no particular feelings for him, that what she's feeling doesn't come from inside her, but from the game. And yet she has all the signs of the lover spurned or ignored, stalking the object of her love, from passing 'furtively' by his hotel to waiting for him outside an antiques shop. There is something almost daughterly about the project, and incestuous, as she begins to think perhaps she is in love with him. This must be the reason she follows him, no? What other reason could there be? 'Only love,' she writes, 'seems admissible.'[12]

+

When I was little, I nearly drowned in my friend's pool. It was the above-ground kind, a not-very-big raised ring of chlorinated water resting on the soggy grass of her backyard. It was filled with toys and floats and a couple of rafts, and I was tadpoling around picking up plastic rings weighted with sand from the bottom of the pool when I tried to get to the surface, but was blocked by a flotilla of rafts with my friends sitting on them. My breath was running out and I couldn't find a way above water that wasn't blocked by plastic weighted with flesh. I did, just in time, but I've never forgotten the panic.

About a year after I moved to Paris, I remembered that day when I couldn't get out from under my friend's raft. The guy I loved had left me to go to law school in the south of France, and in the crush of it I turned to a therapist. I could barely get out of bed most days, the outside world had taken on a swampy aspect that made daily activities feel heavy, like every step I took I met with resistance. All I could talk about, in our sessions, was this guy, but I wasn't making any progress getting over him. One afternoon I reported the dream I'd had the night before. I was in a shipwreck, and was out on the high seas, and desperately clinging to some kind of flotation device.

That's the guy, she said. Or, well, whatever he represents to you. That's why you can't let go of him – he's your raft. You're just hanging on for dear life.

I was hanging on, I think; but the raft was also killing me.

+

So I'm trying to cling to something besides a person, who can leave. I'm in this floating city, walking the streets of Dorsoduro, trying to find what that thing is that holds me together, and above water. There's something intensely religious about Venice, but I have tried religion, and found it to be an impasse. As the child of a lapsed Catholic and a lapsed Jew, neither ever fit quite right, because there was always that other bit that didn't belong. I give Catherine the same background and the same longing to belong; I give her the surname Parrish, and cast her into Venice, a city whose neighbourhoods are organised by *parrocchia*; a simple translation that perhaps neutralised religion from being a concept of inclusion or exclusion to one of assimilating to a place. But I think, on some level, that's not true. We want to be accepted by the people, too.

I go to Santa Maria della Salute, following the advice of Philippe Sollers, who says he lights a candle in a church every time he arrives in a new place 'to guide the hand that writes'. I need guidance for so many things, but if I can just have a little help with the writing, I think, I won't worry so much about the rest of it.

I make it as far as the nave when a clean-shaven young man approaches me and shakes his head disapprovingly. '*Troppo corto*,' he says, gesturing at my skirt. I had worn a cardigan over my tank top, but hadn't given a second thought to the skirt. A man walks past us wearing a tank top and shorts but nothing is said to him. Just as I give in to the beauty of Catholicism it raps me across the knuckles, like the nuns did to my mother, when she was a child. 'Can I just light a candle and then I'll go?' I ask. He frowns, but allows it. Sin may light a candle, so long as it drops a euro in the coffer.

On Shabbat, I visit an actual synagogue for Saturday-morning services. I have picked the Spanish Synagogue, since some of my characters' ancestors were Sephardic Jews from the Iberian Peninsula, stopping in Venice before leaving for Croatia when the Venetian Ghetto was created in 1516. I want to write about the Jews of Venice who refused to be contained in the ghetto, who pretended to be Christian to keep their freedom, but practised Judaism in private in their homes. I wake up early and set out from Dorsoduro on what I hope is the right track, but I get lost, and am late to shul.

The entrance is guarded by two armed men. One speaks English with me. He asks to look in my bag, and when he finds my camera and cell phone, he refuses me entry. 'This is an Orthodox synagogue, signorina.' The thing about Shabbat, you see, is that you're not meant to light a flame or do any work. Using electronic equipment is considered lighting a flame, so even the presence of potential flame-lighters is *verboten*. I try reasoning with him ('But if they're not on then it's not breaking any rules!'), then I try tears ('But I've come so far from Dorsoduro, and got lost . . .') and then I try God: 'But it's Shabbat! I have to observe the Sabbath!'

He isn't fooled, but he offers me a deal. 'Tell you what. If you can find a place to leave these things, I'll let you in. Otherwise, you can come back tonight for Havdalah. But I'm telling you,' he says (condescendingly I thought), 'most shopkeepers around here are closed for Shabbat.' There's no way I'm going to traipse all the way home and back, so I meet his challenge. Around the corner, towards the train station, I noticed an open antiques store, and head back there. I'm in luck: the genteel middle-aged owner speaks enough French to understand why I am holding out my digital camera and cell phone to him.

I return to the synagogue and triumphantly open my bag to the man, when I spot my iPod peeping out from underneath my wallet. Luckily, he doesn't, or he pretends not to, and he lets me in.

+

The word 'ghetto' originates with the Jews in Venice; the Venetian Ghetto was built on the old iron foundry in Cannaregio, which was called the *ghèto*.

Still, here's me trying to get *into* the ghetto of religious identification. Why am I so anxious to be bound to someone else's rules?

+

Sophie Calle is crouching in an alleyway, waiting for the man she's following to come out of the antiques shop he and his wife entered hours ago. It's decidedly stalker-like behaviour and she's feeling pretty foolish. It's freezing cold. He is testing her, she thinks, staying inside for an 'absurd' amount of time just to show her 'You can wait for me, I won't come.'[13]

What *is* she doing? What kind of *flâneuse*-ing is this? If a *flâneuse* is a liberated woman, determined to go where she isn't supposed to, what would it mean for her to follow someone around? I think of Edgar Allen Poe's short story 'The Man of the Crowd' (1840), about an anonymous man, just another face in the crowd, but a particular kind of man, watching the world go by: the classic *flâneur*. Poe's man has his interest piqued by a strange type, whom he follows all throughout the city, only to lose sight of him. You could argue the *flâneur* is the man doing the following or the one being followed, the one making the choices in the city or the one making the choice to relinquish choices in pursuit of something he can't put a name to, only a face.

Calle doesn't take shortcuts; Calle doesn't follow the yellow signs, unless the man she's following does. But her progress through the city is anything but passive. She thought of it as play, not art. So she didn't take enough pictures. She had to go back and fill in the missing ones. The man we presume is Henri B. in those photographs, the ones we see in the book she published, isn't him. From follower she has become tracker, artist, photographer. She would call the project *Suite Vénitienne*, with all that word, *suite*, implies. From the Latin *secutus*, the past participle of the verb *sequoir*, which becomes *suivre*, in French, and *to follow* in English. *La suite* is what's next, what follows, a sequel. It is a series of events, or a series of movements. Classical music comes in suites. Hotel rooms, if you're lucky, come in suites.[14]

Above the antiques shop Calle notices a sign on which it is written 'Show me your home, and I'll show you who you are'.[15] It's got to be a reference to André Breton: 'Tell me who you follow and I'll tell you who you are,' Breton writes in the opening of his novel *Nadja* (1928), as he proceeds to stalk, seduce and abandon a mentally unstable young artist he names Nadja for her exotic Russian beauty. Breton also turns following into a subversive act, in which love is amplified by flight, and contoured by the surrounding city. Literature is full of men who stalk and women who are stalked. It takes an artist like Sophie Calle to turn the tables.[16]

She's not the first or the only artist to follow people in the streets. Vito Acconci made a similar piece in New York City in 1969, following people around the city, sometimes for hours, until they entered a private place. He carried a camera down the street and every time he blinked, he took a photograph. It was a way, he said in his notes, of getting out of the house, of getting around, of being taken out of himself into something larger. These projects make us aware of the publicness of being in public, of the vulnerability of it, of the charged atmosphere, as we avoid confrontation and all it might involve: invasiveness, danger, erotic encounters.

It's different, though, a man following or a woman. There are all sorts of other implications. A woman following a man is subservient. Isn't she? But a man following a woman is passionate pursuit. Throughout *Suite Vénitienne* Calle is herself followed by men; some speak to her, some don't; some are threatening, some aren't. Mostly she likes the attention. (We are so complicit, with our vanity, our need to be noticed, seen. 'Today, for the first time in my life,' Calle writes, 'someone called me a good-looking blonde.')[17] And, as Calle herself has pointed out, Acconci wasn't working in the realm of affect, of the sentiments. Where Acconci's was about performance and being in public, Calle's is much more about privacy and interiority. She records not only where Henri B. goes and what he does there, but her personal responses to the act of following him.

When they finally leave the antiques shop, and walk to a vaporetto stop, she stays close by, looking in shop windows, boarding their boat just as it's about to leave. She stands outside as they sit in the cabin, feeling encircled by the same water, the same Venice, he is.

His Venice is her Venice.

Put me somewhere.

Where you go I will go, and where you stay I will stay. Your people will be my people and your God my God.

The creed of the convert.

+

Following is devalued in our culture; there's something suspect about being a follower, it denotes weakness, or even perversion. We're encouraged to be leaders. To take the incentive, to forge our own paths. But there is something subversive about submission. Calle's work reflects this: it opens up the opportunity for chance within a set of controls. And she does have control. She's relying on another person, but she's still making the calls. He's just sparing her the feeling of being 'lost' in the labyrinth: as long as she's got her eye on him, she's exactly where she needs to be.

This is not the case ten years later, when she goes travelling with a man, ostensibly on equal terms. Her 1992 film, made with her ex-husband Greg Shepherd, *No Sex Last Night*, may or may not recount the unravelling of their relationship. It is unclear how much of the film is staged, and how much is spontaneous. The premise is that they have agreed to drive cross-country together and make a film of it. But when she arrives in New York he hasn't done anything to prepare – the car hasn't been serviced, he's lost his driver's licence, hasn't rented or bought a camera, he forgot to pick her up at the airport. 'I knew he didn't want to leave any more,' Calle says in voice-over, 'but to protect my trip, I organised everything. Even if it's going to be a disaster, we'll go.'

They only film when they are in the car; when they get out of the car we just see still photographs of the hotels, the diners, each other. She speaks English to him and French in voice-over, in a kind of proto-reality-show confessional narrative, except the voice-overs are often layered over a shot of the two of them together, giving us access to what each of them is thinking and what they don't say to each other. 'Why am I here?' he asks himself. 'I'm getting tired of her French in that camera. 'Just say what you're thinking, just say what you want to say.' Her French a place he can't travel. Her mind as well. Every night they stay in a hotel, and every morning Calle takes a picture of their room, and announces, in voice-over, 'No sex last night.'

Greg was drawn to Sophie, he relates in voice-over, after seeing a show of hers in Boston. Inspired by her off-beat approach to art and human relationships, he resolved that one day he would find her and follow her. But before he could seek her out, she walked up to him one day on the street in New York: 'She had found me first.' But now her games make him feel alienated, and mistrustful. He accuses her of constantly 'turning up things' to find evidence against him, of 'invasion of privacy . . . Which you and I know you specialise in.' They are two people thrown together in the pressure cooker of a shitty car driving cross-country. The car keeps breaking down, costing more and more time and money. Their tenuous bond frays as neither of them can give the other what they need. They both know Greg is the problem – he is immature and non-committal, the classic neurotic tortured and torturing creative male – but Sophie contributes to his insecurity by being 'ironic' about everything; he finds her 'judgemental' and shrinks in anticipation whenever she says anything. They both can't wait to get where they're going.

Greg makes phone calls to other women periodically throughout the trip, and sponges money off her to fix the car. In one scene he asks 'Are you OK?' and she nods without saying anything, without blinking even, for about ten seconds, as rain falls down the window and someone plays the harmonica on the radio. She's not acting.

It's hard to see someone you revere heartbroken over some guy who bites the hair off his hands and arms.

+

This is the story of how Calle ended up in psychoanalysis. When she was thirty, her father said she had bad breath, and told her to see a doctor. He made the appointment but when she got there it was a shrink's office. Calle told him there must be some mistake, her father was supposed to send her to a doctor for her bad breath, and the shrink said, 'Do you do everything your father tells you to do?' That was when she decided to be his patient. It was a way of following, and not following, her father's instructions.

The project of following Henri B. is a tug of war; sometimes she relinquishes control; sometimes she grabs hold of it. There's no knowledge at stake, no information to be gleaned, except about Henri B.'s daily existence. She plays the detective, but there is no crime, no reason to survey. She would play with this idea a few years later, when she would hire a private detective to follow *her* throughout Paris. Secretly, she follows the detective.

By then she is better at following. Or at least so we assume; we don't know if the detective ever figures out she's been tailing him. Henri B., however, does. The day after she has waited for hours outside the antiques shop, he spots her following him inside the hospital of S.S. Giovanni e Paolo. Her eyes are what gave her away, he says. He recognised her eyes. She should have disguised them better.

Just before this, Calle has been almost giddy with joy, with nervousness, with triumph. '*I've diverted him from his course,*' she writes. '*He's intrigued.*'[18]

It makes me think of another man Calle 'targeted' with one of her projects, called *The Address Book*. In 1983, after finding an address book lying in the street in Paris (the rue des Martyrs, around the corner from where I was living at the time I started my own Venetian project), Calle undertook to call all of the people listed in it, trying to get an image of the man who had lost it. She made little articles out of these conversations, and published them in *Libération*. The man in question was not pleased, and tried to sue Calle for invasion of privacy. He also tried to get *Libération* to publish nude photos of Calle. That was the one time, Calle admits, that she went too far.[19] She also, as with Henri B., claimed to have fallen in love.

Some people don't like being followed.

Does it come with too much responsibility?

+

She manages to get to Paris by a different train, via Bologna, five minutes before he does. She watches him and his wife get off their train and struggle with their baggage, walking very slowly. One day they will have wheels on their suitcases, and they won't have to struggle. But then, one day they'll all be taking easyJet, and the romance will be gone.

I wonder where Henri B. is now. I wonder what he thinks of Calle. Does he own a copy of her book? Has he been to Venice since, and is his city now transformed? Has he found someone of his own to follow?

CDG> NAR two-hour bus to ANA Hotel, get off in the underground parking garage and take the elevator up, up, up

TOKYO

INSIDE

A good many of the ordinary ways of living go when people begin to live up in the air.

— Maeve Brennan, *New Yorker*

In November 2007, my boyfriend at the time (I'll call him X, like Sophie Calle) was informed he was being transferred to the Tokyo office of the bank where he worked, effective January. The discussion went like this:

— No.

— …

— Quit your job. Find another job. You hate being a banker anyway.

— …

— We can't move to Tokyo. How can they just move you to Tokyo?

— …

— How long are they moving you there for?

— Indefinitely.

— No. No.

My reasons were many. But above all, I didn't want to leave Paris. I had worked so hard to get there, and stay there, every year was a new fight to renew my visa, to get teaching work to support myself, to balance teaching with research, with writing. Then there were the professional challenges facing me that year: I had to study for my orals exams, which would take place in New York in May; this required reading and taking notes from the roughly seventy books I had on my lists. I needed stability, I needed continuity, I needed a reference library. An image flashed through my mind of me lugging seventy books onto an airplane.

On the other hand: Tokyo! I had never been to Asia; I didn't know when else I would get there. I had always imagined that I would go there one day. I saw myself at some vague point in the future, as a middle-aged woman, there with my husband, our kids away at university. Maybe this was an opportunity I shouldn't let pass me by. His company would pay for me to travel back and forth. And he promised he would look for another job in Paris as soon as he could, that we would enjoy Japan while we were there, and then go home.

So I said OK.

+

Rumour has it there's a mental ward in the Hôpital Sainte-Anne in Paris for Japanese tourists who are catatonically disappointed to find the actual Paris is dirty and loud and rude, when they were expecting it to be all croissants and *macarons* and smelling of Chanel No 5. They call it 'Paris syndrome', and its physical effects are said to be comparable to what Stendhal described on his trip to Florence: 'When leaving Santa Croce, I had heart palpitations, what one calls "nerves" in Berlin; life was exhausted in me, I was walking in fear of falling down.'[1]

But there is no mental ward in Tokyo for Parisians light-headed at the hideousness of Tokyo. For the first week, I was convinced we were living in the shit part of town. They put us in Roppongi, the *gaijin* (foreigner) ghetto of flyovers and tunnels and steel bridges you had to climb to cross the four-lane highway of a main street. The buildings were almost uniformly covered in bathroom tiles which looked as if they haven't been cleaned since they were thrown up in haste after the Second World War. It hurt. It really hurt. Our building was in a complex called Ark Hills, owned by the slick, wealthy Mori corporation who own just about everything in Roppongi and its environs. Nearby there was a sad orange-and-white imitation of the Eiffel Tower that looked more like an oil derrick.

As I began to venture into the city, I found most of it looked like this as well. Its governing aesthetic was pure functionalism. I don't know what I was expecting, so I can't say why I was disappointed. I was hoping for something different. Something – less industrial. A city I could feel at home in, even if only temporarily. A city I could explore the way I always do: on foot.

But Tokyo is not a walkable city; it is too big, even neighbourhoods are too big to amble in. We lived at a Y-shaped intersection of two main highways (Y for yen, for money, for wealth), one leading to Shibuya, the other to the Imperial Palace. All the places I wanted to explore – Shinjuku, Harajuku, Nakameguro, Omotesando, Asakusa – lay beyond, far from us and, for the most part, from each other, connected by long stretches of pedestrian-unfriendly highways. We could walk to Azabu, an upscale neighbourhood full of embassies, but that was about it. After two weeks, I wanted to scream. But I didn't.

Hold it together. Give it a chance. Keep an open mind.

We lived in one of those long-term business hotels, the kind they call an apart-hotel, in a sixteenth-floor eyrie with a view that looked like Midtown Manhattan. Every day at five o'clock a little tune like a children's song would play on the loudspeakers attached to the buildings, wafting up from the canyon. As evening came on the buildings captured the warm orange of the sunset on their windows, and at night they twinkled with protective lights, a million red eyes blinking in the dark. In the morning helicopters drifted across the sky like mosquitoes.

Everything was automated. The flowers on the balcony watered themselves. If you were in the kitchen and fancied a bath, there was a button on the wall that would turn on the tub taps in the bathroom and automatically turn off when it was full. If the water cooled while you were lying in it, you could reheat it. The 'shower toilets' (as they're called) had a whole range of functions that included seat-warming, arse-cleaning, music-playing, and self-flushing. Ours opened automatically when you approached it, which is a better idea in theory than in practice. Even if you're just getting a towel from the cabinet, the toilet begins to beep and whirr expectantly, as if you've woken a sleeping dog. I was constantly setting it off. I would deactivate the cover-lifting function, and X would reactivate it, and so on and so forth. The banker's life in Japan: the things that were nice were unnecessary, and the things you'd want to be nice were not.

A week after we got there, the world financial markets crashed. A renegade trader at X's bank lost all its money. From one day to the next it was *la crise*. There were no jobs to be had back in Paris.

We were marooned in Tokyo.

+

Well, not marooned. I came and went, as planned. But his absence transformed Paris, made it temporary, instead of the place I lived. When I was there, I wanted to be in Tokyo, and when I was in Tokyo, I wanted to be in Paris. I had been split between New York and Paris, but now I was strung across three continents, and unhappy in all of them.

+

I kept a journal.

22/01/08

The day after a massive downturn in the stock market. I study the faces of the be-suited people surrounding me at Starbucks, who consult their laptops on their coffee breaks, but I see no trace of the previous day's catastrophe on them. Is it imperceptible to the untrained eye?

The impact has yet to reverberate across the ocean to America, where the markets were closed yesterday (today for them) in observance of Martin Luther King Day. Tomorrow we will know more. The American credit bubble is responsible for this mess – how will it play out over there?

+

I emailed my sister.

23/1/08

I am daily frustrated by not speaking the language, although I'm learning little phrases and taught myself the numbers. I think I will enrol in a language class. I miss Paris a lot – it's so ugly here. And I miss you guys. I spoke to M&D on the phone the other day and it was so nice to hear their voices. Paris feels like the next town over from NY compared with Tokyo – I feel so far away. But this is a once-in-a-lifetime and never-in-most-lifetimes opportunity, so I need to get everything I can out of it, and be here for as long as it makes sense for us. And hey – if ever I fly from Tokyo to NY I will have flown around the world.

+

I made a Dada cut-out poem out of an article in the *FT*.[2]

led markets about close. rally
Japan no Asian cuts, surprises
recession optimism a buying no drew
eco- interest investors sprang figures
already further Tokyo

+

I felt the distance in my bones. All those hours spent flying over Siberia. The trip took me so far from where I'd started; it was the wrong way round the globe. I should have flown to Tokyo from New York. Maybe with a stopover in California. NY > LAX > Tokyo.

Everything was drab in the winter light. The sky looked dingy, like a white towel that got washed with the darks.

And out in the streets of Roppongi, dense crowds of people in puffer jackets, ads for whisky and beer, a shopfront for a business called Brawny Weeds. 'For rent an apartment, call Brawny Weeds.' Hello Storage. Someplace called the Birdman. A cafe called Almond with a sickening pink-and-white candy-striped awning. Everything was covered by a canopy of highway. There were lovely ornate street lamps, and trees that did try; and I tried in turn, to find scraps of beauty, you can see it in my photos. I would zoom in on details – that's where they say God is, right? I was trying to surprise a little Shinto god, dwelling in the city.

+

I wrote in my journal.

13/02/08

I don't want to be here. This is wrong.

+

Ark Hills describes itself as a 'multipurpose city complex which fulfils work, play and relaxation, all the elements of urban life'. And it's true, there was everything you might need: supermarkets and specialty food shops (selling grapefruits and melons on satin beds in boxes, like precious jewels, selling for one hundred dollars each – cheap for jewels, dear for melons), everyday things like a pharmacy, a doctor, a dentist, several banks, a heliport, a concert hall. There was a barbershop called Angel Foot that advertised all manner of hair-removal services. I took a picture of a picture of a Japanese woman tending to a Japanese man on a sign that read EAR HOLE. I bought French *Elle* at a bookshop called Maruzen, and sometimes books in English, mass-market paperbacks of Murakami and whoever had recently won the Booker. There was a fake French cafe called Aux Bacchanales where all the French traders went to drink, where I sat and tried to pretend I hadn't left. But it felt less like a Parisian cafe in Japan and more like a Japanese imitation of a French cafe in New York.

The synthetic, corporate environment felt constricting. It didn't feel like part of Tokyo. Tokyo was out there, I was sure of it. But how to get at it?

+

I learned to conjugate where we were in space based on the history of the neighbourhood. Ark Hills was at 1-12-32 Roppongi, Minato-ku. The first part of the address corresponds to the '*chome*', or arrondissement, in Minato prefecture. The *chome* is then divided up into different sections, of which we lived in the twelfth. The third part of the address specifies the building is the thirty-second to be built in that section.

So if you're walking down the street looking for a particular address, it's unlikely you'd know where to find it unless you knew how the neighbourhood built up.

How do you navigate a city where the streets have no names?

+

That five o'clock song implants itself in my head. *So so la so so so mi do re mi mi re* and what is the rest?

+

I wrote in my journal.

16/02/08

Today was a pretty good day. X took me to Yodobashi Camera and then out for *katsu-don* (pork cutlets and rice topped with a fried egg) and beer. Like a little kid he's saddled with and has to please, except with alcohol. It was

one of those Japanese-style Automat-type places where
you pick out what you want from a sort of vending
machine and pay except all it gives you is a ticket and
then you pick up your food from the counter. Men on
stools hunch over Formica tables and slurp up their
noodles loudly and with great smacking of their lips.
There was a man from the camera store wearing an
armband that said 'interpreter'.

+

There were other nice things. I found a street full of shops in
Harajuku selling cheap women's fashion, with names like Jet
Lag Drive, Flower Monsoon, Kolor, all the salesgirls standing in
the doorways singing their song of welcome. '*Irrashaimaseeeeee!*'
Shops full of little-girl clothes for grown women, round collars
and frills. I bought a ruffled sleeveless top that I wore as a dress
but back in Paris realised was far too short to get away with.

Every now and then we heard of something that sounded so
exciting, so fantastic, we wanted to find it at once and do it so
that we could feel we were experiencing all the city had to
offer. Like the kitten cafe rumoured to be located at the top of
Isetan department store. We went up there one day and,
needless to say, found no kittens, only boxes of dolls dressed
like samurai.

+

It's a Japanese folk song, I learned. It plays everywhere in the
whole country, every day at five.

+

Food was a problem. I haven't been a picky eater since the third grade, when my mother asked me to *keep an open mind* about a white substance that turned out to be mozzarella and on the whole keeping an open mind has generally rewarded me with something delicious. But in Japan I realised my mind can only open so far. The highest form of Japanese cuisine, *kaiseki*, I found inedible. Everything had a strange smell, like the ground-up contents of a rabbit cage was made into a broth, and then the rest of the meal was simmered in it. The tea tasted like the air in a room that had been closed up for a very long time. There was one root vegetable, some kind of radish, which tasted like the underarms of an old man's tweed jacket.

I went to the supermarket and couldn't read the labels. Is this brown liquid soy sauce or teriyaki sauce or some as-yet-undiscovered sauce? Is this bag of white granules sugar or salt? (With the predictably disastrous consequences in my cup of coffee the next morning.) Bags and containers of ginger-coloured stuff – gunk, paste. Made of what? good? bad? Bags and bags of dried fish (ugh). Rows of brown substances in jars in the supermarket. What are they? What could I have them with? It seemed as if there were some amazing culinary world right beneath my eyes but I couldn't access it.

We went to a French restaurant in the Roppongi Hills mall so often we made friends with the sommelier. For Valentine's Day, X took me to a restaurant that specialised in tofu. There was only a tasting menu, and one of the dishes consisted of a white, tofu-like ball, in a little shot glass, which the English translation on the menu identified as 'milt in an orange reduction'. 'What is milt?' I asked, regretting it almost immediately. Best not to know. *Keep an open mind.* X googled 'milt' on his phone. 'Fish testicles,' he answered. I spat mine out. He ate the pair.

Through trial and error, I found that some Japanese food was really delicious. The afore-mentioned *katsu-don. Okonomiyake*: a kind of everything-but-the-kitchen-sink omelette topped with mayonnaise. We managed to find a really good curry house in Roppongi, where they serve skateboard-sized slabs of nan dripping with butter, and where the food was so good it almost didn't matter that the restaurant was thick with smoke, it being illegal to smoke outside in Japan (except for in appointed smoking shelters) but legal to smoke inside.

I ate like a teenager.

And I liked the small touches, the unexpected details. If I went out to buy a bento box for lunch from the nearby deli it would come wrapped in coloured paper with a bow. There were beautiful stone walls in Azabu, lining the hilly streets on which clusters of trees grew, evergreen. The walls seemed ancient, though they couldn't have been very old, not even a century. They referenced a much older Japan that is no longer visible, that I couldn't feel, or didn't know how to feel. We started visiting apartments – you can't stay in an apart-hotel forever, or can you? – and some had a view of Mount Fuji. Its proximity was confusing. *Are we there, then?*

+

Through the looking glass, I became a student of reversals. In the taxis, whose drivers wore white gloves and whose seats were laid with lace, the doors opened and closed themselves. On the metro, men with paddles pushed you into overstuffed carriages. What you can do for yourself is in one context done for you, in another imposed on you.

+

The months accumulated, and X stayed in Tokyo. I passed my orals in New York, travelled back to Paris, saw friends, tried to keep my life full without him in it. I looked at real-estate listings in shop windows, thinking of the flat we'd move into when he finally came back, a nice big one-bedroom, somewhere on the Left Bank (X hated the Right). But after hearing all his stories of Michelin-starred restaurants and titty bars with brokers footing the bill, it dawned on me that X didn't want to come back to Paris. That, in Tokyo, French bankers were *le shit*. What I wanted really didn't matter.

+

It was hot, so hot, the hottest summer I could remember, and that included those stifling drowsy summers on Long Island when the world swam in the heat rising from the sidewalks and the caterpillars dropped from the trees in exhaustion. The air felt pressurised, pushing on my skin from every direction, entering every pore. I bought a parasol to shade myself, like the women I saw on the street, but it didn't help much, and was just one more thing to carry. I sprayed myself often with a little can of atomised mineral water from the pharmacy in Paris.

We moved to an apartment in Akasaka, to another Mori property on the other side of the Y intersection. This was not an apart-hotel but an apartment. But though the furniture was ours, it still felt temporary, an airplane-seat apartment like the ones I lived in in New York. For a short while you live the drama of your life in them, and then you leave and can barely remember them, since they have no particular attributes. Our new home's neutrality, in its institutionality, its mimicry of home, made it not an apart-hotel but a hotel-apart.

The hotel: the home of the foreigner, the misfit, the impossible-to-assimilate.

I spent my days in the air conditioning, avoiding the soul-melting oven of the outside world, or, when I started to feel stir-crazy, went down to the Starbucks in the lobby of our building. I read Roland Barthes in a corner with an iced coffee, to a background music of baristas singing *grande cappuccinôôô!*, one to the other, until the precious drink was offered to the customer with both hands and a presentational *arigatogosamaaaaaasu!*

By then I had that children's song down pat.

Barthes was fascinated by Japan, which he visited in 1966 and wrote about in a book called *Empire of Signs* (1970), a culmination of his work on semiotics, understanding language as a self-referential system with no concrete connection to the things it represents. Japan, and Japanese, marked for Barthes a system unto itself, totally 'detached' from our own, that does not yield to him any 'truth' about Japan, nor about our symbols for it, but rather the limits of symbols themselves. A lot like writing, which can only strain to describe so far, before the words themselves become plastic, and meaning is created on the page, not beyond it.

Japan forced Barthes to confront the emptiness of language. The void. The absence of a transcendental signifier, or a way to break the code. 'The dream: to know a (foreign) language and yet not to understand it.' To be relieved of the burden of meaning. For the outsider, Japan is a proliferation of unreadable signs. The language, strokes of meaning organised architectonically, throws up a physical barrier to the Western tourist; trying to remember a kanji, for me, is like running into someone you met at a party years ago, trying to place them. I would confuse the kanji for Tokyo

東東

with the one for city

市

and sometimes even the simple one for person

I could not summon the ability to tell them apart. Not that I needed to. But I wanted to.

The character for woman, *onna*, is supposed to be a figure with breasts sitting down.

女

For Barthes, Japanese was a protective veil against all the ways people present themselves through language. But these illegible signs came at a moment when I was trying so hard to become myself in Barthes' language, to situate myself within it, to prove I could do it. And now this new language, in which I could not get a foothold.

+

I signed up for intensive, one-on-one Japanese classes at a language school in Meguro. My teacher, Hayashimoto-sensei, was a proper Japanese lady, impeccable in her silk twinsets and pearls. Lauren-san, she called me, rolling the 'r'. I liked her very much.

The logic of Japanese: every part of speech followed by its corresponding preposition, or rather, postposition. Subject followed by subject preposition. Direct object followed by direct object preposition. Verb. I learned to build sentences the way I used to play with those stackable logs as a kid. This one layers this way, this one fits on top.

> Watashi wa Roppongi ni ikimasu.
> I am going to Roppongi.

> Watashi no kuruma ga akai desu.
> My car is red.

'Yo!' they add at the end of a sentence, for added emphasis. *Watashi no kuruma ga akai desu yo!* My car is red, you know it! Or they say 'ne', to express doubt, or the wish for agreement. *Watashi no kuruma ga akai desu, ne?* My car is red, no? (If there were other inflections, I didn't catch them.) I would sit and puzzle over the word order, trying, and failing, to commit it to memory.

I did my homework at the second-floor terrace at Tully's Coffee on Akasaka-dori, across from Biz Tower. On the street the people went by. Pretty girls in frilly dresses and espadrille wedge heels. Junior high school kids with their uniforms untucked. Women of all ages carrying parasols to shield themselves from the sun, even at five in the afternoon. (And ... there's the song.) Middle-aged men in Hawaiian shirts with interesting facial hair. Dehydrated-looking young men in suits. Stylish women in tight black trousers with Dean & DeLuca tote bags. Workers in blue jumpsuits with Aladdin cuffs coming out of the *konbini*. Young guys with messenger bags slung across their torsos and blond patches in their hair. Women wearing lacy half-socks with sandals.

+

I think, in retrospect, it was too much all at once.

(God, I can't wait to go back some day.)

+

It seemed as if everyone walked as slowly as possible. Like the street scene was in slow motion. My life slowed down with it, as I tried to think of the right preposition to follow the right part of the sentence.

Hayashimoto-sensei was very encouraging, but I could only stumble over my words, trying to match nouns to prepositions. *Watashi wa boyfurendu to Kyoto ni Shinkansen de ikimasu.* I am going with my boyfriend to Kyoto by high-speed train.

Most of the sentences I could say featured the word *boyfurendu*.

+

What bothered me most was the certainty I felt that there was a great city out there, full of places I wanted to discover, but I didn't know where to look for them. I didn't know what there was out there. I didn't know where to go, where to walk.

+

We spent our weekends buying furniture at Bo Concept.

I decided what kind of chairs we should have. He liked the tables with drawers in them but we couldn't afford those.

Then the week would start, and he would go back to work.

+

I googled 'interesting things to do in Tokyo'.

I googled 'English-language bookshops in Tokyo'.

I found one in Nakameguro called Cow Books.

I drew a map.

I went to Nakameguro and I couldn't find the bookshop.

I went home frustrated and overheated.

I headed out the next day and hailed a cab.

I showed the address in Japanese to the cabbie.

He didn't know where it was.

He plugged it into the GPS.

GPS didn't know it either.

We drove around and around for a while. Forty euros later, he found it. Cow Books was nice.

I have gone somewhere.

+

Barthes had the same problem I did, but he was more willing to accommodate himself to it. Tokyo is just a different system. It could be learned ethnographically, he says. 'You must orient yourself in it not by book, by address, but by walking, by sight, by habit, by experience; here every discovery is intense and fragile, it can be repeated or recovered only by memory of the trace it has left in you: to visit a place for the first time is

1

thereby to begin to write it: the address not being written, it must establish its own writing.'[3]

Roland you scoundrel, if I could walk this city I would.

+

When I did venture out I stuck to nearby places like the Tokyo Midtown mall, or the Roppongi Hills mall. Of course the American girl heads to the mall. But these are super-malls, not only in size but in concept, with a variety of things to do and see and buy all under one air-conditioned roof. Roppongi Hills (pronounced *Roppongi Hillis*) and another Mori-porium, Tokyo Hills, include parks and museums, high-end restaurants, shopping, art exhibits (we saw one by Ai Weiwei – the entrance to Roppongi is guarded by a Louise Bourgeois spider), hotels, offices, a movie theatre. They are enormous, temples of consumption of the very highest quality. But with all the rain-walls and Zen gardens and wooden walkways mimicking a provincial *onsen*, it all gets a bit tacky, as if Fifth Avenue mated with one of those malls in Miami filled with expensive bars and restaurants and had a monstrously oversized Japanese child. I couldn't afford most of the shops, so I lingered in Muji, buying attractively simple things made of clear plastic and wood, things in which to put other things.

Occasionally I got stuck behind a pair of girls, walking stiltedly, without bending their knees, their feet slightly turned in towards each other, knock-kneed. They didn't seem to have any kind of actual physical impediment causing them to walk that way.

I asked some expats about it. 'It's because they learn from a young age to keep their knees together to keep perverted men from looking up their skirts,' said one. Another blamed it on the formal Japanese way of kneeling on the ground, called *seiza*.

But her friend refuted this right away. 'No one can sit like that for very long,' she said, 'and in any case it makes no sense that it would make them unable to bend their knees when they walk.'

It's supposed to be cute, someone else told me. They call it *x-kyaku*, or x-legs. *Kawaii* (cute)! Japan outdoes all other cultures in cute. For most women *kawaii* dictates a certain performance of giggly femininity that I find grating. They dress themselves like porcelain dolls, all lace and ruffles, their eyes wide as they clomp pigeon-toed down the street. At a party we went to, I watched as X opened a bottle of champagne surrounded by Japanese girls. *Eeeeeek!* they squealed in anticipation as he eased the cork out. A few covered their eyes; one clung to his arm.[4]

I knew I was coming up against my own cultural prejudices, but, like Barthes, I couldn't 'read' Japan, and was left feeling foolish for even trying, and hating myself for hating it there.

+

21/03/08

I am trying to listen. To let it signify. What it signifies I can't understand. I study the language but it's like studying a few grains of sand to imagine the ocean floor. I give myself over to fragments; what else can I do?

+

28/03/08

I refine my maps. I go to random places. I go to Starbucks.

+

Japanese has three alphabets, not counting borrowed Roman letters: hiragana, katakana and kanji.[5] The first two are created of syllables rather than letters; kanji are the pictograms borrowed from Chinese. The 46-syllable hiragana (**ひらがな**) I learn diligently, but by the time we get to the 48-syllable katakana (**カタカナ**) I am exhausted. I didn't think I could commit to more than one alphabet, so I decided I would be a hiragana-only girl. It was once the language for women, who weren't taught the classical learning necessary to read kanji, and though things have changed, I wasn't planning on sticking around long enough to learn the 50,000 kanji that are said to exist. I would be a medieval Japanese woman, reading and writing in hiragana. Many of the great works of early-Japanese literature were composed by women in hiragana – *The Tale of Genji*, *The Pillow Book*, *The Confessions of Lady Nijo*. It was called *onnade*, women's writing. Occasionally they would throw in some kanji to indicate their learning, and references to classical Chinese poetry. Virginia Woolf called for a woman's sentence 'to hold back the male flood';[6] for centuries in Japan the shape of a woman's sentence was columns of hiragana.

Some days the world got the better of me and I was too depressed to go to class. 'Please tell Hayashimoto-sensei I am ill and cannot come to class today,' I would tell the receptionist on the phone. It's hard to articulate why I wanted to stay home. The heat, yes. A headache. But often nothing tangible. The woman in the kanji is stuck inside because when kanji were invented, that is where the woman belonged. I am not trapped inside; I trap myself. I could go outside but I can't. I shower, I put on make-up, I put on my shoes, but I cannot bring myself to open the door and walk out of it.

When I finally made it back to class Hayashimoto-sensei would teach me the vocabulary for whatever ailment, real or hypochondriacal, I had claimed. Stomach ache. *Harawoitameru*. **はらをいためる**. Headache. *Zutsuu*. **ずつう**. Migraine.

Henzutsuu. へんずつう. I like that the word for migraine is the word for headache with *hen* in front of it. *Hen* means strange, odd, peculiar, suspicious. As in, I don't just have a headache, I have a *peculiar* headache.

+

I couldn't make friends. I alienated myself from the kind of people who were supposed to be 'my' people – artists, graphic designers, editors – by complaining about how much I hated Tokyo, how I wanted to go back to Paris, how you can only emigrate and assimilate once and I already did it and it was hard enough and I want to go home.

I was very boring.

People who love Tokyo *love* Tokyo. People who love Tokyo are crazy about Tokyo. People are this way about their cities. They can't understand how you could not love it there. If you don't love Tokyo there must be something wrong with you, you have no eye for detail, no sense of humour, you're too *negative*. For me, living in Japan was like writing with my left hand. I see some people do it fluently. But I can't make anything legible myself.

I resented X for moving there, I resented him for staying there, but you can only resent your partner so much before it becomes impossible to live with them. So the rest of the resentment I foisted off on Japan.

+

At Cow Books, they had a copy of Yoko Ono's *Grapefruit* book, initially published in Tokyo in 1964 and full of endearing instructions for better living, like her 'Map Piece' of 1962, in which she asks the reader to draw an imaginary map, mark a place they'd like to go, and then go walking somewhere using your imaginary map as a guide to the real territory. 'If there is no street where it should be,' she says, 'make one by putting the obstacles aside.'

I have an image of myself putting the obstacles aside in Tokyo. What would that even look like? I can't identify what is obstacle, and what city.

+

Living in Tokyo brought up all these feelings of powerlessness, of having to wait around for other people, as if I had no autonomy. It felt as if I were five years old again and antsy, on line with my mother at Marshall's, trying to relieve the weight of standing for *so long* by leaning on, climbing on, wrapping myself around the sweaty metal railing that demarcated the waiting line. It felt like being stuck in the back of my father's office while he finished up for the day, staring at the rolled-up blueprints and photographs of his buildings, organising his paper clips and staples and pushpins. It felt like sitting through breakfast at the diner, as the sun beat down through the venetian blinds onto the cheap pinewood windowsill, which smelled like earwax, and on which several fly carcasses were scattered. It felt like waiting for my mother at the dentist, in a pinewood-lined waiting room which smelled of antiseptic, where I was encouraged to play with a cardboard treasure chest full of cheap plastic toys. It was like visiting my great-grandmother's apartment in Queens in the early 1980s. The same dimness, discomfort. The same feeling of needing to maintain a strict boundary between myself and the environment: I don't want to eat that. I don't want to drink that. I don't want to sit there.

I thought of Micheal O'Siadhail's poems about Japan and learning Japanese. *Tongues: Unless you behave / As little children /*

These kingdoms too shut their gates. It's about learning a new place, a new tongue, as a child, open, absorbent. I resisted being a child again, so soon after leaving my French childhood, not long after leaving my own. Yearning towards adulthood, responsibility. And here, beginning all over again.

+

One day I discovered a canal, lined with cherry trees. In season, the petals pink and white on the water, it must be so beautiful.

I felt a longing for something I couldn't put a name to.

+

Dum dum da dum dum dum dum dum dum dum da dum

+

While we were there, the legendary Japanese anime director Hayao Miyazaki released his film *Ponyo*. I hadn't really seen any of Miyazaki's films; I suppose I thought they were for kids. But we saw the trailer, and something about adorable Ponyo spinning in her bubble, or yawning sleepily in her bowl — struck me the right way. I asked Hayashimoto-sensei to help me learn the words to the very catchy theme song.

Ponyo ponyo ponyo sakana no ko!
Aoi umi kara ya ate kitta.[7]

I couldn't understand much of the trailer, which was in Japanese, but I could make out that it was a Japanese retelling of *The Little Mermaid*. Ponyo is a little goldfish who wants to live on land. She swoops up out of the sea during a storm and becomes a

little girl, and makes friends with a little boy. Her parents –
some kind of giant mer-queen, the other a human with magic
powers who lives underwater – discuss whether to reclaim her
or let her stay. Meanwhile she frolics on land with her new
friend Sosuke. *Paku paku chu-gyu! Paku paku chu-gyu!*[8] Ponyo
gets to stay a girl instead of a fish because she's so damn *kawaii*.

It was the first thing in Japan I felt unadulteratedly happy
about. I can sing a song in Japanese! And I'm enchanted by a
little fish-girl called Ponyo.

+

So so la so so so mi do do re mi re
Mi mi so la do do la so so la so do!

+

After years of passing, or trying to pass, for French, it was
psychologically difficult to be openly American again. This was
in part because of the expectation, in France, that immigrants
will assimilate. Whether or not this is a good immigration
model is beside the point; the point is, after years of practising
my 'r's and making other, more subtle adjustments, I could just
about pass for French. Whereas in Tokyo, there is no way either
of us would blend. But X didn't have to; French bankers were
highly valued. Had I been his wife, raising our internationally
schooled child, there would have been a community of wives
in place for me. But there is less respect for the non-wife, the
one with no place to go all day. He didn't expect me to blend,
but he made it clear I was a problem.

He was extremely concerned about the way we stood out.
The way *I* stood out. In the winter my nose is always running.
He got embarrassed whenever I pulled out a tissue. Either

you're not supposed to blow your nose in public, or you're supposed to excuse yourself before you do, I never learned the exact protocol, but sometimes I couldn't wait or there was no one to apologise to. I dabbed at my nose as delicately and unobtrusively as I could. *Dirty gaijin*, he called me.

Pretty early on it became clear that it was not going to be easy being a woman in Tokyo, especially a non-Japanese one. I signified in a different way. I was either invisible – men bumping into me in the street, or brushing my papers off my table at Starbucks with the back of their coats – or I received a distinctly negative form of attention.

X had a habit of pulling me into his lap on the metro, so we used up only one seat. He thought it was considerate. We were going to Yodobashi to replace the lens on his Nikon. I was planning to see how far I could get us with my Japanese. I was wearing a skirt. My legs were crossed. I didn't even see the man until he had already slapped me.

His hand connected with the inside of my thigh. It was swift and authoritarian and made what was, I'm sure, a very satisfying sound. It stung like hell.

A diminutive middle-aged man, mostly bald, wearing a navy-blue windbreaker, was halfway down the carriage, walking away as if nothing were out of the ordinary. I swore at him, but he didn't turn around. The episode was finished; the day closed over it.

'Did he really just slap me?' I asked in disbelief.

'You shouldn't have had your legs crossed,' X said. 'Your leg was sticking out into the aisle.'

My fault, then, for sticking out.

+

Best to stay in.

+

In Sofia Coppola's 2003 film *Lost in Translation*, Scarlett Johansson plays a familiar figure in American literature. She is the culture-shocked American abroad, trying to connect with the local culture but unable to. Like me, Charlotte has come to Tokyo with her partner, and is left to her own devices while he goes off to work. Like Charlotte, I would spend my evenings staring out at the Tokyo nightscape from our apartment on the twenty-sixth floor. There was something lofty and unconnected about my life there, much like Charlotte's life in the Park Hyatt.

Charlotte needs a project, a direction, but has none at hand. She wanders around her hotel, listens to self-help tapes, tells herself that her life is now, that it is happening now, but that she can't connect to it.

Neither could I. I was depressed. A fish out of water in the land of raw fish. I couldn't rally myself to find a university library where I could research my PhD thesis. I just sat in our apartment, *flâneuse*-ing around the Internet, longing for Paris.

Watching the film again, in Japan, I was struck by the institutional quality of Charlotte's hotel. I thought I remembered it being more chic, but it looks like any other hotel in any other city in the world.

Different to my own, my hotel-apart. It is home but not my home. It is not meant to be a home but a temporary home, a mimicry of home, a promise of what home could be like in Tokyo, that is, certain kinds of homes, the kinds of homes foreign banks pay for traders and their wives to live in.

I am not a wife and this is not a home.

The Tokyo setting intensifies the familiar story of the American abroad, and gives it an arrestingly contemporary cast. If Paris was the capital of the nineteenth century, and New York the capital of the twentieth, Tokyo is the undisputed capital of the twenty-first century; but it is alienating in its contemporaneity. It's too contemporary for Charlotte, who realises, as she looks out in scene after scene on the Tokyo night, where red lights blink in an announcement of their own presence, that her life is now, that it is happening now, but that she can't connect to it.

The hotel should be the refuge of the *flâneuse*. A place to rest your weary dogs. Or it is a trap, to keep you from walking and exploring. Stay in, have room service, take a bath. To sit in the window and look out, contemplative.

From my hotel-apart I can't get a read on Tokyo. I can't find its topography with my feet, and there is no skyline I can see. I live plunged into the middle of its needling black buildings with their twinkling red lights stretching on into the infinite city.

Writing on *Lost in Translation* and the final episode of *Sex and the City*, in which Carrie, defeated by an afternoon of attempted *flâneuserie* foiled by dog shit and violent French children, falls asleep (or pretends to) in her hotel room waiting for her artist boyfriend to get home from work, Maggie Lange blogged for the *Paris Review* that 'The cities outside the lodgings are an afterthought' to 'putting their men on imaginary trial'. This isn't true. The city is unsurmountable. The city is antagonistic. If anything the girl is confined in her hotel room by the city: it holds her in. The man is the reason she's there. If he is on trial, it is for bad partnership.

All my walks have led me to this space, these sixty square metres.

+

According to the beliefs of Japanese folk religion, your spirit can go walking while you sleep. In the ninth chapter of *The*

Tale of Genji, the Lady Rokujo – Sixth Avenue Lady – goes and kills the Lady Aoi while both women are asleep.

Mono no ke, they're called, these spirits. Like the Miyazaki film I watched at home one night while X was out carousing, *Princess Mononoke*.

And that night while I slept my spirit walked out of Akasaka, clear out of the city, boarded a plane, and went and curled up in my bed in Paris.

+

Charlotte acts the tourist in an attempt to connect with Japan, or at least with its past. But Japanese culture does not come neatly wrapped up for her consumption. It is incomprehensible, unreachable. 'I saw these monks today and I didn't feel anything,' says Charlotte, after a day trip to Kyoto, on the phone to someone at home who doesn't understand. She listens to the self-help tapes, she reads philosophy, but nothing gets her any closer to connecting with her own life. Japan, too, provides a variety of models of people searching for true meaning: the Zen practice of flower-arranging, the traditional wedding in Kyoto, the kids playing video games in the game centres, even the American actress in Tokyo at her press conference, promoting her latest action film ('I really believe in reincarnation, so that's part of what drew me to *Midnight Velocity*').

Charlotte and I differed in one big way. She was lost in general, unsure what she wanted to do, or be. I was older, more sure of myself. I had already learned that self-discovery is a lifelong experiment. It doesn't happen in one trip to a city. But unlike me, Charlotte makes a friend in the blurry city. That last scene in the film when Bill Murray whispers something into her ear that the audience doesn't hear is genius. Whatever there is to be 'learned' from travelling and wandering can't be summed up in a film or a book, but whispered from one person to another, when they have unexpectedly broken through the selves they thought they were, alone together in an unfamiliar city.

+

My work suffered. I couldn't concentrate. I couldn't accept not knowing what was going to happen, when X would quit his job, when we would move back to Paris, both of us, full-time. I obsessed over this unreachable resolution.

+

A film called *Tokyo!* came out, three short films about the city.[9] I liked the first one best, 'Interior Design', by Michel Gondry. It was a bit like *Lost in Translation*, actually. A young couple comes to Tokyo. He's a film-maker. She doesn't know what she's going to be yet. He says she lacks ambition, but that isn't quite it. They have no money and they're staying in a friend's tiny one-room apartment – with the friend, and occasionally her boyfriend, still in it.

Everything is untenable. But the film-maker boyfriend shows his film, and everyone loves it, and soon the young woman gets left behind. Jobless, ambitionless, she visits depressing apartment after depressing apartment. 'No boyfriends, no pets,' says the owner of a cube. Another has a dead cat outside the window and still another is full of cockroaches.

Then the film takes a weird turn. As she looks in the mirror, she notices her torso is gone, supported only by her spine. As the day wears on, her legs turn to wood, and she limps down the street, more than knock-kneed, de-kneed.

Suddenly, she stops walking altogether.

She has turned into a chair.

女.

But that's not where it ends! She can turn back into a woman – a naked woman – when she runs.

Earlier in the film, back when she was all woman and not part chair, her boyfriend told her about the spirits that emerge from cracks in the walls and run around the city, flat as a board, after dark.

In a postmodern take on the *mono no ke*, she has become the spirit of the chair – or her spirit has hardened into a chair.

Someone brings her home off the street, thinking she is only a chair, and when he is at work she sleeps in his bed, waters his plants, plays his banjo, bathes in his tub. She seems happy.

When the guy comes home, he finds the chair in the tub, full of bathwater. He calmly dries it off. When he works at the computer, she peeks over his shoulder. When he looks behind him, she ducks, and is a chair again.

+

Sophie Calle did a project in Japan called *Douleur Exquise*. Exquisite pain (the French kind). She was awarded funding by the government in 1984 to study there for three months. She didn't want to go. She didn't want to leave behind a relationship. She was away for ninety-two days. Then he left her. She writes, in her notes, 'I decided to make the project about my pain, rather than my journey,' and structured it as a series of photographs stamped with the countdown from when she arrived in Japan to when he jilted her. The pillow of one side of a hotel-room bed, made, unslept-in. '67 days to unhappiness.' The slept-in side: '66 days to unhappiness.' A photograph of a blue dress and a pair of jeans. '7 days to unhappiness.'

This part of the project is followed by a photo essay, in which she and several others recount the moments they were most sad. It begins with a sad twin bed in a hotel room, with a red telephone on it, the kind they had in the 1980s, with the dial face and the handle you pick up, with a spiral cord you twirl nervously in your fingers as you talk to the man you love. He was supposed to meet her in India at the end of her trip. Instead she received a message at her hotel in New Delhi that read: 'M. cannot meet you. Accident. Paris. Call Bob.'[10]

Bob knew nothing of any accident that would have kept M. from travelling. M. had gone to the hospital for an infected finger, that's all.

It turned out he had met someone else.

98 days ago, the man I loved left me.

The 25th of January, 1984. Room 261. Imperial Hotel, New Delhi.

Enough

+

And yet over time – surprising everyone including myself – I grew to love Japan. On my last visit I stepped outside the airport and it was as if the world had shifted into high definition. So crisp. Had I really looked at it before?

It took some time to find places I could connect with. The temples around Asakusa. The parks, Harajuku, with its cosplay characters, or Ueno, where I saw a giant statue of a fat man in a kimono with a dog, a bonsai exhibit, and a tabby cat asleep in the sun, lying on a pavement clean enough to eat off. A temple where there were hundreds of little wooden signs hanging from a fence, onto which people had written their prayers. In Kyoto the palette made me feel deeply calm, all deep greens and greys, the opposite of Tokyo with its harried pace and bathroom-tiled buildings. (To-kyo restated as Kyo-to, and vice versa.) There were bathroom-tiled buildings in Kyoto, too, but there was so much else that it didn't matter. The Kamo River quietly moved through the centre of the town, its banks lined with walking paths and restaurant terraces. Kyoto was livable, manageable, aesthetically interesting, and, most of all, a place to walk. I never saw it during cherry-blossom season, but I hope to one day. I lost myself on the grounds of the temples, endlessly photographing the details on doorways, the fish in the water, a cobweb on a tree, trying to capture the exact quality of the light.

I had been trying to find the city on street level, but that's not where it was. To *flâneuse* in Tokyo I had to walk up staircases, take elevators, climb ladders, to find what I was looking for upstairs, or on rooftops. You can't just walk through the city waiting for beauty to appear. This isn't Paris.

It's no place for the shy. That retiring *kawaii* thing is a surefire way to miss out on the best of the city, standing knock-kneed on the sidewalk.

+

As my relationship to Japan grew more and more rich, my feelings for X soured. As if I couldn't love them both at the same time. We suddenly stopped functioning. He wasn't the person I wanted to see those things with. All the resentment I had focused at Japan came sloshing out of place, and soaked him.

We had a crushing fight at our French restaurant after I offhandedly gestured at a woman sitting a bar stool away from him. He got very angry that I had gestured at a stranger. 'You don't *do* that,' he fumed, while I grew indignant and not a little confused. 'First of all she probably doesn't speak French, so she has no idea what I said, and second of all I don't think she even noticed that I gestured at her because *you are sitting in between us*.' The fight escalated and I left him there on his ridiculous bar stool. I walked home by myself, in my heels, so angry I couldn't feel how much my feet hurt. When I woke up the next morning, I found him asleep under the dining-room table.

I went over and over what had happened, trying to understand. He thought I embarrassed him so he made a scene. I made a scene because he accused me of making a scene. Barthes: 'The scene is like the Sentence: structurally, there is no obligation for it to stop; no internal constraint exhausts it, because, as in the Sentence, once the core is given (the fact, the decision), the expansions are infinitely renewable.'[11] And round we go. I did this because you did that because I did this because you did that. How to break out of it, except by leaving?

We almost broke up then. But we didn't. Instead we got engaged.

+

Then there were the earthquakes. He loved them; I feared up. He liked the idea that whatever was below the surface was forcing itself up into the world. I just wanted everything to calm down and stabilise. The first one we had, I ran to the doorway and sat down, and waited while the building creaked and swayed, as if we were on a boat. We were on the twenty-sixth floor of a building barely three years old; the foundation was constructed on springs absorbing the energy. It didn't feel the way I thought it would because we were up in our high-rise boat in the sky, protected from the earth, its shifts, its caprice.

He was giddy with the joy of it until we found out late how serious it had been. In the north of Japan, in Iwate prefecture, an *onsen* collapsed and three people died.

+

Dead words, dead tongue, dead of disuse, my mouth stuck shut. My withdrawal is in my posture, the articulation of my spine saying I have given up on you, I don't care if you like me or not, I don't like you either. I reject your codes, so dead, so exclusionary. You don't belong to my world. I don't even know what you're talking about.

We are at a stalemate, we are at an impasse, I said in your language, which I have come to speak, *ta langue, ta langue dans ma bouche*, and you've brought me to this place where my new tongue lies flat in my mouth. A crack in the road, the sidewalk blistered, how long has it been since I left New York concrete for Paris cobblestones? Why am I here, where I can't ask for aspirin, or sleeping pills, where the yogurt aisle is a tofu aisle? I can't think straight, I can't make one thought lead to another, I just tell you I hate it, and hate it, and I mean you, and before we know it I'm breaking things and jumping up and down and screaming at you in your tongue, in my tongue, in my mother tongue. My mother spoiled me, you say. But you have spoiled us. I never thought we'd be here.

+

The thing about fault lines is that they are such a cliché.

The fractures in the bedrock. The fault zone. The instability underneath it all. The shifting tectonic plates entirely out of anyone's control. Too much tension builds, and we quake.

Fault. Faulty. Your fault. My fault. At fault.

OED: 'fault: a defect, imperfection, blameable quality or feature in physical or intellectual constitution, appearance, structure, workmanship, etc.'

Who bears the fault?

How much can the fault bear?

Not long after, back in Paris, I ended it.

cross the Seine, north on Boulevard du Palais, cross the Seine, left right left right left on rue de Rivoli, continue for 10 minutes, past the Louvre, past the mini-Arc de Triomphe, into the Tuileries. Here there once stood a palace

PARIS

PROTEST

Ten thousand citizenesses, armed with good muskets, could make the Hôtel de Ville tremble.
              – Gustave Flaubert, *Sentimental Education*

It's 1848. Once again Paris is in a revolutionary fever, in a swelling of indignation that will surge across Europe, and this time the rebels' gambit actually pays off. On 24 February, King Louis Philippe abdicates and, with the help of his American dentist, flees to England, he and the queen dressed as commoners, and calling themselves 'Mr and Mrs Smith'. The people lose no time crashing the Tuileries Palace, looting and sacking and destroying. They take turns sitting on the throne before they throw it out the window, then burning it on the site of what was until sixty years before the Bastille prison. Two days later, the Second Republic is declared.[1]

During the uprising, on 15 May – a day that will be important for other reasons, but we'll get there – George Sand, now well and truly famous throughout the land, attended a rally in favour of Polish independence. On her way, she came upon a crowd of people being harangued by

a woman in a window. 'Who is that woman?' she asked
someone in the crowd. 'George Sand,' they replied.

She watched the funeral procession for the men who died in
the uprising, this time not from the balcony of her tiny flat, but
with François Guizot, the recently ousted prime minister, at his
home. She recounted to her adopted daughter Augustine: 'This
morning from Guizot's window, while chatting with Lamartine, I
saw the cortege pass by. It was beautiful, simple and touching [...]
a throng of four hundred thousand people between the Madeleine
and the July Column; not a single policeman, not a single constable,
yet so much order, decency, calm, and mutual consideration that
not one foot was stepped on, not one cap crushed. It was admirable.
The people of Paris are the best in the world.'[2]

Sand was enraptured by the Fête de la Fraternité which
took place on 20 April, a massive demonstration that culminated
in fireworks at the Arc de Triomphe. In a letter to her son she
called it 'the most massive human event ever produced!' 'But
then,' her biographer Belinda Jack comments drily, 'scenes of
huge, peaceable crowds always elicited hyperbole from Sand.'
I can understand that, being deeply moved by a show of
solidarity. It's very powerful to unite a group of people in
public defence of an idea. But it's also very dangerous, as Sand
recognised.

That 15th May, the demonstration supporting Poland began
at Bastille, and headed towards the Place de la Concorde. Part
of the group went across the river to the temple-like Palais
Bourbon, where the Assemblée Nationale was meeting (and
where it meets to this day). There, the splinter group declared
the assembly dissolved, and marched onward to the Hôtel de
Ville (these are not small distances) where they tried,
unsuccessfully, to set up an insurrectionary government. The
ringleaders were rounded up and imprisoned.

Sand was aghast. She followed the march for three hours,

she told the Prefect of Police, Caussidière, believing, like many in the crowd, that it was a demonstration to support Poland. 'No one could have predicted the scenes of violence and confusion which would break out in the heart of the National Assembly,' she said. Most of the Assemblée Nationale were in favour of a resolution supporting Poland, and this pleased the crowd, who were then astonished to find a violent sub-group within their ranks, one that did not 'in any sense' express 'the wishes of the multitude'. But she equally descried the over-enthusiastic, even sadistic, police crackdown on the demonstrators. She concluded by warning Caussidière against 'confus[ing] order, this official word of the past, with the mistrust which embitters and provokes. It is very easy to maintain order without attacking individual liberties. You do not have a right to conquer the people.'[3] Sand knew not to trust zealots, no matter whose banner they marched under.

+

Living in Paris, I'm always aware of the people's ability to explode into rebellion, given the right circumstances. Writing about the May 1968 uprising for the *New Yorker*, the Canadian short-story writer Mavis Gallant describes her ambivalence towards the events of May, her admiration for the bravery of the students tempered by impatience for the 'false siege psychosis' the population indulges in, creating a crisis situation that does not abate for months. It's true anywhere – any social demonstration will be equal parts sincere and self-mythologising. But the Parisian readiness to stand up and march, to speak truth to power, and to make visible one's dissent, has always impressed me; it's part of why I wanted to live here. I can't claim to be exempt from the desire to mythologise it. But I'm aware that this is a dangerous thing to do.

'Streets are the dwelling place of the collective,' Walter Benjamin wrote in his *Arcades Project*.[4] In the street we can stand together in favour of an idea. Marching is an instinctive response to feeling wronged, or desperate, or compelled to make a statement. It makes us feel stronger to be part of a group. It feels good. Marching is a political act, but it's a social one as well. We have so few occasions for doing the same thing at the same time, and when we do it we feel we belong to something bigger than us.

After a nineteenth century punctuated with revolutions and a twentieth century strewn with wars and strikes and student revolts, the Parisian *manifestation* eventually codified into an institutionalised kind of resistance, replacing the frenzied construction of barricades with a slow-moving political trudge. Where they walk to and from is very significant: left-wing marches begin and end at places with revolutionary or Republican significance, like Bastille, or Nation, or République, mostly in the east of Paris. Occasionally they'll snake along the Left Bank and end in front of the Assemblée Nationale. The right-wing marches, on the other hand, begin or end in the moneyed quarters of the 7th, or the Latin church at Maubert-Mutualité in the 5th.

The '*manif*' is a rite of passage for most people here; their parents took them when they were kids, and was part of their coming of age during high school: cutting class to go to a protest is the French *lycéen*'s version of rebellion. They march in a few at university, and as adults they probably take in one a year. Highly organised affairs, *manifs* usually represent the interests of several groups who have banded together to appear more imposing. Some enterprising vendors will show up with their barbecues and cook up merguez sausages you can buy for a euro; others sell beer in plastic cups. Assuming there's nothing particularly tragic on the agenda, it can be quite a jolly affair.

When a French friend attended the 15 February protest against the Iraq war in New York in 2003, she was shocked that it ended with the police charging the crowd on horseback; she and her friend had to duck into one of the shops on First Avenue.

Not all Parisian manifestations finish as peacefully as they begin. Protests against an employment law in 2005 that began with students wearing stickers and marching for job security ended up attracting anarchists and rabble-rousers – the *casseurs*, French for 'people who break things' – who are never far from a good protest. Wearing hoods and keffiyehs to hide their faces, they smashed shop windows, set cars on fire, mugged people in the street, threw things at the riot police, and destroyed a legendary bookshop on the Place de la Sorbonne.

In 1986, a young man named Malik Oussekine was accidentally killed while in proximity to a *manif*, when the police mistook him (or so they claim) for a *casseur*. The students were marching against fundamental changes to the French university system: tuition was going to be raised by the equivalent of two hundred euros (nearly a 100 per cent increase), and a policy of selection would be put in place whereby universities would have the power to accept certain students, and not others, which goes against the idea of university as a public right: anyone can attend any French university, so long as they have a high school diploma. Two hundred thousand students demonstrated on 17 November, and then nearly 500,000 on 4 December. A group of students occupied the Sorbonne the next day, and when they were chased out tried to build a barricade at the corner of the rue Monsieur-le-Prince and the rue de Vaugirard. Oussekine himself was apparently not demonstrating, but coming out of a jazz club in the early hours of the morning. The police pursued him on motorcycles and beat him to death.

+

When I first moved to Paris, I kept my distance from the demonstrations. You never know what you might get caught up in. I could hear my mother's voice in my head: *Don't forget that you're an immigrant. Don't make trouble. Keep your head down.* I think of my father's experience of 1968; he was in graduate school in Philadelphia, getting his master's in architecture. It was the end of the semester. Some students (as he tells it) came into the studio and tried to get everyone stirred up about the protests at Columbia. But my father and his fellow students went right back to drawing. Sorry, they said. We've got to finish our final projects.

I've always wondered if I would have done anything differently. Probably not. Once the movement was already under way, what would it matter if there were one student more or less sitting in Dodge? Then, too, my father's cousin, Andrew Goodman, had been killed by the Ku Klux Klan in 1964 when he went to Mississippi to work for civil rights. That was recent family history, in 1968. I can understand my father's impulse to stay out of harm's way.

For most of us on the tail end of Generation X, it took September 11th and the ensuing war on terror, with its twin invasions of Afghanistan and Iraq – one for each tower – to dislodge us from our couches and get us out into the street. Though I was horrified by the Bush government's blind, teeth-gritting march to war, I didn't immediately join the protesters. Somehow it all seemed too nefarious, fuelled by the interests of corporations and arms dealers, for any of us ordinary citizens to have an impact. What would be the point? I thought. No one in power is going to listen to us shouting *No blood for oil!* in the street. They're just going to dismiss us as hippies and idealists.

During those confusing days in the run-up to the invasion of Iraq, it was hard to know who to listen to. I remember a general feeling of helplessness and frustration in New York – our city had been attacked, feelings were running high. We needed a real conversation, I remember thinking, for an anti-war movement to really take off. (This would later prove to be a massive failure on the part of the American media.) What we didn't need, from either side, was empty rhetoric.

So it was inadvertent that I ended up in a demonstration against the war, that winter of 2003. I was walking home from the library, heading north on University Place from Washington Square Park, trying to lace my way through a group of protesters on the sidewalk, when the police showed up and kettled me along with the marchers. They pushed us into a people-blob and surrounded us with linked arms, creating a nightstick barrier from which we could not escape. One minute I was a graduate student with a backpack full of library books, the next there was a nightstick pushing against my stomach, right under my ribs. The police weren't distinguishing between marchers and bystanders, or between a peaceful demonstration and a rowdy one.

I'm embarrassed to say it was that day, at that moment, physically restrained by a group of riot police, that my ambivalent feelings about marching resolved into something like a belated epiphany. Because of this war, innocent people were being caught up in a fight they had nothing to do with, and were going to suffer a lot more than a nightstick under the ribs. I had left the house that day feeling distant from the protesters, but by the time I finally made it home, I was one of them.

We need the mass movements, we need people to get together and march, or even just stand in one place, not only for those in power to see what the people want, but for people who are decidedly not empowered to see you out there, and to shift, just a little bit, the pebbles of thought in their minds. The protest is not only to show the government that you disagree, but to show your fellow citizens – even the smallest ones – that official policies can and should be disagreed with. To provoke a change. To disrupt easy assumptions.

You show yourself. You toss in your chips. You walk.

+

I marched in my first French *manif* on 29 January 2009.

Of the 65,000–300,000 people who marched that day (depending who you asked) many were there to protest the way the government had handled the economic crisis. Some were there because they were game for any opportunity to show how much they hated Sarkozy. Some were there because it was a good excuse not to go to work. But this *manif* was unusual, because for the first time in years, the professors as well as the students were on strike. My colleagues were uniformly against the reforms to the university system put in place by then-Minister of Education Valérie Pécresse, which would favour research in the sciences, and disadvantage those of us in the humanities. They did not address the real problems in the system and would only serve to eliminate jobs, funding and in some cases entire institutions.

Some professors started an ongoing march in the old Place de la Grève [Strike Square], in front of the Hôtel de Ville, and called themselves the '*ronde infinie des obstinés*', or the 'unending dance of the stubborn', and they walked in a circle for seven weeks. It was well intended, but met with the predictable jokes, compounded by the unfortunate slogan they had scrawled on the ground in the centre of their circle: *I think, therefore I am useless*.

In a more savvy bit of demonstrating, a group of professors organised a marathon reading of Madame de Lafayette's seventeenth-century novel *La Princesse de Clèves*. For eight hours, students, professors and passers-by were invited to read a portion of the novel aloud. *La Princesse de Clèves* is a book with weighty anti-Sarkozyian implications: in 2007, Sarkozy, then running for president, had expressed bafflement about the fact that the novel was on the required reading list for several competitive civil service examinations. An in-depth knowledge of seventeenth-century French literature might not seem all that useful for someone who works behind a desk at the tax office, but there was general outrage at the idea that great literature should be made to serve some useful purpose, here in France, the land of the *exception culturelle*. The film-maker Christophe Honoré was inspired by Sarkozy's ignorance to make a twenty-first-century updating of the story, set in a posh Parisian *lycée*, and the film's star, Louis Garrel, was one of the readers at the Panthéon protest in 2009. His presence lent another neat revolutionary *frisson*, since he also starred in *The Dreamers*, Bernardo Bertolucci's film about May 1968. In solidarity, I put the novel on my syllabus in a world literature class I taught that year.

Those of us from the English department had a delightful array of discipline-specific signs: 'I Am Not a Number, I Am a Teacher', 'For Us the Bell Tolls' and 'University Strikes Back'. We joined the French department, who had their own signs: '*Fac culturelle, pas fac poubelle!*' and '*Quand on cherche, on ne compte pas!*' We began in the Place de la Bastille, where we stood still for a very long time, as all the groups slowly arrived and took their places. I was pretty wound up, excited to chant some slogans, ready to pump the air with my fist, but no one else seemed to be; there was no chanting, it was overcast, and everyone was freezing cold. Hours and hours later, we had still only moved about half a mile up the Boulevard Beaumarchais, when it started getting dark, and I decided it was time to head home. The sky deepened from blue to purple as some kids at the back began to set off flares, filling the air with smoke, creating a red glow around the protesters and turning the lamp posts along the boulevard into a string of suns, burning in the haze. A pile of poster boards was set alight as I walked back through the Place de la Bastille, with a group solemnly gathered around it, holding flags and banners aloft. The smoke rose up around the July Column, and the red haze intensified. I took a photograph, and it was as if the nineteenth century had appeared, like a ghost, on the film.

A week later we were out in the streets protesting again. The energy was high, the press was everywhere, and everyone was happy to be out marching on such a beautiful day. We began at Jussieu, walked past the Jardin des Plantes, down to Censier, up rue Claude Bernard, right on rue d'Ulm, past ENS, and then up to the Panthéon, where the march came to a halt. We were supposed to finish in front of the education minister's compound, but the police had blocked off all the streets leading to the ministry. So the cortège continued up rue Victor Cousin ('*A la Sorbooooooooonne!*' cried the leaders), left on the rue des Écoles, right on Boulevard Saint-Michel.

Here things got out of hand. Half of the marchers took off leftward on the Boulevard Saint-Germain. The other half stayed on Saint-Michel, where the demonstration ended not long after. But there was no way to know that we had gone with the wrong group until later, when it became clear that we were following a group of anarchists who were marching us down the boulevard right into the traffic, running between the cars, which honked at us in complaint. (Or: honked in support?) It was exhilarating. *This* was a Parisian protest!

Upon realising what had happened, I felt a little silly. This was not a *manif* in favour of anything or against anything, only a deviation, led by a bunch of troublemakers. I had become exactly what I had avoided back in New York – someone who was more interested in the ritual than the content. It was only too easy. There was brute power in walking, all together, in a pack of people; belonging to a mob for the first time in my life, I felt uneasy. It was too easy to be led who knows where, by who knows whom, to do who knows what.

+

In 1848, Sand wanted to do more than just watch as history unfolded: she believed she understood the people at every level of society, as well as their leaders, and this was her chance to make a difference in people's lives. To live in ethical cooperation with your fellow creatures, she believed, you have to join the collective project. As the unofficial minister of propaganda, she would take a major role in shaping the new government's message. She threw herself assiduously into the life of public service, providing input on who should be named to various cabinet positions, and Ledru-Rollin, the new minister of the interior, actually listened to her. She started her own journal, *La Cause du Peuple*, and wrote articles for the new government's *Bulletin de la République*, in which she exhorted the people of France, no matter where they lived, to pay attention to what was happening in Paris. 'Citizens,' she wrote, 'France is embarking on the greatest endeavour of modern times: the foundation of the government of *all* the people, the organisation of democracy, the republic of all rights, of all interests, of all intelligences, and of all virtues . . . !'[5]

She saw, and tried to make her readers see, how much was riding on the upcoming elections. She met with the legendary statesman de Tocqueville in those early months of the new Republic, and he recalled, in his memoirs, her telling him: 'Try to persuade your friends, monsieur, not to push people into the streets by unsettling or irritating them; in the same way I want to counsel patience to those on my side; because – believe me – if a battle breaks out, you will all perish.'[6]

With the new government, it seemed as if women would have the opportunity to advance their own goals, calling for economic independence, childcare, the right to employment. They wanted more from this revolution than to see real women with real needs abstracted into allegories for the nation, bare-breasted Mariannes promising *liberté* for all except those who resembled her. But most men still agreed with the novelist and pamphleteer Claude Tillier: 'Who ever saw a political idea dwelling under a gauze bonnet?' Few nineteenth-century men, it seemed, could agree with the utopian Socialist Charles Fourier, who declared: 'The degree of emancipation of women is the natural measure of general emancipation,'[7] or applaud Victor Hugo's 1853 statement, at the funeral of Louise Julien, who was imprisoned and exiled for protesting Louis Napoleon's *coup d'état*: 'If the 18th century proclaimed the rights of man, the 19th proclaims the rights of women.'

Flaubert gently mocked the feminists in *Sentimental Education* (1869), in the form of the spinster Mademoiselle Vatnaz, for whom 'the emancipation of the proletariat was possible only through the emancipation of women'. She wanted 'the admission of women to all types of employment, investigation into the paternity of illegitimate children, a new legal code, and either the abolition of marriage or at the very least 'a more intelligent regulation of the institution'. And if these rights were not granted, Mademoiselle Vatnaz avers, 'they would have to conquer force by force. Ten thousand citizenesses, armed with good muskets, could make the Hôtel de Ville tremble.'[8]

Still, Sand herself could not stand up for women's rights independent of anyone else's. A few women's groups asked Sand to run for office, and she refused. 'Society has much to gain by the entry of some of our sex into the administration of public affairs,' she wrote, but 'the mass of poor, uneducated women would have nothing to gain by it'. This is hard to swallow. Universal male suffrage was put into law for the first time since the Revolution, and though the writer Delphine de Girardin, who wrote under the male pseudonym 'the Vicomte de Launay', militated for women to be included ('In their fine promises for universal suffrage, they forgot women'), others, like Sand and her friend Marie d'Agoult, who also wrote under the male pen name Daniel Stern, thought women's suffrage should be gradually attained, rather than suddenly introduced. Society would have to be fundamentally reorganised, Sand believed, before women could profit from that power. Once women had won equality in the home, then they could seek equality in the outside world. Sand worried, in a letter from April 1848, that women were making themselves look ridiculous by asking for the vote; it was too much, too soon.

It was France that Sand defended, a Socialist France with opportunities for all. But Paris was the city where she stood up for her own rights, and saw others, as well, rise up for theirs. Like Flaubert's Frédéric Moreau, Sand was inspired by 'the ardour of the crowds'; the stirring of revolution made her aware of 'the consciousness of a vast love, a sublime, all-embracing tenderness, as if the heart of all mankind were beating in [her] breast'.[9] Of all the places Sand wrote about, and dreamt about, it was in Paris – workaday, dirty, infuriating, beautiful Paris – that a new world had the best chance of being realised.

Things did not turn out as Sand had hoped. The elections that were held just after the Fête de la Fraternité, on 23 April, were disappointing. The people she championed did not turn out to vote, and the new assembly ended up nearly as conservative as the old one. A Socialist state was not to be. Sand's ambivalent stance towards the feminists didn't matter for long; the feminist clubs that formed in those early months were outlawed on 28 July. The few advances made on behalf of the workers – notably in the form of workshops providing employment – had been eliminated by June. So the people rose up again. It took two days for the army to quell the uprising.

Sand burned out as a politician very quickly. Within a year or so, the inefficacy of politics got to be too much for her; she was too pragmatic, and yet too idealistic.[10] She would always prioritise diplomacy. As conflict and conservatism reigned, Sand retired from politics, and left Paris. She was running out of money, and afraid her son would be arrested because of his involvement in the rebellion. She framed her concern with the way the rebellion had got out of hand in terms, once again, of her limited freedom of movement in the city: 'All during the month of March I could come and go on my own in the whole city, at any hour, and I never met a worker, a ruffian, but he stepped out of my path on the sidewalk, and did so with an affable air of goodwill. By the 17th of May I could barely step out of my home in broad daylight accompanied by friends: "order" reigned!'[11] Her stance on the Commune in 1871 would be held against her by Socialists for generations to come. 'Poor people!' she said. 'They will commit excesses, crimes, but with what a vengeance will they be crushed!' Paris became, in Sand's words, 'a hideout for bandits of all stripes, oppressing a troop of cowards and imbeciles, who will finish by destroying the haven they've sullied!'

Perhaps she resented the Commune because it represented 'a return of the *citoyen* [citizen] to the detriment of the *promeneur* [walker]'.[12] The newly reorganised, aestheticised, sanitised city was presented in the media as having been under threat by the figure of the Communard. But the figure of the female revolutionary was depicted as even more threatening. For the *flâneur*, the street may have become a 'de-politicised space', but for the *flâneuse*, this was neither possible nor desirable. During the Commune, a specious report from an American journalist, in which he claimed to have seen women throwing the nineteenth-century equivalent of Molotov cocktails into the basements of Parisian buildings, led to the creation of the figure of the *petroleuse*, or 'woman who sets things on fire'. Revolutionary women were perceived by their contemporaries to be totally uncontrollable, much more dangerous than any group of men. At one point during the French Revolution, women were outlawed from publicly gathering in groups of five or more. Sand would have been aware of all of this, and it fed her outrage that women did not have the same freedoms as men, in private or in public. 'There is but one sex,' she wrote to Flaubert. 'A man and a woman are so close to being the same thing that I hardly understand the many distinctions and subtle arguments on which society feeds in this matter.'[13]

Sand's contribution to the revolution of 1848 is still not appreciated in its subtlety. She recognised that both the people and their government had constructed airtight mythologies to justify their actions, and understood that the clash of polarities was not the way forward. She occupied some third space of protest and mediation, as she demonstrated in her dealings with the Prefect of Police.

She should have taken the women's side; she should have lent her name to their cause. Maybe if she had, she'd be remembered with less ambivalence. But she stayed behind no lines; she cut across all perspectives.

+

I was in Paris when it happened. Slowly people began to gather in a park near Wall Street, to hold meetings, to put up tents, to protest the abuses and greed of the financial system. Soon they had a library, a kitchen, a place to charge your phone, a first-aid tent. Whose streets? Our streets! they cried. Hundreds of people were living in Zuccotti Park. They managed to point out better than any speech, any exposé, any op-ed, what was wrong with the US, where 40 per cent of the nation's wealth is owned by 1 per cent of the population. We, the 99 per cent, have been plunged into a shitty economy by the 1 per cent, who are making money off of us, every minute more. New York used to be a vibrant, diverse place; now it's become a sandpit for corporate interests. It was stirring to see the videos of the people's microphone, waves of rhetoric rippling back through the bodies of the crowd, and the protesters marching across the Brooklyn Bridge, then being arrested by police.

The Occupy movement's ideals were beautifully captured in that early poster of a ballerina balancing in *attitude* on the charging bull statue in front of the New York Stock Exchange – the bullishness of the market charging over all the other components of a life, from the arts to health care to housing; the dancer a triumph over the market. Her pose reminds us that it's all supposed to be a question of balance, from the branches of government through the economy to the complicated urban ballet we all take part in every day. *What is our one demand?* the poster asked, and no one ever said, definitively, what it was. It was more interesting to leave the answer open.

The answer was also, somehow, impossible to articulate; it was bigger than words – that's why it needed a trespassing kind of movement. But that physical openness created space for authoritarianism to storm in and declare it illegal. The police cracked down on the tent city, confiscating books, arresting people for loitering, especially those wearing Guy Fawkes masks, citing an 1845 New York City law banning masked gatherings in public. The attacks spread to Occupied spaces across the country, from cities to universities, and we all watched on our computers, horrified, as campus police pepper-sprayed undergraduates at close range. And although the police intimidation was all too real, by a certain point genuine disgust at police tactics was overshadowed by performative outrage, like someone laughing too quickly at a joke. No one was innocent of the charge of playing politics.

+

Watching the tents being disbanded from Paris, where Occupy didn't really take off ('We're always protesting,' my French friends said, 'and anyway who wants to live in a tent?'), reminded me of the energy, and the failures, of the 'events' of May 1968. What starts off peaceable never ends that way, and then it's over and everyone moves on. All that remains is legacy.

As far as mythologised collective uprisings go, you can't do much better than 1968 in Paris. It all began at Nanterre University, a modern campus in the western suburbs of Paris, built in the mid-1960s. Within a few years, it would earn the nickname 'Nanterre Rouge' for its radical leftist activities; the nickname persisted nearly forty years later, when I went to teach there, and found a campus dotted with brutalist cement buildings, many of which have by now fallen into disrepair, some propped up on iron columns under which walkways have been created, others set back from the asphalt by steps which do not invite undergrads to congregate, eat lunch and flirt. It's very modern, but not very nice. And in the mid-1960s, the rules were as draconian as the architecture.

In March 1968, a group formed called Les enragés ('the Angry Ones') to protest the fact that male students weren't allowed to stay the night in the female dorms. The minister of sport was visiting the campus to inaugurate a new swimming pool, and a feisty student called Daniel Cohn-Bendit interrupted his speech to hassle him about a recent report published by the minister of youth: '400 pages on the young and not a word about sexuality!'[14] Cohn-Bendit was almost expelled and became a folk hero to the students; they protested in his defence until the university was shut down, and then they went to protest in the Latin Quarter, in the heart of Paris ('Latin Quarter meeting place, Latin Quarter vicarious myth,' writes Antonio Quattrocchi in his iconic account of the events) and got themselves arrested while other students occupied the Sorbonne, always the Sorbonne, 'Sorbonne mater dolorosa where the dark ancient rites of initiation and consecration are performed. Sorbonne mater dulcissima, where the golden fruits of scholarly minds blossom in secluded cloisters, well protected from the winds of history and the infinite infections of vulgarity. Sorbonne the citadel. Sorbonne the fortress.'[15] The rector of the university closed it down, and allowed the police to come in and disperse the students. After several days of marching and skirmishing with police, the students' leader, with Daniel Cohn-Bendit at his side, articulating their demands in a voice hoarse from shouting: Amnesty for all demonstrators. Reopening of the universities. And the disappearance of all police from the Sorbonne.

A week after the students' protests began, the unions declared a general strike for Monday 13 May. One by one, that week, the factories went on strike. On Thursday, at the Renault factory just outside Paris, one young worker (this is Quattrocchi's account) said 'I have had enough', and got up from his machine. One by one his colleagues joined him, and within half an hour their workshop was empty.[16]

That's all it takes: one person to stand up and say I've had enough. Revolutions are made by individuals. Pass the *pavé*.

But of everything I've read and seen about 1968 – from academic studies to popular films – it's Mavis Gallant who best captures Paris during that eventful time, not only because her descriptions are so vivid, but because she refuses to romanticise what's happening around her. Gallant observes 1968 from an ironic distance, which is, I think, the only ethical way for a writer to respond. The barricades, for instance – they are not the spontaneous expressions of resistance thrown up by students, she and a friend realise through investigation; the rocks are too big to have been dug up from the pavement, they must have been carried by truck.[17] She sees through the pose everyone is frenetically trying to maintain: the high school students who don't really know why they're marching but beg to stay out late; the well-meaning marchers who talk to Gallant, a foreigner, 'as if I were a plucky child recovering from brain fever in a Russian novel. Turned out she thought I was an Algerian, and that was her way of showing she wasn't racist.' There are the people in the neighbourhood who create a false siege mentality, claiming there is no bread and milk in the Sorbonne neighbourhood, which a quick call to a friend proves isn't true, and the violence of the counter-protesters, the wealthy bourgeois out on the Champs-Elysées shouting 'France for the French!' Gallant writes that the Place Maubert is like 'one of those dumps that smoulder all the time, with a low fire that you can smell for miles. Blackened garbage, singed trees, a burned car. Don't want to see more. Walk down the Seine. Keep turning my ankles – so many holes in the ground, and so many stray wood, stone, and iron *things*. Nothing has a shape or a name.'[18] With the piles of garbage everywhere, the whole city looks like it's been knocked over, like a giant overturned garbage can.

Even still, in the black-and-white footage you can find on the Internet, it looks amazing. People clustered on balconies. Students up on the Lion de Belfort with 30,000 people massed around in the Place Denfert-Rochereau. You watch the video and hear what it sounded like, and it sounds just like a march today. The din of far-off traffic and voices. Someone beating on a drum like the regular chugging of a train. Someone blowing a whistle with an insistent staccato beat. The increasing roar of the crowd as it gets closer. The sing-song cry of the sirens. The chant: *lib-ér-ez! nos! ca-ma-rades!* People silhouetted against the smoke, in balletic leaps as they hurl paving stones, running away from the police, getting into fistfights. Masses and masses of people, walking together with arms linked. A shot of hands waving in the air, punctuating their demands, like something out of Fosse, here and there a cigarette between the fingers. Imagine that. A revolutionary gesture with your smoking hand.[19] People on the balconies up and down the Boulevard Saint-Michel, excited without understanding why. Gallant recognises that this kind of civil disobedience so easily becomes a form of entertainment. In the early days of the student uprising, Gallant describes the atmosphere as 'Electric, uneasy, but oddly gay. Yes, it is like a holiday in a village, with the whole town out on the square'; as the crisis dragged on through the month of May, 'Everyone enjoyed the general strike so much that no one has gone back to work, from the sound of it.'[20] Flaubert noticed this feeling as well. 'There was a carnival gaiety in the air, a sort of camp-fire mood,' he wrote of the revolution in February 1848; 'nothing could have been more enchanting than Paris in those first days.'[21] He captures the performance of certain values that such an uprising makes necessary, certain words to pronounce, like a Shibboleth, to prove your stripes: 'it was necessary to criticize the lawyers all the time, and to use the following expressions as often as possible: "Contribute one's stone to the building . . . social problem . . . workshop".'[22] The same in 1968, the same in 2011; all that changes is the vocabulary. Gallant laments the inauthenticity of her era: 'Everything tatty, a folklore now – China, Cuba, Godard's films. Our tatty era.'[23]

And we look to 1968 for authenticity, just as they looked to the Communards. And to whom did the Communards look?

To 1848.

+

There are two elements of the protest: the march and the barricade. The forward movement and the resistance. A demonstration can't become a protest without the forces of order saying no to their no. Both play their part. The barricade is a symbol of revolution, but the police kettle is just another kind of barricade. The very things that stir our heart in a revolution may be co-opted by the forces of order – or the other way around. Gallant sees a man beating with a stick 'the three-plus-two rhythm that used to mean "Al-gé-rie fran-çaise" but now stands for "CRS S-S"': 'Algeria for the French' or 'CRS = SS'; the blind imperialism of the French in Algeria, or resistance to authority: the same catchy beat.[24]

Napoleon III tried to learn the lessons of the 1830 and 1848 revolutions, recognising that whoever owned the streets of Paris would own the battles that took place there. To this end, he asked his personal urban planner, Baron Haussmann, to take these mass uprisings into account in his redesign of the city. Walter Benjamin describes the way he did this in the *Arcades Project*: 'Widening the streets is designed to make the erection of barricades impossible, and new streets are to furnish the shortest route between the barracks and the workers' districts. Contemporaries christen the operation "strategic embellishment".'[25]

But wider boulevards just call for larger barricades.

Barriers never do their job; there is always someone willing to go the long way around. Which, I am convinced, is the only reasonable way past them: steam right through, by all means, but that is the way towards violence and armed conflict. Find a way around. '*On s'en fout des frontières*,' they chanted in 1968. We don't give a shit about borders.

There has to be an element of surprise, if the doings of many people are to put paid to apathy, to burst through their everyday habits and worries, and reroute thought. There has to be a feeling of pushing against boundaries. In 1968, reading the accounts, you can see them – students, workers, everyday people – searching out that tipping point, where it all turns over. Something in the city, the charged energy between the people marching, pushing everything forward. Tip – tip – tip – there it goes – or almost –

And then it doesn't. The police are there to make sure it doesn't. They don't need to remake the city. They just need to quash the gatherers. Or delegitimise them.

+

'It is far too early to tear down the barricades,' wrote my mentor Jane Marcus in the 1980s, encouraging the 'good girl' feminists not to put away their tents quite yet and 'slip quietly into the establishment.'[26]

+

It all comes down to a question of borders, a subject to which I am, by now, very sensitive.[27] The more I read Gallant's account of 1968, the more I realise it wasn't about students, or dorms, or mores. It was about immigration.

+

What Gallant does find heartening in 1968 is the students' defence of Cohn-Bendit. By mid-May the government was calling for his expulsion not only from Nanterre, but from France. Having been born stateless, the child of German Jews who had fled the Nazis, despite having lived in France nearly all his life, his 'Frenchness' was up for debate. 'I hear them chanting, "*Nous sommes tous des juifs-allemands*",' Gallant writes ('We are all German Jews'). She can't believe her ears. 'This is France, they are French, I am not dreaming . . . It is the most important event, I think, since the beginning of this fantastic month of May, because it means a mutation in the French character: a generosity. For the first time, I hear a French voice go outside the boundaries of being French.'[28] That they are able to identify to this point with the Other, a people so recently expelled from France, handed over to be exterminated, is an incredible leap of empathy. Could this empathy be the real legacy of 1968? Whatever their motivations – whether they were caught up in the joy of it, or in the cult of personality around Daniel Cohn-Bendit, or just trying to piss off their parents, or the police, or call them out for not standing up twenty years earlier, the youth of 1968 walked up the Boulevard Saint-Michel shouting *We are all German Jews*. Perhaps in another ten years they'll shout: *We are from the banlieue, too.*

+

I thought of that after the *Charlie Hebdo* attacks, when I stood alongside one and a half million people in the streets near République, in mourning, solidarity and defiance, in the biggest *manifestation* in Paris since the liberation in 1944. How much fracturing and dissent was covered over that day? A few people talked about how they wouldn't go, that they refused to march behind Sarkozy, or Netanyahu, or Ben Ali, that they rejected the binary invented by the media, pitting freedom against extremism, 'us' against the terrorists, calling it a 'superficial consensus' that wilfully tried to forget 'the fractures, the profound divisions in France'.[29] And yet none of us on the ground that day would have claimed that the group was unified in anything other than a desire to speak up and shout back, as we walked with our children, and our dogs, and our signs reading *Je suis Charlie, Je ne suis pas Charlie, Je suis Ahmed, Je suis les frères Kouachi, Je suis manipulé, Je suis Charlie Juif Musulman Policier*. We were everybody, we were everything. We were an entire city of opinions. We argued with each other along the route, and in the cafes, and when we went home that night. The key is to keep arguing.

We stood for an hour on Boulevard du Temple, a street Sand most certainly strode down in her defiant trousers. We shuffled forward a few inches at a time, the crowd chanting *Char-lie* and *li-ber-té*, occasionally bursting into the Marseillaise, repaving the ground with our good intentions while singing the bloodiest of national anthems. *Marchons, marchons, qu'un sang impur abreuve nos sillons* [March on, march on, *let impure blood water the furrows of our land*]. If you're going to sing the song, you have to face what it's saying. The fractures are right there in its lyrics, its xenophobia, its violence. Can we *détourne* it, reroute it, remake it, in the way we receive it from those who left it to us? There's a children's verse to the French national anthem, about how they will rise up once the adults are dead and gone: *We will have the sublime pride of avenging them or following them*. Who knows what the children are learning as they march with us today.

Here there was once a prison. Here there were once theatres. Here lived Gustave Flaubert. Here they tried to kill a king. Here Daguerre took a photograph, and it is thought to be the earliest surviving picture of a person. I took a picture of a woman in a long black dress, in a black hat, covered with netting, motionlessly, looking at the crowd. She looked like an apparition from another century. So singular and alone, a black mark of mourning against the building. I thought of Sand when we'd finished the march, and gone upstairs to our friends' flat on the Boulevard Voltaire to watch the hundreds of thousands of people who were still marching as night fell, and I remembered Sand's description of the funeral procession for those who were killed in the February 1848 uprising, all the people packing the streets between the July Column and the Madeleine, except here it was all the boulevards from Nation to République.

I thought of Sand, too, a few days earlier, when I went to the Place de la République to see the impromptu shrine that the statue of Marianne, symbol of the Republic, had become. People had drawn pictures and scrawled slogans in French and English on the marble base of the statue, *Criéz fort, L'engagement, ce mot qui donne un sens à la liberté, Liberté de penser et aussi d'écrire, C'est l'encre qui doit couler et pas le sang, What kind of society are we building?* They had left drawings, pens galore, piles of flowers, tea lights that never seemed to go out. That first night all these people climbed the statue and hung from it defiantly, as if it were a barricade. And when the madmen came for us on 13 November 2015, once again we gathered at Republique, and decked Marianne with posters and flowers. Official gatherings were forbidden. There was no march. But we found each other, and held each other, in the square.

One day this will all be a memory.

And one day beyond that it will be a plaque.

And one day they'll all walk past it, with something else to protest, or prove, and maybe they will think of us.

east on Boulevard des Invalides which becomes Boulevard
Montparnasse which becomes Boulevard Port-Royal

PARIS

NEIGHBOURHOOD

I'm learning to see.
— Rainer Maria Rilke, *The Notebooks of Malte Laurids Brigge*

Yesterday the complete filmography of Agnès Varda came in the mail. The box weighed at least two kilos, the size of a small cat. I've been a devoted fan of the most lovable director of the *nouvelle vague*, with her exuberant spirit and medieval monk's haircut, ever since I first saw *Cléo de 5 à 7* (1962), a film which tracks, minute for minute, a young woman's movements around Paris, mostly in and around Montparnasse, in real time. *Tout(e) Varda*, the filmography's called, a pun on the French words for *all* and *quite* – *all* of Varda, *quite* Varda. The postman tracked me down on a Saturday afternoon in a cafe near my apartment, where I was having lunch with a friend, and brought the package over. The cafe manager was amused. *C'est bien de se faire livrer son courrier ici!* How convenient to get your mail delivered here!

I opened the package right then and there. Eleven DVDs, two films per DVD, with assorted *courts métrages*. A little booklet of photographs and liner notes. And some kind of little envelope of stuff that I left for later.

When I got home I opened the little envelope with great curiosity. It turned out to be a trove of postcards and Varda-esque trinkets:

1) A DVD in a paper sleeve called *Les trois vies d'Agnès et Quelques Veuves de Noirmoutier.*

2) A DVD in a paper sleeve called *inédits et inattendus, dont Nausicaa 1970.*

3) A postcard of a woman walking barefoot next to a cement wall that is bare except for a poster which is partially torn off, so that we see only the smiling face and curled hair of a blonde woman. Turn the card over and it says: *Sophia Loren au Portugal, Povoa de Varzim, 1956.*

4) A postcard providing the recipe for *gratin de côtes de blettes* with bits of trivia worked into the recipe, e.g. *Step 8: Place in the preheated oven ('It was as dark as an oven; the sky was dressed this evening like Scaramouche.' Molière).*

5) A postcard, or possibly a sticker, featuring the poster art of all of Varda's feature-length films.

6) A postcard with a drawing that looked like something you'd see on a tarot card, of a woman standing on a tower, looking out into the distance, and waving a red handkerchief. The card reads: 'But where is Agnès hiding . . . and her cat?' There is a little cartoon Agnès drawn onto the woman's dress. Her cat is upside down on the tower. At the bottom it reads: 'Anne, my sister Anne, do you see anything coming? The poor woman replied – I see two knights, but they are still quite far off.' It's true, there are two men on horseback wending their way to the castle. But Agnès and her cat are already there, if you know to look for them. I promptly hung this card up on my mirror.

6) A film negative showing two women in red dresses and feathered headdresses.

7) Another card with cats drawn on it which says, 'There's a little Chris Marker in all of us.' On the back are quotes from the late Chris Marker, the legendary film-maker and a good friend of Varda's ('Television is great. It moves, it's lively, it's like an aquarium full of parakeets'). One cat is Chris Marker's avatar, Guillaume-en-Egypte; it also appears in *Les plages d'Agnès* and speaks with the digitised voice of Marker himself.

8) A stencil of the Ciné-Tamaris mascot cat, Zgougou.

9) A little piece of wood with a hand on it, with finger pointing, on which is written: 'Qui commence?' On the back is a little red bead. I realise this little wooden thing is the spinner for some kind of game, or perhaps for any game, to be spun on its bead to decide who goes first.

10) Another card with a cartoon Varda in profile. Her eye is a plastic googly one, and her nose is made of a thin silver chain. On the bottom is written: 'Instructions: hold the card horizontally while gently shaking it.' When you shake it the chain moves, as if Varda is nodding her head.

What *were* all of these things? I wondered, choosing *Cléo de 5 à 7* from among the smooth DVDs lining the box, cracking open the jewel case, feeding the disc into the machine in the living room. Whose idea was it to cram all that in with the films? They added up to exactly the kind of clutter I militate against in my flat, wary of accumulating too much stuff (read: crap) in a very small space. Yet I was charmed by these trinkets. These *charms*. I liked to imagine they were replicas of tchotchkes you could find in Varda's own overstuffed house in the rue Daguerre. Especially the postcards.

Varda and her postcards. If you know a few of Varda's films, you might have noticed that she has a thing for postcards, tarot cards, playing cards, passport photos, daguerreotypes – any kind of talismanic image. Varda lends them (or in some cases restores to them) an esoteric strangeness. She started out as a photographer, and this is how she got into cinema: images spoke so loudly she had to give them words. Even as a screenwriter and director she has stayed with images; she includes many still photos and paintings in her films, and sometimes reconstitutes them with live actors. There's a famous shot in her first film, *La Pointe Courte* (1954), with Philippe Noiret's and Silvia Monfort's faces forming a hard right angle to each other, her profile covering half of his face; the camera holds them tightly together for a moment, in black-and-white sculpturality, and, commenting on this image in her autobiography-cum-documentary, *The Beaches of Agnès* (2008), she announces, seeing cubism reflected there, 'Braque!'

Postcards are the wanderer's flare signal, shot up into the dark, an announcement of presence. Postcards have distance built into them. You buy them in one place, and send them to another, an emissary from wherever you're visiting. This is their purpose. We believe in the connection of postcard to place so deeply that the postcard becomes proof that we have been there. Varda uses this subterfuge in her feminist musical film *One Sings, the Other Doesn't* (1977); the young Pauline lies to her parents, telling them she needs 20,000 francs to travel with her choir to a festival in Avignon, when in fact the money is to send her friend Suzanne to Switzerland to get an abortion. Pauline goes to a postcard shop in Paris and buys a postcard of Avignon, and somehow – I suppose they used to have services for this – gets it sent to her parents from Avignon. Suzanne, meanwhile, pretends to go to Switzerland, but in order to save the money for her bills she has an illegal abortion in Paris instead.

The postcard can make up part of a personal archive, rerouted on its journey from one person to another, becoming a souvenir, or a slender journal, on the back of which we may jot down our impressions of a place only for our own memories, intercepted decades later by a curious grandchild, or a stranger at a flea market. Varda collects old postcards of places she has lived, but she only buys them as far away as possible from the places in question. 'Buying postcards of Noirmoutier in Noirmoutier,' she writes, 'where's the fun in that!' Where is the fun, then? In a slight rotation. A postcard of New York bought in Paris. A postcard of Paris bought in Tokyo. Last time I was in New York, I bought a necklace with a charm in the shape of New York State. 'Isn't that kind of silly?' my mother said when she saw it. 'But she's not going to wear it here,' my sister said. 'She'll wear it in Paris. It will make sense in Paris.'

Some things only make sense out of context.

+

Tarot cards are the first image we see in the film. Cléo is waiting for the results of a biopsy and fears the worst; deeply superstitious, she wants to believe in some kind of knowledge beyond that of science. She is out of place from the moment the film begins; she would not otherwise be in a clairvoyant's office. Something is not right inside of her; this slight displacement inside sets in motion the rest of the film. The tarot reader explains that she is looking for Cléo in the spread: 'The cards speak better when you appear.' And she draws a card with a woman on it, standing in a luxurious faux Louis XV drawing room: candelabras and brocade drapes and ornate tables and picture frames. She is a woman of some wealth and social standing. Or else she's a courtesan.[1] She is framed by a velvet curtain, as if she were onstage. But there is no actress card in the tarot deck, and no courtesan card, either. She could be the Empress, signifying feminine power, rebirth, connecting, according to traditional readings of this card, with 'higher planes of consciousness through nature'. Or she could just as easily represent The World, always depicted by a woman alone, and read to contain promises of travel, of discovery, a sense of closure to the past and the beginning of something new.

The fortune-teller sees a 'departure, a journey'.

FORTUNE‑TELLER

It is difficult to see, we must do another
spread.

The second drawing contains a surprise: a young man, talkative, amusing. 'Ah,' she warns,

FORTUNE‑TELLER

. . . but something is going to go wrong, I
see a shock, an upheaval: it's your disease,
which you are taking very seriously.

She cautions Cléo not to exaggerate, take another card, wait and see. The card Cléo draws is Death. She cries out in horror. The fortune-teller reassures her, tells her the card does not necessarily promise death, but rather, a profound transformation. Cléo scatters the cards on the table and says she's seen enough: the moment they took the blood sample she knew. Though she is genuinely aggrieved, there is something artificial about Cléo's tears.

The camera tracks her as she walks out of the fortune-teller's flat, lingering on the transition from inside to outside. There are several flights of stairs, winding down to the street; Varda slows this shot, cut, cut, cut on Cléo's face. (Jump cuts: the line breaks of cinema.) I pause and re-watch the scene a few times, counting the cuts, trying to understand what is so fascinating about her face moving over and over the screen. I think it's because of the subtle differences in her face, the emotions playing over it; it's not the same shot over and over, or if it is, it's unevenly cut. I never noticed it before, but the film is somehow about these shifts and gaps, what the French call *décalages*; this really resonates, as someone who lives *en décalage*.

That's what gets me about all of her films. Varda's images are dynamic, always in movement, even when the camera is resting. If *La Pointe Courte* seems rigid, even academic, because of the flat, detached way in which the actors were instructed to read their lines, visually the film is in an uproar over the manifold textures and patterns at large in the world. The same is true of Varda herself: even with her lens trained on one place, she can find, there, an infinity of other places. 'I think people are made of the places not only where they've been raised, but that they've loved; I think environments inhabit us,' she said in a 1961 interview. 'By understanding people you understand places better, by understanding places you understand people better.' In *Cléo de 5 à 7*, she would explore the force a neighbourhood exerts on Cléo, but not in a static way – rather, the way something inside Cléo herself shifts as she moves through the neighbourhood, as the neighbourhood moves through her.

+

The film was shot in 1961. That was the year of the Tokens' 'The Lion Sleeps Tonight', the Shirelles' 'Will You Love Me Tomorrow', and Dion's 'Runaround Sue', a year when, in Hamburg, a group of four Liverpudlians were recording their first album. Dalida and Jean Ferrat topped the French charts. *Yé-yé* music was about to break through as the dominant sound of France in the sixties. At the cinema you could have gone to see *Last Year at Marienbad, La Notte, Splendor in the Grass* or *West Side Story*. Foucault published *Madness and Civilisation*, and Franz Fanon published *The Wretched of the Earth*. De Gaulle was (still) in power, France's economy was booming, and Algeria had been fighting for its independence since 1954; they would finally get it the following year, in 1962. Varda is careful to contextualise Cléo's story within these larger events; in one scene, in a taxi, Cléo hears on the radio that a group of French generals who tried to stage a *coup d'état* in Algeria have been found guilty, twenty people have been killed in a demonstration there, the farmers are protesting in Poitiers, and the workers in Saint-Nazaire.

Godard, Truffaut and company were inventing a cinematic vision of the streets of Paris that was modern and photogenic, yet also somehow nostalgic. But it was nostalgic for the present, above all; the fast cars and onslaught of advertising gave the impression that the world was moving so quickly that the present was always just moments behind the now, *en décalage* with itself. Godard's producer wanted to capitalise on the success of *Breathless* the previous year by producing another film with a similar new-wave aesthetic. He wanted a director who, like Godard, could make Paris look good, a place where adventures could begin, and he wanted someone who could do it on the cheap. Godard suggested Varda, who proposed a relatively short film about a beautiful young woman, a singer with several hit singles to her name, who, while waiting for the results of a biopsy, walks apprehensively through Paris for two hours, eventually meeting a soldier about to leave for Algeria, who comforts her and puts her fears in perspective.

To save money, Varda decided to film in a single day, the spring equinox in March 1961 – outclassing Godard by lending an Aristotelian unity to her production, as Paris changed from winter to spring. Alas it was not to be; the necessary financing could not be secured in time, so they decided to film on the summer solstice, 21 June: the longest day of the year. In the end, Varda didn't regret it at all.

The film takes place in thirteen chapters, as Cléo spends an afternoon walking through the incessant noise and grime and gossip of Paris, from five to seven in the evening (or more precisely from just before five until six thirty: Varda's practical joke). In a neat symmetry, the thirteen chapters take Cléo from the 1st arrondissement at the beginning to the 13th at the end.

'What did Paris represent for me?' Varda wondered years later.

A vague fear of the big city and its dangers, of losing myself there, lonely and misunderstood, indeed, shaken to my core. These are the provincial's thoughts, of course, and mainly come from books. I remember this character in a book by Rilke, who seemed dislocated, I remember seeing old people, solitary people in the street, buskers doing strange things (piercing their arms, swallowing frogs). These small fears quickly conglomerated into the fear of cancer which, in the 60s, took root in everyone's minds.

In Cléo, Varda blends this 'vague fear' of the city with the concrete fear of death and mortality. Varda thought of the Northern Renaissance paintings of Baldung Grien, depicting beautiful women in the grip of horrific skeletons. Ageing, death and disease threaten the blonde, nubile bodies of his German models: the skeletons lay hands on their naked flesh, or tug ominously on their gossamer skirts and hair. To translate this mortal fear into cinematic form, Varda says, 'I imagined a character walking in the city [...] The fear of being mortally ill. Is beauty then no protection, not mirrors, not the way other people see us?' She dreamt up a young singer called Cléo, short for Cléopâtre, though her real name (we learn much later) is Florence. A proto-*yé-yé* girl, Cléo is all teased blonde updo, saucer eyes, and totally unrealistic corseted figure. Varda calls Cléo a '*cliché*-woman: tall, beautiful, blonde, voluptuous'. *Cliché*, in French, means 'photograph'.

Varda has explained that the emotional thrust of the film is about Cléo's journey from image to subject, the pivot from being 'the object of the look' to 'the subject who looks'. The looks she receives at the beginning of the film shore her up, makes her feel beautiful, desirable, but she finds another kind of validation from within through an afternoon spent wandering in the city. Seeing the familiar sights of her neighbourhood with this new awareness of death and the impending decay of her beauty, Cléo sheds her synthetic self and finally reaches a state of calm self-awareness. The city refuses to let her wallow. It forces her gaze outward.

As Cléo stops thinking of herself purely in terms of how others see her, the camera stops watching Cléo only from the exterior, and begins to represent the world from her point of view. The film specifically challenges the idea that a woman could not walk the streets the way a man does, anonymously, taking in the spectacle; a woman *is* the spectacle, goes this argument. Looking, not simply appearing, signals the beginning of women's freedom in the city.

The real moments of agency in the film are when Cléo disappears from view: this is when she sees, instead of being seen. Varda herself takes this freedom a step (pardon the pun) further. It is Varda we imagine behind the camera, even if she is not the camera operator, Varda who determines where the camera will go, and when, and what it will capture. It is powerful to see the evolution of a *flâneuse* in front of the camera, but every step Cléo takes reminds us of the one *behind* the camera.

Could the film take place elsewhere? In London? In Tokyo? Maybe, but it wouldn't scan the same way. Paris is a city of mirrors. It's full of them – in the foyers of buildings, on the streets, on the sides of buildings (or maybe they're one-way windows that look like mirrors to passers-by. I imagine the people inside spend their whole day mocking the vain Parisians who nonchalantly cast a glance into the window-mirror as they walk by, which is exactly why I studiously avoid looking at myself in them, lest there be someone there to notice and judge). The city is so photogenic it almost doesn't have a bad angle, and it's always ready for its close-up. Even the people on the cafe terraces are mirrors of a kind, watching the people who walk by, reflecting on their faces their approval, or disapproval, or complete disinterest.[2]

Cléo has no embarrassment whatsoever about stopping to admire herself in every mirror she sees, at least in the first half of the film. Even leaving the fortune-teller's building, she stops to look in the mirror in the lobby, comforting herself that as long as she is beautiful, she is safe. 'Being ugly, that's what death is. As long as I'm beautiful, I'm ten times more alive than everyone else.'

As she walks into the cafe we hear the switch from the street to the cafe, from the hum of engines to the chatter of voices. Cléo's in a kind of daze, as if she doesn't really see where she's going. There she joins her governess/personal assistant Angèle, and she bursts into tears. Angèle removes Cléo's belt and holds a hanky to her nose, calling her *ma petite fille*. They leave the cafe – drinks are on the house – and on the way home for a music rehearsal, Cléo spots a hat shop with a little furry cap in the window. She tries on half the hats in the shop, hats that must have looked absurd even to a 1960s audience. One sits like a starfish on her already starfish-like updo, one cascades over in feathery tentacles, one perches like Peter Pan's.

(Unmistakably Varda taking the piss out of women's fashion.) '*Tout me va,*' Cléo sighs, *Everything suits me*, and is comforted. We watch her from outside, through the shop window; the city is reflected on its surface, and in the shop mirrors, slowly moving from being a reflective surface for Cléo to a character in its own right, Cléo's co-star.

+

Varda would have liked that the postman was willing to come and find me in a nearby cafe – very flexible, very small town of him. *Ça fait très quartier.* It's exactly the way you'd like to think an idyllic Parisian neighbourhood should operate.

They say that Paris is made up of a thousand villages. In fact, this is administratively true. Each arrondissement has its town hall, its local government; each micro-neighbourhood has its markets, its Monoprix, its Franprix, its post office, its branches of the major banks, its high street shops. But – and this may be a controversial opinion – each village is a lot like every other village in the city. The spiral layout of the post-Haussmannian arrondissements confirms this impression, as if the 1st arrondissement were the model for all the others as they spin outward from the centre, self-replicating until they hit the *périphérique.*

But every neighbourhood has its own specific feeling, even if, superficially, they can all look alike. You know when you step out of your neighbourhood: you can feel it. I seem to recall Georges Perec writing of one of his walks around the city that he can sense the moment when one neighbourhood gives way to the next without consulting the blue-plated street signs, and that this sets apart the Parisian from the visitor. The Situationists noticed this as well: 'The sudden change of ambiance in a street within the space of a few meters; the evident division of a city into zones of distinct psychic atmospheres.'[3]

Things happen in your neighbourhood that don't happen outside of it. There's a sense of community; I may not know the people in my building, but I know the fruit guy, the wine guy, the woman at the post office, the woman at the pharmacy, the people who run all the cafes within a five-minute radius (and there are at least four). I suppose this is the case in any neighbourhood in the world; I suppose this is the very definition of a neighbourhood. But when it happens in Paris, it feels special. Perhaps it's because everyone is so bad-tempered all the time that the moments of civic harmony stand out and shimmer. Or maybe I feel this way because I'm an adopted Parisian, and love the city with the vehemence of the convert. But probably it's because it makes me feel like this is home.

Perec calls this 'putting a mawkish face on necessity, a way of dressing up commercialism', but then he never moved to a foreign country.[4] It's not mawkish when it's a question of survival; you have to construct a community out of something. It's when people make a gesture that goes beyond necessity that it becomes neighbourly, like the time the woman who lives downstairs came to my door with an uncooked quiche in her hands, asking to use my oven (hers had broken), which is maybe an urban French version of asking for a cup of sugar, or to borrow the lawnmower.

Neighbourhoods are important to Varda. She's a deeply Parisian director, though she's originally from Belgium, and in 1977 she made a documentary about her street, the rue Daguerre, in the 14th arrondissement, called *Daguerréotypes*. The camera introduces us to the kinds of people who live and work there, the people who own the boulangerie, the accordion shop, the grocers, the butcher. Often we see them through the glass of their shop windows. Or Varda asks them to speak about their lives, what they do, where they're from. She comments, in voice-over, 'In the 14th everyone comes from somewhere else. Its sidewalks smell of the countryside.'

One of the three exterior arrondissements of the Left Bank, the 14th is bordered on the south by the suburbs (Paris *extra-muros*), and on the west by the train tracks leading into the Gare Montparnasse. Dividing it from the rest of Paris along the north is the Boulevard Montparnasse, where cafes cluster by cinemas and crêpe stands, and which eventually becomes the stately Boulevard Port-Royal. To the east it is demarcated by the rue de la Santé, named after the notorious prison (where Jean Genet was once an inmate) that currently stands there, on the site that until the seventeenth century was occupied by a hospital, transferred in 1651 to the present-day location of the nearby Hôpital Sainte-Anne. There are stretches of the 14th, like the avenue de Maine, which seem to go on forever. The 14th borders the once shabby and now stylish 6th arrondissement, as well as the once shabby and now less shabby 13th, and the once shabby and now bourgeois 15th. And everywhere it is studded with hospitals – Cochin, where I had an operation once, Sainte-Anne, La Rochefoucauld, Saint-Joseph, too many to name. Even the prison is called the Santé (Health). As Cléo remarks towards the end of the film, standing on Boulevard de l'Hôpital in the 13th:

CLÉO

This neighbourhood is full of hospitals. As
if one were better cared for in the 13th and
14th arrondissements . . .[5]

Varda moved to the rue Daguerre in 1951, when Montparnasse was full of artists' studios. She was a young photographer, and no doubt the reference to Louis Daguerre, inventor of an early form of photography, appealed to her. The living in her flat was extremely rough. For the first three years there was no heat, except for a coal stove, and no indoor toilet. There was no telephone, either; Varda had to trespass on the generosity of a nearby bistro to make and receive calls. But it included a little courtyard, and in time she took over the whole house, making it much more comfortable. Varda's husband, the film-maker Jacques Demy, came to live there in 1958, and soon the house was their base of operations in Paris, the site of many a film shoot, and a haven for visiting friends. In the days before the Veil Law legalised abortion in 1975, Varda says she and Demy lent their home on two separate occasions to clandestine surgeries. She still lives in that same house; she's even set up a shopfront where you can buy her films on DVD.

Cléo lives in Montparnasse, too. When she and Angèle head for home in a taxi, she gives her address as 6 rue Huyghens, which on the north links the Boulevard Raspail, one of the main arteries of Montparnasse, with the cemetery on the south end. Their taxi driver is a woman, which fascinates them.

CLÉO
And at night, you aren't afraid at night?

TAXI DRIVER
No, I'm not afraid of much.

She says she got into an altercation once with a bunch of kids who didn't want to pay their fare, but she chased them off. The driver is a *flâneuse* on wheels: she knows the city, she's completely independent, and she knows how to defend herself.

When the driver asks if it's all right to put on the radio, Cléo replies, '*Vous êtes chez vous*': she is at home in her taxi, at home everywhere she goes. She's the first independent woman Cléo notices in the film. Angèle finds her inspiring and courageous. Cléo, not yet on her journey, doesn't.

In her long career, Varda has filmed her neighbourhood so many times that the late film critic Roger Ebert dubbed her 'Saint Agnès of Montparnasse'. In the director's commentary to her short film *Le Lion Volatil*, she addresses the camera with tarot cards hanging on the wall behind her, and as she speaks, she shuffles through an assortment of postcards. She displays one for the camera of the Lion of Belfort, the immense lion reposing in the centre of the roundabout at Denfert-Rochereau, a replica of the sandstone statue in Belfort, sculpted by Auguste Bartholdi to commemorate the Prussian siege of 1870–71 (which makes it the 14th arrondissement's Statue of Liberty). In 1933, the city circulated a questionnaire: What could be done to the monuments of Paris to embellish them? André Breton replied: give the Lion de Belfort a bone to gnaw on and turn him so he's facing west. Varda does just this in the film, which is a love story about an apprentice fortune-teller and a mysterious man who works at the Catacombs. Turning a famous postcard lion a few degrees to the west is the kind of adjustment Varda adores.

Varda frequently walks in front of the camera like this, either as narrator, subject or onlooker, except for one scene in *The Beaches of Agnès* where she's dressed like a potato. She is physically memorable: short of stature and prominent of proboscis (an attribute we share), her round eyes take in everything and her face wears an eternally knowing expression. But it's her hair that most people notice. Since the late 1950s she's had the same bowl-cut hairstyle, something between a medieval monk and Joan of Arc. It began dark, and as it greyed she dyed it a brilliant shade of aubergine. Halfway through *The Beaches of Agnès*, it becomes even more idiosyncratic: as the hair dye grows out, she leaves a round grey circle at the crown of her head, making her look even more like a monk, the kind that shaves his head at the crown and lets his hair grow on the sides.

It's a wonderful, almost punk use of hair dye not to disguise the onset of age or to attempt a different hair colour, but to highlight the artifice. It wouldn't be going too far to suggest that her films do the same, combining elements of naturalist storytelling with documentary techniques, blending truth and fiction and pointing it out to the viewer. She refuses the constraints of story, shape, genre and hair colour.

I didn't choose the neighbourhood I lived in for many years, down the other end of Port-Royal. I moved there in order to be closer to a boyfriend, who lived in the rue Mouffetard. I spent most nights at his place and rented mine as a kind of office/storage facility, a place to put all my stuff while I waited for us to get a flat together. Then when he took a job in Tokyo, and moved out of his flat, this became my primary residence in Paris, the place I would come home to when I wasn't staying with him in Japan. At first it still felt like his neighbourhood, but as time went on I seemed to inherit it. After we broke up, it stayed my home. I lived there for eight years, longer than any place I'd ever lived, apart from the house I grew up in.

It's strange the places we end up wedging ourselves. What does our neighbourhood say about us? What is the value of a neighbourhood? Mine is a mirror of my past choices. Pick your path and see where it goes. Pick a subject and see where it leads. Most assuredly you won't be able to predict anything along the way. This is Varda's version of cinematic *flânerie*. In spite of her well-feathered nest in the rue Daguerre, Varda is a vagabonding sort of person, and a vagabonding sort of director; she's tracked her subjects from Los Angeles to Cuba to Iran, filming hippies, Warhol muses, Black Panthers, Communist revolutionaries and feminist folk singers. Even her very latest film, a short called *Les Trois boutons*, shows a young girl *flâneuse*-ing her way down the rue Daguerre in Paris, buttons falling off her dress, creating the life she wants to live. Perennially open to inspiration by objects as well as people, Varda shows herself, in *Les plages d'Agnès*, hunting through the *brocantes* of Paris. 'I love flea markets,' she tells the camera. You never know what you'll find there, or how they'll alter the course of your project. In 2000 she made a documentary about the age-old occupation of gathering food from what is left on the ground after the harvest, called *Les glaneurs et la glaneuse* (*The Gleaners and I*).

I call her a *flâneuse*. She calls herself a *glaneuse*.

Her curiosity guides her; she follows whatever clues are laid down in front of her, so that her films, especially the documentaries, are often collections of observations and serendipitous encounters. In *Les plages d'Agnès*, she goes to visit her childhood home in Brussels, which is now owned by a couple she's never met. She wants to see where her bed was and those of her sisters, but the husband, a man about to retire and move to the countryside, just wants to show her his train collection. She accordingly films the man proudly showing off all of the different trains, the milk train, the post train, the passenger train. It's worth two million Belgian francs, he says, identifying himself as an amateur lover of trains, a *férrovipathe* – an invented term which can best be rendered in English as 'trainophile'. Varda hoots behind her camera, and repeats the term, amused by the turn of events: she went looking for her childhood, and instead found a model-train collector. This leads to reflections on other kinds of trains, other journeys, forced rather than nostalgic ones; her family left Brussels 'amid the rumbling of bombs and ambulances' when Agnès was almost twelve. The train-loving man living in her childhood home wasn't on the itinerary, and yet he became the itinerary.

+

And so we get in the taxi with Cléo, picking up bits and pieces of Paris from the back seat, snatches of the river, the bridges, the churches, the park. As the car stops at lights Cléo is confronted twice with African masks in the windows of Saint-Germain art galleries. The car is surrounded by students from the Beaux-Arts (where Varda studied) wearing masks, celebrating 21 June with some kind of wild ritual that involves shaking the car, banging on the windows. Cléo is getting jittery and carsick, as if every bump, every jostle of the car is shaking loose something inside of her that she has worked very hard to secure. They pull up to the corner of Boulevard Raspail and rue Huyghens and Cléo is home, walking through a courtyard to a free-standing building housing a *très* Montparnasse loft (in real life the studio at this address was the home of Emile Lejeune, painter and friend to the avant-garde musicians of the group Les Six). Why do they come home in the middle of the film? I wonder. Why not start at home and voyage out?

Her studio looks like an enchanted room out of a fairy tale, completely at odds with the modern city outside. Everything is white; there is a four-poster bed in the corner; kittens run and trip across the area rug.

CLÉO

I'm suffocating

she says when she walks in the door, stripping down to her slip. Her lover, José, comes to visit. Inserting herself into a relationship, however low-commitment on his end (does he have a wife? I wouldn't be surprised), has the effect of narrowing her life inward, and the whole film constricts down to the bed where she receives him. This seems purposeful on Varda's part, not just a reference to Cléo as a courtesan, whose business arrangements are carried out from the bedroom, but rather to show the way seeing herself as José's doll keeps her immobile.

Her composer, Bob, has her sing the new song he's written for her, and the thing inside of Cléo that has been threatening to drop finally does. The song is beautiful, haunting, the kind of masterpiece typical of Legrand, subsequently so famous for his score to Demy's *The Umbrellas of Cherbourg* (1964).

CLÉO

I am an empty house without you
I am a grasping, empty body without you
I cover myself in wrinkles without you
And if you come too late,
they will have buried me in the ground:
Alone, ugly, and pale without you.[6]

The camera gets closer and closer to her until her studio disappears and all we see is Cléo's face with a black background behind her casting her into a visual abyss. It is as if Cléo has entered a different psychological space to the others. She commits totally to the song, it brings her to tears, and then she freaks and lashes out at the musicians.

CLÉO

You unnerve me to exploit me . . . I want to
be alone.

She pulls off her wig to reveal a natural blonde bob, puts on a black dress, her new hat, and leaves. The song has forced her out. It is the exact middle of the film.

This, then, may be why she comes home; Varda needed to divide the film in half, to show the two different Cléos in the city. And the song, then, and its grim confines of isolation and abandonment, is the key to her transformation. As long as she is beautiful – or conforms to certain standards of beauty – people will look at her. As long as there are people to look at Cléo, she exists, and she's not alone. Her disease threatens her beauty, and then where will she be? *Sans toi*; completely alone. The song – like the tarot cards – seems uncannily to predict that future. Her perfectly made-up, corseted, belted, bewigged pop-star look is a mask – but who the real Cléo is, who she is underneath, she no longer knows. She has to look for herself in the cards.

+

In her description of Cléo's origins, Varda talked of being inspired by a 'character in a book by Rilke, who seemed dislocated' by the city. She is doubtless referring to Rilke's only novel, *The Notebooks of Malte Laurids Brigge* (1910). A classic twentieth-century narrative of a destitute young Danish poet wandering around Paris, hoping to write, the *Notebooks* are a philosophical meditation on illness, death and fate. Brigge is disillusioned by the city from the first sentences: 'Is it here, then, that people come to live? I'd have thought it was more of a place to die. I've been out walking around. I saw hospitals. I saw a man slip and fall. People gathered around him, which spared me the rest of whatever there was to see. I saw a pregnant woman. She was pushing herself along a high hot wall, touching it from time to time to be sure it was still there. Yes, it was still there.'

It turns out Rilke's wall runs along the front of the Val de Grâce military hospital, in the Boulevard Port-Royal. I know that wall. It stops a block away from the rue Berthollet, where if you turn left and then make the second right you'll be on my old street. Many nights I walked past that wall on my way home and looked at the dome of the baroque chapel, lit up gold against the thick navy sky, and felt so thankful to be able to walk past that sight whenever I liked. Rebuilt since Rilke's day, the hospital is a modern 1960s affair, all cement cubes, the kind you find anywhere in the world, built in the universal language of hospital architecture. There are some military insignias out front and I wondered, when I walked past, about the people inside – are they all in the military? or veterans? What does the hospital specialise in? Is it public or private, nice or grubby? (These are the kinds of things you don't know when you're not really from a place.) There's a sign out front that says *Visitor parking from 15h–20h*, or did I read that wrong?

I used to pass that wall twice a day, to and from teaching in the 16th arrondissement. In the mornings, to save time, I'd catch the 91 bus to Montparnasse station, then take line 6, my favourite, because when it goes above ground in the 15th you can peek into the windows of the Haussmannian buildings, before the train heads across the river and into Passy. As we crossed the river I would stand at the window to look at the Eiffel Tower as it rounded into view, so massive from so close by. I'd try to catch a glimpse of Sacré-Coeur in the distance, up on its hill. On foggy mornings I couldn't see it at all. In the afternoons, I'd get off at Montparnasse and walk the fifteen minutes home, rain or shine.

Now, looking back, I see my old self reflected in the biscuit-coloured stone of that wall, in its textures and its grain, in the soot that gathered in its fissures and nicks and notches. *Will it be this way always?* I wondered at the time. *It feels like it will always be this way. Like I'll always be teaching in the 16th and living in the 5th, like I'll walk past the Val de Grâce every day for the rest of my life.* I wanted so badly for that to be it. That route – that job, that apartment, that neighbourhood – was exactly the life I had dreamt of when I moved to Paris. I had friends, I had a boyfriend, I loved my job and my home and my journey to work.

The reality was less durable. The job was part-time with no hope of being renewed eternally. My visa and my right to work, and therefore the source of my meagre income, would expire imminently. My boyfriend lived in Tokyo. The relationship was bad, and doomed from the start. I laid down a layer of need over it, until I couldn't do without it, and I couldn't see what was underneath that need. Each piece of the puzzle had been meticulously assembled, and I defended it furiously. I had to. Because each piece – to mix metaphors – covered an open wound. I myself was a mixed metaphor, the wanderer who wanted to be a settler.

Things came to a head when the building I lived in was being refaced, and a metal exoskeleton of scaffolding went up. It blocked the light in my bedroom, and there were workmen on the terrace all the time, making my dog bark uncontrollably for hours on end, as they scraped and drilled the stucco from off the building's facade. The dust seeped in, and the fumes used to strip the paint from the shutters made me ill, with headaches and vomiting for hours until I finally went to a hotel. Then, within the space of a week, an unrelated upstairs leak caused water to drain into the walls of my kitchen, loosening the shelving joints so they collapsed and every single one of my plates, spices and a jar of honey shattered into a gooey, dusty, spicy sharp mess. I wanted to scream and scream until they came to take me away. Then, at least, I would be someone else's responsibility. It felt like everything I had worked so hard to build had been wiped out.

These are things that happen. These are the things that happen. All the stuff you have accumulated can be ground to dust in a moment. Those are not the things that matter. I came here with a suitcase, the refrain of the immigrant. When you first arrive, you waver, flicker; you are denuded of context. You quickly cover yourself with new things, a new persona. But you will live in a state of heightened sensitivity; you will always feel exposed, as if you're missing your top layer of skin. The slightest paper cut is agony.

This was the thing I had to learn the hard way, over the years. Although I loved the way it felt to be inspired by Paris, set at an angle to it, able to appreciate the ways in which it was different from home, the initial joy of displacement eventually wore off.

I wanted to settle into a slot in Paris that corresponded to the slot I had vacated in New York. I wanted a job at the university, a home, partner, children. The same thing everyone back there wanted for me, but in French. I kept hoping the slot would open up, and I would gratefully slide into it. I was not a rebel. I was just someone who happened to have moved countries. Displaced, dislocated, I wanted to be re-placed, re-located.

+

Where Cléo's face registered her anguish as she left the fortune-teller's apartment, now her face is set in determination as she walks out of her door. In the courtyard a little boy – a mirror for Bob? – plunks at the keys of a toy piano, the notes of the song we've just heard, as the soundtrack picks up its motif in troubled, fluttering arpeggios. She bursts out of the gate, breaking out of the fairy-tale tower in which she had imprisoned herself, and for the first time in the film she's on foot and without a destination.

She walks up her street, away from the cemetery, towards the Boulevard Raspail. She catches sight of herself in a mirror on the street, tears off 'this ridiculous hat' and grimaces at her reflection. 'I can't even see my own fear, I always think others look at me but I only look at myself, it wears me out.' She walks past a flower stall without pausing – those beautiful things, for sale past the moment of their death – and heads for the Dôme Café at the corner of the Boulevard Montparnasse. She puts one of her songs on the jukebox. All around her, people have their own conversations, their own stories. They speak Spanish, talk about Algeria, surrealism, painting, poetry. There are cubist paintings on the walls, by local geniuses perhaps, or in imitation of local geniuses, and although they echo the African masks in the gallery, in this context they're not frightening. Is it because in the gallery they were (only?) mediated by the art market, while in the cafe they are decoration? Is it because by 1961 cubism has lost its radical edge? Or perhaps there's another reason: by this point in the film the African masks and the art they inspired have already begun to be placed into another context, from one of frightening taboos to one of independent choices. Cléo is now a very different woman from the one who sat in the taxi. Independent choices are scary too, but not as scary as the feeling of faux safety Cléo had in the car.

The world is less scary when you have some control over where you go in it.

Postcards, playing cards, tarot cards, cubist paintings – all images that speak silently. All are a particular kind of fiction: the reader creates a narrative from them, like images on a film storyboard. Their story is subjective, their meaning open-ended. They do not foretell an irrevocable future; what they show can change from moment to moment, for they reflect the emotional state of the querent. They are just one of the many mirrors Cléo consults. There may be some certainties – medical ones – but for the duration of the film, things are not certain, they haven't gone in the wrong direction yet. Cléo is still drawing cards, so to speak. And once she reroutes her day, good things happen to her, promising things, that will allow her to take on the challenges of her illness.

She walks through the cafe to see if anyone is paying attention to the music. No one is. She keeps her sunglasses on. She overhears some people talking about an artist's model she knows, Dorothée, and she decides to go and see her at the studio where she works. (*This* is a true neighbourhood moment

– when you realise you and the people at the next table have friends in common.) Now we walk with Cléo. The camera no longer films her solely from the outside, but begins to show us what it looks like as she goes. There is no music; only the sound of her footsteps on the sidewalk. We experience first-hand the way people look at her, and the way she looks back at them. Men, women, old, young, Cléo meets their gaze head-on. Varda cuts in shots of all the people who cross her mind – images, one after the other, frozen, judging, like the tarot cards.

CUT TO:

A man in the cafe // the fortune-teller // the people Cléo passes in the street // Bob with a kitten on his shoulder // the monkey clock // José // Angèle // Cléo's wig perched atop the mirror.

Her footsteps are joined by the sound of a ticking clock, whose noise recedes as she refocuses her attention on her immediate surroundings.

+

I don't mean to make her walk through the city sound only positive, inspiring, validating. If the city is the cure, it's also the malady. What she sees on the streets at first is a series of revolting penetrations: a man who swallows frogs and spits them back out again, a man with a thin rod piercing his bicep, a bullet hole in the glass window of Le Dôme where, later, they say a man's been killed. There's something abject for Cléo about these violations of flesh. But the men are all right; that's the key thing. A man can pierce his arm muscle clear through with a metal rod and survive. The frogs make it out of their human aquarium alive. As for the man in the cafe: we don't actually know if he died, or if there was even a man concerned. Gossip loves a tragedy. *I'm learning to see*, Malte Laurids Brigge says, several times. Like Cléo, he sees things he doesn't want to see, begins to understand what he would have preferred to leave obscure.

+

As Cléo enters the studio where her friend works as a life model, we see Dorothée perfectly still, silent; there's almost something sacred in the room, silent except for the sound of the art students' chisels as they work. The camera – standing in for Cléo – circles slowly around the room, and as it comes into Dorothée's field of vision she turns her head, looks directly at the camera, and greets her, cheerfully. It's a startling moment, as we don't usually get to hear the artist's model speak. Another collapsed archetype; another image that says more than it seems to.

Cléo is amazed that Dorothée has no problem posing nude. She couldn't do it, she says; she'd be too worried someone would spot a physical defect. Dorothée says they don't see her when they look at her. They see something else, some idea they're looking for . . .

DOROTHÉE

So it's as if I weren't there, as if I were sleeping. And I get paid for it!

The two drive around in Dorothée's boyfriend's convertible, and Cléo playfully engages with the 14th arrondissement as it passes by. The streets begin to speak to her as she becomes aware of the city in a new way.

DOROTHÉE

> The names aren't very inspired around here
> . . . rue du Départ, rue de l'Arrivée . . .

CLÉO

> I would like it if the streets had the name
> of living people. Piaf Street, Aznavour
> Avenue. They could change the names when
> they die.

If you had the sound off, it would look just like any other *nouvelle vague* film: the open top of the convertible, the highly aestheticised black-and-white shots of 1960s Paris, with its billboards, its neon, its joyous embrace of all things modern. Except for the fact that it's two women, on the road together, no man in sight, no guns, no brooding, complicated lovers waiting for them at home with a cigarette and a scheme. Godard famously once said, 'All you need for a movie is a girl and a gun.' Varda proves that all you need is a girl.

The film is in constant movement now. As they approach the Parc Montsouris at the bottom of the 14th, Cléo puns on the name of the park, which sounds like it's saying *souris*, smile.

> *C'est comme* cheeeeeese!

she says, as if an English photographer were taking her picture. (She hasn't lost all of her instincts for self-presentation.) Dorothée is a refreshing tonic.[7] She reminds Cléo of the time before they were famous, when they and Bob used to hang out in Montparnasse trying to make something of themselves; she brings Cléo down to earth. But undoubtedly it is the soldier, Antoine, bound for Algeria that night, who best puts things in perspective for her.

+

As she walks through the park, she comes upon a flight of stairs. The camera waits at the bottom, the soundtrack silent, as Cléo walks down the steps, whistling. Then she begins to dance down them, as if she were the star of a Busby Berkeley musical, one step at a time, singing.[8]

So much is happening during this moment. For one thing, she has no audience; she's singing and dancing for her own entertainment, just for the love of it. But also, she's singing one of her hit singles, one that we've heard on the radio earlier in the film. But we're hearing a different verse this time, one about *'mon corps precieux et capricieux'* ('my precious capricious body'). It's no longer Cléo herself who is capricious, but her body. It can't be relied on. She stops singing at the bottom of the steps, and walks along quietly, hands behind her back. We follow her from behind. She's alone. She has no audience. The singing and dancing was for fun, for the love of it. But she can stop the performance.

Varda does love her symbolism, and so it is as Cléo walks over a Japanese bridge in the park that she meets a man, wearing the bottom half of a soldier's uniform; the water all around them serves as another mirror, but one that, were it to be broken, would quickly restore itself. The soldier is chatty; Cléo forgets to snub him. They talk for a while, and she finds herself confiding all sorts of things to him: her medical woes, her real name. He tells her he's been on military leave for three weeks, but that he's going back to Algeria that night. He comforts her and she him; he helps her to laugh at herself, at him, at her fears. Both archetypes (like the tarot cards), the little princess and the good soldier, they quickly prove that who they are and what they mean depends on more than mere appearances.

+

To Antoine she confides that her real name is Florence: another Varda-esque displacement. He plays with this, free-associating.

ANTOINE
Florence is Italy, the Renaissance,
Botticelli, a rose; Cleopatra is Egypt, the
Sphinx, the asp, a tigress. I prefer
Florence. I prefer flora to fauna.

On the bus they go past the Place d'Italie, in the 13th arrondissement.

ANTOINE
Florence. It's almost home for you.

As they drive, Antoine tells her that the trees that grow there are Pawlownia trees, that they flourish in China and Japan but they come from Poland. We hear Varda's playful love of displacements here too, in Antoine's observations of the city, as if Varda herself were accompanying and comforting her heroine – which she is, and has been doing the whole film. An Italian guitar quavers the melody of the film's main theme.

+

Antoine prompts one more reflection on images and their meanings when he asks for a picture of her to take to war with him. She gives it to him, not like a star giving out a signed photograph, but bashfully, like a young girl giving one to her sweetheart. Derrida, in *The Post Card*, writes that postcards are the confirmation of the ineluctable distance between one person and another: 'I want to address myself to you, directly, without a courier, only to you, but I can't [*je n'y arrive pas*, literally *I don't arrive there*], and it's the very depths of misery. A tragedy, my love, of destination. Everything becomes a postcard.'⁹ The photograph is as well, and so is film; as Barthes points out, the image is the uncrossable distance between then and now, we can't arrive back there. Time can't unspool; it only goes forward, leaving our earlier selves, and the people we've loved, imprinted on the past. Every photograph, every film, is haunted by death; 'every photograph is this catastrophe'.¹⁰ The city is the inverse of this imprint: some leave their names to a street (there are a handful of streets in France named after Jacques Demy) but as Cléo would have it the streets would only be named after people who are alive, and changed after their death, lending the streets a sad kind of mutability. Most of us, alive or dead, won't leave our names anywhere. Our apartments, our streets, the places we've loved, we leave invisible traces there, perceptible only to the most sensitive of our descendants, who may feel the slightest atmospheric shift as they walk over some subway grate or threshold, without knowing why or who has crossed there before them. 'Environments inhabit us,' Varda said.¹¹ These places that we take into ourselves and make part of us, so that we are made of all the places we've loved, or of all the places where we've changed. We pick up bits and pieces from each of them, and hold them all in ourselves.

+

And sometimes we hold on with both hands to things we really want to release.

This is a hard thing to admit. How do we know what to keep, and what is just an old idea we had about ourselves?

+

We have no objectivity on our own lives, so we turn to the cards. We like games of divination, just as we like divining rods. Lead the way. Tell me where there's gold. I used to do something I saw in a movie once. I would pick up a book – *Pride and Prejudice* is the one I used a lot, hoping for some of Elizabeth Bennet's good sense – open it to a random page, and put my finger down, and whichever word it landed on I regarded as prophecy or counsel. This is called stichomancy, and it is an ancient divining practice. But there is no book, no tarot card and no GPS on earth that can tell us where to go next. I think of Marcel Duchamp, who according to André Breton once flipped a coin to decide if he should go to New York or stay in Paris. 'And this without the *slightest* indifference,' Breton wrote. [12]

But I think what Varda's films suggest is that nothing, no situation, is ever static. Everything is always changing. Beauty, life, meaning is about the unexpected, in Varda's universe; it comes from flux. What matters to Varda, the film critic Phil Powrie observes, 'is not where you are, nor where you are going, but movement, transformation, becoming'. [13] Inside the hospital gates Cléo is disoriented; she has never come on foot, only by taxi. On learning that her doctor has most likely left for the evening, she decides not to bother looking for the doctor, but to sit with Antoine in the garden. She has reconciled herself, even if only momentarily, to not knowing the future.

Varda has said that the first feminist act is to gaze, to say, 'I am looked at, but I can also look.' Her films do just this, looking askance at the world and our places within it, we gleaners, *flâneuses*, vagabonds, neighbours. There is no such thing as objectivity. *L'objectif*: French for the lens, through which we can only see one way, even if we turn it on ourselves. This is a comfort; if it's true then nothing can be objectively bad, not even illness.

The doctor does show up, driving by in his convertible.

DOCTOR
Don't worry too much. Two months of
radiation therapy will set you right again.

The car pulls away and the camera with it: Cléo's shock rendered in movement, a quick back zoom travelling. Travelling shots for a travelling director.

+

And so although what she's been fearing for two days has actually come to pass, Cléo is no longer afraid.

CLÉO
It seems like I'm happy.

She and Antoine say nothing further, and there is no music, just the bells of the chapel ringing, and their footfalls on the gravel. The camera walks in front of them, framing their two faces as they hold each other's gaze, and the film ends.

anywhere at all, cross the street, open your eyes

EVERYWHERE

THE VIEW FROM THE GROUND

There is too much space in the world. I am bewildered by it, and mad with it.

        – Martha Gellhorn, Letter to Stanley Pennell

Robert Capa has his camera on the ground, angled up at Martha Gellhorn, who stands among the ruins of the Greek temple of Cerere in Paestum, Italy. Or perhaps he's simply standing a little ways away, down the steps that surround the temple on all sides, and is resting his camera on one of the stone walls for stability. Either way, it's a strange angle; she looks larger than life. The composition frames her within the stone structure, the same height as the Doric columns, a living caryatid, her head just meeting the architrave, as she concentrates on a book. It is as if she belongs there, here, in this Greek temple in Italy, mistakenly attributed to Ceres, goddess of fertility. But looking at the photograph, it's clear both subject and photographer know this is actually a temple to the goddess of wisdom. Grey-eyed Athena turned grey-trousered Gellhorn, in the city once known as Poseidonia, the city by the sea. She pauses, but she could take off at any moment, in who knows which direction, propelled by whatever it is she's reading, some stray thought, some unknown impulse. She squints in the sunlight, scrutinising her guidebook, if it is a guidebook. But she is not a dutiful American tourist abroad: this is Martha Gellhorn, famous war correspondent, permanently home-building, permanently homeless, novelist, runaway, divorcee, a brash, sassy reporter, a broad abroad.

Gellhorn and Capa had driven down from the film set of John Huston's *Beat the Devil* in Ravello, where Capa was working. It was April 1953; she had spent the winter in a bitterly cold Italian farmhouse near Rome with her son, Sandy. She and Capa had been friends since they met in Spain in 1937. Dashing and Hungarian and twice a refugee, having fled Horthy to Berlin and then Hitler to Paris, he called himself 'Robert Capa' to sound like an American film star (real name: Endre Friedmann). Seventy years later, Susan Sontag would write that 'virtually everyone who has heard of [the Spanish Civil War] can summon to mind' Capa's iconic photograph of the Republican soldier who's just been shot, 'the grainy black-and-white image of a man in a white shirt with rolled-up sleeves collapsing backward on a hillock, his right arm flung behind him as his rifle leaves his grip – about to fall, dead, onto his own shadow'.[1]

As an American living away from America, Gellhorn was attuned to outsiders; she knew she was one by choice, but she was drawn to those who don't get to choose, to the exiled, the cast-out, the marginalised; she began her career documenting the devastation wrought by the Great Depression in the United States, interviewing Americans who had become strangers to themselves through deprivation. Her upbringing in St Louis, Missouri, was at once traditional and socially aware. She came from a relatively well-to-do family; her father was a doctor (the only specialist in gynaecology and obstetrics in all of St Louis), and her mother was a suffragette and activist – well known as a campaigner in Washington, and a friend of Eleanor Roosevelt's. Both of her parents were half-Jewish, although this does not seem to have registered in young Martha's mind until she was an adolescent. Her biographer, Caroline Moorehead, speculates that her 'suppressed awareness of bigotry and racial slights may explain the later intensity of her feelings'.[2]

When they met in Spain, Capa was twenty-five, Gellhorn thirty. The European Jew posing as an American; the American Jew come to learn something about Europe – they were naturally *simpatico*, both interested not only in documenting history but in capturing portraits of people in extreme situations. They knew they had encountered each other, and so many others, because the cruel men who were trying to rule the world had ripped up its fabric, starting wars that cast people adrift, out of their homes and into each other's lives. Looking at Capa's photographs, reading Gellhorn's reports, the way they each capture the individual within the historic event, it's clear they were evolving what would become their key styles together, and that these ways of telling about war and history would set the standard for the rest of the century. Gellhorn, in particular, would be driven throughout her life to turn what she saw into something else. Writing helped her process the trauma of what she witnessed; she called it her 'mind and spirit's purge: there are things to be eternally rid of'.[3]

But her reporting would always be just one way of doing this: fiction-writing would be another. Capa would persist in taking pictures in colour, though that wasn't what people wanted from him. And Gellhorn went on writing novels, though it was her journalism that won her accolades. Fact and fiction were both indispensable ways of seeing.

+

Capa had arrived in Spain in 1936 with his partner, Gerda Taro, who set about documenting with her Rolleiflex the impact of the war on the people she saw around her on the streets of Barcelona. She was accidentally killed by a Republican tank a few months after Gellhorn arrived. Perhaps Gellhorn took her cue from Taro. Reporting from Madrid, where you could walk to the front line, right there in the middle of the city, Gellhorn wrote about her daily walks around the besieged capital, detailing the everyday impact of war on the city and the people who lived there. She wanted to know how people lived in those circumstances, what it felt like, what they did, how they coped.

She would later describe her war reporting as 'a gesture of solidarity'. But in order to go to war, she often had to detach herself from her home life – first from her family, then from her husband, eventually from her son. Although she could never stay for long in one place, she tried again and again to make homes for herself, and abandoned each of them in turn – like Sandy, whom she adopted in Italy, and would frequently leave in the care of friends, nannies and assorted caregivers. All in all she set up house eleven times in seven different countries, buying houses, or renting them, or building them. This homemaking seems at odds with all the travelling, as if she needed a reliable spot to return to, a nest between flights. But it also suggests Gellhorn felt a strong double pull in both directions, home and abroad. She would contend her whole life with the immenseness of the world, its great and overwhelming promise. 'There is too much space in the world. I am bewildered by it, and mad with it. And this urge to run away from what I love is a sort of sadism I no longer pretend to understand.'[4]

She saw travel and *flânerie* as extensions of the same impulse: to *flâner*, she told Victoria Glendinning, 'is as necessary as solitude: that is how the compost keeps growing in the mind'.[5] She offered her own definition of the word, which she called 'the best French verb': 'It is a need for occupation, done sitting down or moving.'[6] Gellhorn directly contradicts the solitary, disassociated image we have of the *flâneur*, and redefines it as oriented towards some goal, some revelation, some way of recording and sharing what she had seen. Faced with war and suffering, she could not stand by and watch. She preferred to 'jump into the general misery, where you have almost no choices left, but a lot of solitary company'.[7] In her dedication to exposing misery, Gellhorn turned *flânerie* into testimony.

According to Moorehead, Gellhorn 'drove herself into brick walls searching for a balance between love and independence, society and solitude, outwardness and inwardness, and was beset by a profoundly American indecision between the road and the homestead'.[8] She could not stop making homes; nor could she stop leaving them, even when they contained Ernest Hemingway, her first husband, or Sandy. The term we use for marrying and having children is the opposite of wandering: we say we're 'settling down', as if, meeting with a natural course of resistance, we eventually slow and become still. Is there a happy medium between being vagabond and a wife, between solitude and 'settling down'? For Gellhorn there wasn't, as she pinged between extremes. The testimony she produced was born of her unwillingness to compromise.

+

Over a lifetime of work as a war correspondent, Gellhorn put herself where the blood was spilling and the filth and despair were proliferating. If there was a story somewhere, she had to get it, and she got it in (as she later recalled) 'Spain; Finland; China; World War II in England, Italy, France, and Germany; Java; Israel; Vietnam'.[9] When she couldn't get accredited by the US Army to report on the D-Day invasions, because women journalists were banned from embedding, she disguised herself as a nurse and stowed away on a ship. (She was eventually caught, arrested, reprimanded by the army, and barred from France.) Hemingway loved how fearless Gellhorn was, but he resented the competition and missed having her around the house. He sent her a telegram at the Italian front in 1944: 'ARE YOU A WAR CORRESPONDENT OR WIFE IN MY BED?'

It was a golden age for women daring to journey out, and travelogues from Rebecca West, Emily Hahn, Olivia Manning, Gertrude Bell, Jane Bowles, Freya Stark, Dorothy Carrington and Alexandra David-Neel were piling up in the bookstores, their stories something more and something else than what gets called 'travel writing'. Gellhorn was one of these travelling, wilding, writing women, driven by a desire to see 'more of the world and what's in it'. Many of the others were travelling with or in the wake of their husbands, who had been posted abroad for some official reason. Whereas Gellhorn was often more daring even than her husband: when she wanted to go to China, she had to drag Hemingway along. She wanted to see the Sino-Japanese conflict for herself. He was happy in Cuba. He had good reasons, he protested, for not wanting to go to China; for example, his uncle had been a medical missionary there and was forced on one occasion to remove his own appendix on horseback. An adolescence spent reading Somerset Maugham and Fu Manchu and being forced to contribute dimes to the cause of converting the heathen of China had given Hemingway – usually up for any sort of

THE VIEW FROM THE GROUND 251

adventure – a strong aversion to the place. And yet, in early February 1941, off they went, by way of Hawaii, calling it their honeymoon. By then a seasoned war correspondent, Gellhorn wanted to get a sense of Chinese life from the ground up: 'Opium dens, brothels, dance halls, mah-jong parlours, markets, factories, the Criminal Courts: it was my usual way of looking at a society.' Months later, when her hands were covered in 'Chinese rot' and she had to slather them in evil-smelling pomade and wear oversized white motorman's gloves, Hemingway was unmoved: 'who wanted to go to China?' In an essay about this trip, written many years later, she dubs him 'Unwilling Companion', or 'U.C.' It's the only time she wrote about him, after their divorce.

But it was Hemingway who inspired her to go to Spain. Along with John Dos Passos, Lillian Hellmann and Archibald MacLeish, he was setting up a company called Contemporary History, which would exist in order to drum up funding to make a documentary about the war in Spain, to be directed by Joris Ivens. Spain was the front line in the fight against fascism and totalitarianism, and it was, Gellhorn increasingly believed, the 'Balkans of 1912', the next troubled zone that was about to erupt into global war. She was squarely on the side of the Republican forces attempting to put down Franco's reactionary uprising.

For most of her life she had been against war, and would not have been interested in seeing one fought. In *The Face of War*, her 1959 essay collection of war writing, she talks about meeting some young Nazis in Berlin in 1934, and speaking with them, trying to understand them as Socialists, empathising with the German position, as she says all right-thinking people did at that time. 'I was a pacifist,' she wrote, 'and it interfered with my principles to use my eyes.'[10] She was blinded by the idea of maintaining peace at all costs. But a mere two years later, her eyes were back in working order, and she set out for Spain. 'I am going to war with the boys,' she wrote in a letter to a friend. In New York an editor at *Collier's* gave Gellhorn a letter identifying her as a special correspondent for the magazine. She did not, however, see herself as a foreign correspondent; rather, she was a novelist (the author of a novel that later embarrassed her, *What Mad Pursuit* (1934), who had done some work as a journalist. She travelled from France and turned up in Spain with a backpack and fifty dollars in her pocket.

When she arrived in Madrid, in March 1937, it was 'cold, enormous and pitch-black, and the streets were silent and perilous with shell-holes'; it was very clear she had arrived in the middle of a war, but a war fought on the streets of the city. Shelling rained down several times a day from the rebel forces, who were camped in the hills on three sides of the city. 'It was a feeling I cannot describe; a whole city was a battlefield, waiting in the dark. There was certainly fear in that feeling, and courage. It made you walk carefully and listen hard.'[11] As if to highlight the surreal juxtaposition of daily life and carnage, she observed that you could take a tram to the front line, near the university. She followed the male correspondents around (respectful of these 'experienced men who had serious work to do'), and used their transportation passes to get around. She learned 'a little Spanish and a little about war', and spent time with the wounded. Those first few weeks, she was also rather busy beginning an affair with Hemingway, and befriending another American war correspondent, Virginia Cowles, with whom she would later write a romp of a war play, *Love Goes to Press* (1946).

But soon, a 'journalist friend' (Hemingway) suggested she use her writing to contribute to the war effort (the *causa*). Her talent seems very obvious to us, her readers, in retrospect, but in spite of her youthful bravado, Gellhorn didn't see herself as being an expert at anything – not journalism, not novel-writing, and certainly not Spanish politics, especially as she lacked the credentials to get in to meet with the key players. '[H]ow could I write about war,' she asks, looking back years later, 'what did I know, and for whom would I write? What made a story, to begin with? Didn't something gigantic and conclusive have to happen before one could write an article?' But her journalist friend said she could write about Madrid. 'Why would that interest anyone? I asked. It was daily life. He pointed out that it was not everybody's daily life.'[12]

She did not expect that *Collier's* would accept the first piece she sent them, but they did. It begins as a portrait of a city under siege, with observations on shopping, theatres in wartime, the opera, hotels that were now hospitals. Then she turns her gaze to describing the way the houses looked after the bombings, the children in the hospitals, mutilated and starving, the smell of the trenches, the precise sound of a shell as it left a gun and whizzed towards you, the feeling of waiting for the shell to hit alone in a room that 'got dustier and dustier as the powdered cobblestones of the street floated into it'.[13] As the street came inside, she had to get outside into the street, 'practising on the way how to breathe. You couldn't help breathing strangely, just taking the air into your throat and not being able to inhale it.' In this strange version of a city, the street, in the form of its pulverised cobblestones, entered the lungs.

After her first few articles, *Collier's* added her name to their masthead. In a series of reports, Gellhorn described her daily walks, detailing the everyday impact of war on the city and the people who lived there. She wrote about how strange it was to find a war just down the road, how to pass the time they 'went visiting at the nearest fronts (ten blocks from the hotel, fifteen blocks, a good brisk walk in the rain, something to circulate your blood)', and 'strolled to University City and Usera, to the Parque del Oeste, to those trenches that are a part of the city and that we knew so well', amazed that '[n]o matter how often you do it, it is surprising just to walk to war, easily, from your own bedroom where you have been reading a detective story or a life of Byron, or listening to the phonograph, or chatting with your friends'.[14]

She described the people as simply waiting, for the next shelling, or for something else to happen. People 'standing in doorways and around the square, just standing there patiently, and then suddenly a shell landed, and there was a fountain of granite cobblestones flying up in the air, and the silver lyddite smoke floated off softly'.[15] One man can't bear waiting in a doorway, in a group, and says he thinks it's over, but in any case he must go. '"I have work to do. I am a serious man. I cannot spend my time waiting for shells. Salud," he said, and walked out calmly into the street, and calmly crossed it.' His decision to move inspires all the other people to move along as well, navigating the bombed-out square, 'pock-marked with great round holes, and littered with broken cobblestones and glass. An old woman with a market basket on her arm hurried down a side street. And two boys came around the corner, arm in arm, singing.' Here she addresses the reader, or herself, or the Madrileños, all together in the second person: 'You couldn't wait forever; you couldn't be careful all day.'[16] They – return to the third-person plural, return to detached, yet empathic, description – had to get on 'with the routine of their lives, as if they had been interrupted by a heavy rainstorm but nothing more'. She walks around the city, noticing who's where, what disruptions have there been to people's lives, how are they reacting to the ongoing shelling. Three men are killed in a cafe in the morning, while they are reading the paper and having coffee, but by afternoon the clientele has returned. The bars in Madrid's version of No Man's Land are still crowded at the end of the day, even if there are dead animals on the pavement, and 'crisscrossing trails of human blood'.[17] Women brave the shelling to get groceries for dinner. And inside a shoe shop, as explosions go off outside, a clerk calmly suggests to some girls trying on sandals that perhaps they should move to the back of the shop, in case the front windows should break.

Then there is the passage that must truly have brought home the tragedy of the conflict to Gellhorn's readers.

An old woman, with a shawl over her shoulders, holding a terrified thin little boy by the hand, runs out into the square. You know what she is thinking: she is thinking she must get the child home, you are always safer in your own place, with the things you know. Somehow you do not believe you can get killed when you are sitting in your own parlor, you never think that. She is in the middle of the square when the next one comes.

A small piece of twisted steel, hot and very sharp, sprays off from the shell; it takes the little boy in the throat. The old woman stands there, holding the hand of the dead child, looking at him stupidly, not saying anything, and men run out towards her to carry the child. At their left, at the side of the square, is a huge brilliant sign which says: Get out of Madrid.[18]

The passage is proof of Gellhorn's deep empathy, her willingness and even her obligation to look, and to record. But from this awful observation comes, perhaps, an important truth about war. You can be killed at home as easily as anywhere else – you are not safer at home with your things around you than you are out in the unfamiliar world, though – to paraphrase her first husband – it is pretty to think so. We take a certain amount of solace in the idea of home. But a home can be used against you.

Gellhorn had left her family behind in the US in pursuit of the freedom to come and go as she chose, and found herself hooked by a husband who tried to reel her in like one of his marlins. They bought a house in Cuba, and the responsibility of it drove her to despair. 'I got very gloomy,' she wrote to Eleanor Roosevelt, 'thinking now I am caught, now at last I have possessions (and I have feared and fled them all my life), and what in God's name shall I do with this palace now that I have it. So I felt that the world was at an end, I had a house and would never write again but would spend the remainder of my life telling the servants to scrub the bathroom floors and buy fresh paper for the shelves.'[19]

And then the pleasures of the house would sneak in on her, the 'sun streaking over the tiled floors, and the house itself, wide and bare and clean and empty, lying quiet all around me', and she would feel 'very serene and safe again'.[20] That word, 'safe', could mean so many different things to her – it could mean what it usually does, or it could contain all the guilt and self-loathing she could summon at being home and safe when others were not.[21]

+

Gellhorn had no patience for what she liked to refer to as 'all that objectivity shit' – the idea that a responsible journalist has to be neutral, and report her subject from all sides.[22] Objectivity was boring, not to mention unattainable. She was more interested in capturing the feel of a time and place. 'How is it going to be possible ever to explain what this is really like?' she asked in an essay for *Collier's*. 'All you can say is, "This happened; that happened; he did this; she did that." But this does not tell how the land looks on the way to the Guadarrama, the smooth brown land, with olive trees and scrub oak growing beside the dry steam beds, and the handsome mountains curving against the sky.'[23] Capa told Gellhorn that 'in a war [. . .] you must have a position or you cannot stand what goes on'.[24] Gellhorn didn't have just one position; her orientation was always adapting, as she ranged around Madrid. 'Disaster,' she wrote, 'had swung like a compass needle, aimlessly, all over the city.'[25] She described the world in geographical terms, but any objective sense of direction had become impossible. She met an architect who was carrying his 'day's ration of bread' in a newspaper. 'He was very careful all morning, climbing through ruins, jumping flooded gutters, not to drop the bread; he had to take it home – there were two small children there, and come death and destruction and anything else, the bread mattered.'[26] This is a kind of micro-reporting, telling the world not what happened at a meeting between generals, but how much a loaf of bread mattered to an architect and his children.

+

I saw the Capa photograph of Gellhorn at Paestum at the International Center for Photography in New York, in a show about his colour photography. Although Capa is best known for his work in black and white, he started experimenting with colour in 1941. It was an eccentric medium at the time. Colour film was expensive and took a long time to develop, making it impractical for war reporting, so editors rarely wanted it, and Capa's colleagues turned their noses up at it. 'Photography in colour? It is something indigestible, the negation of all photography's three-dimensional values,' said Henri Cartier-Bresson. After the war, however, magazines no longer wanted dour images of destruction and suffering wrought in many shades of grey; they wanted loud popping colour, and Capa did all he could to keep up with the demand, travelling to Israel, Norway, Budapest, Moscow, Morocco, France, as well as Italy, to shoot spreads of magical places most people would never visit, places that imagined a world untouched by war. Some of the images in the ICP show had been published in magazines like *Holiday* and *Life* in the 1950s, but many had never been seen before. These colour pictures weren't of the subjects he was known for and therefore, as the exhibition notes said, were considered irrelevant to Capa's 'canon'. I think that fiction was Gellhorn's colour photography. Not in the sense that it presented a world in Technicolor, like the brilliance of the Oz portion of Victor Fleming's musical (released on 15 August 1939, two weeks before the war began), but in the sense that it filled in what readers had been left to imagine: she could not only narrate the slice of the architect's life during the war, but create a story for him.

Although she downplayed her abilities before the literary god she had married, she still needed to funnel the real world into an invented one, that nevertheless bore its likeness. She wrote self-deprecatingly to Hemingway in 1943 that journalism was bad for him, but good for her. 'It gives me many things for my eyes and mind to feed on, and they need to feed on actual sights rather than reading, simply because they are not first-rate, but that is their best food. It gives me a chance to meet people I would never otherwise meet, and I want to know them . . . Besides, deviously, everything I have ever written has come through journalism first, every book I mean; since I am not Jane Austen or the Bronte sisters and I have to see before I can imagine, and this is the only way I have of seeing.'[27] What novelist wouldn't feel hemmed in, married to Hemingway? *I'm not Austen or the Brontës – or Hemingway*, she might have added; I am no threat to you. But still: she insists on imagining. Journalism was a way towards fiction, a necessary step in between life and fictional life. And maybe, though it might not incite 'direct action' on the part of her readers, she hoped 'it makes a sort of climate, that it makes a little more receptivity in people who read it'.[28] But fiction held pride of place.

Like Capa's colour photographs, fiction took too long to develop to be 'newsworthy'; the reporting she had done came to serve as a sort of fieldwork for the characters and situations she would create in her fiction, where she would develop the psychological impact of history. *The Trouble I've Seen* (1936) is a collection of linked short stories drawing on her work with Roosevelt's Federal Emergency Relief Association during the Great Depression. As Rachel Arons wrote in the *New Yorker*, 'though it predated, by several decades, the literary reportage of Ryszard Kapuściński or the New Journalism of the nineteen-sixties that brought creative-writing techniques into the realm of nonfiction, *The Trouble I've Seen* foreshadowed those journalistic movements: it read like a novel but gained power from that journalistic advantage Tom Wolfe called "the simple fact that the reader knows all this actually happened".'[29] For Capa and for Gellhorn, colour may have been closer to life not only because most of us live in a world of colours, not shades of black and white, but because it was also, with its brilliant, Kodachrome colours, more spectacularly artificial. There is no sharper truth than that of fiction.

In those early days she sometimes went too far, and blurred the lines between fiction and lies. In 1936, she published an article about witnessing a lynching. This event turned out to be something she had heard about, but not actually seen, the conflation (she told Eleanor Roosevelt) of two different accounts she had heard while travelling in the American South with her lover, Bertrand de Jouvenal (Colette's stepson and former lover, but that is another story). She did not let on for many years that she had not been in attendance that day when 'a group of men, shoving and pushing, got Hyacinth's limp, thin body up to them. He half lay, half squatted on the car roof.' There is no doubt that Gellhorn places herself at the scene; she notes that everyone was so still 'you could hear the mosquitoes whining' as they threw the rope up and over the tree. 'I went away and was sick,' she writes.[30] Gellhorn was ashamed not of having pretended to have been there, but of not having spoken up, when the article was picked up and reprinted and earned her an invitation to testify before a Senate committee as they drafted an anti-lynching bill, though she declined.[31] She would not give false testimony before the law. And she would spend the rest of her life trying to really *be* there.

The ethics of it are tricky to parse. We rely on journalists to be at least truthful, even if pure objectivity is impossible. But a first-hand account is always going to be more titillating for readers than something invented; we love the thrill of something that *really happened*, we prefer our fictions to be *based on a true story*. Had she written a short story about a lynching, she would likely still have been praised for her daring. But writing about the event as though she had witnessed it first-hand shifts the focus almost imperceptibly from what happened to her own presence. In that sense Gellhorn's work – not only this piece of writing, but all the rest as well, true or false or a blurred combination of the two – points up an uncomfortable truth about reportage as testimony. The drive to speak for those who can't speak for themselves is, on some level, a drive to let your own voice be heard. She did not imagine, she wrote, that she would go on to become a professional in the field, 'an unscathed tourist of wars'.[32] There is a fraught politics at work here, something cutting in the notion that war has its tourists, who can come and go as they please, that there is a class of 'professionals' of the field of war, who make money and fame off the suffering of others. But Gellhorn also shows us that self-interest can be a form of empathy, as she plunged herself again and again into other people's hearts and minds, even to the point of making things up when she should have drawn a clearer boundary.

It was the Second World War that forced her to confront the fact that the act of witnessing would not leave her unscathed, that getting to see events first-hand exacted a price. Gellhorn would write three novels about that war: *A Stricken Field* (1940), a novel set in Prague under the Nazi occupation in 1938, which was inspired by her time in that city, and features an American female journalist reporting on the demise of Czechoslovakia as Europe turned their backs; *Liana* (1945), set in the Caribbean, about a mixed-race girl, the French husband who exploits her, and the exiled French tutor she loves and whom she thinks will save her; and *Point of No Return* (1948), a novel that, as Heather McRobie wrote for the *TLS*, 'allows American optimism to disintegrate inexorably in the face of European darkness'.[33]

This last novel, in which she transforms what she witnessed of Dachau into the experience of a young Jewish-American soldier liberating the camps, is one of Gellhorn's most successful attempts at putting her reportage in the service of her fiction. The point of no return, she writes in an afterword, forty years after it was first published, is the moment when a pilot has gone too far to turn back, 'a specific time limit, stated in hours and minutes. When reached, the pilot must head the plane back or it would have insufficient fuel to stay airborne and land in England. Turn or die.'[34] Dachau, Gellhorn wrote, was her own 'point of no return'.[35]

She was told about the camp in 1937. It was not the worst of the Nazi death camps, she said, but it was the first to be set up, in 1933. She spent the whole war waiting to see Dachau liberated: this was her own 'private war aim'. 'By bumming lifts across Germany, as the Allied troops advanced', she got there a week after the first American soldiers discovered it (and a week after Lee Miller took her now famous, deeply disturbing photographs of the Death Train). Afterwards, Gellhorn saw 'the human condition, the world we live in, changed'.[36] In her novel, her hero, Jacob Levy, leaves Dachau, gets in his Jeep, and runs over three German civilians crossing a nearby road, because they had lived their lives not even a mile away from the camp as if nothing were happening. 'They knew, they didn't care, they *laughed*.'[37] From Jacob's enraged perspective, there is no such thing as an innocent bystander. Through Jacob, Gellhorn implicates all Americans in the lynching she recounted, not least herself, driving peacefully through the South with her French lover.

+

While *Point of No Return* is important, and under-read, *Liana*, though not a great work of literature, seems to me to be a text where she was trying to figure something out, trying to understand something about why she couldn't stay in one place, why she could not rest until she had seen all there was to see in the world, then seen it all again. *Liana* is about a lot of things: Empire, and the impact of war on people far away from any front. Race, and white domination, and the inheritance of slavery. Gender, and the inequalities of love between men and women, especially when complicated by race. It's a novel that might not have been written if Gellhorn hadn't been excluded from the European front because of her gender, and sent by *Collier's* to the Caribbean in the spring of 1942 on a submarine-hunting mission (Gellhorn hopped to it, studying up on 'military and naval tactics and strategy, artillery, insignia, and the geography of the islands').[38] But when I read *Liana*, I also see

Gellhorn reflecting on the way people are so changed by what they live through that they can't go back to where they started, or even, in some cases, go forward at all.

The young mixed-race woman at the centre of the novel has been taken away from her family to be first mistress and then wife to Marc, the wealthiest man on the island of St Boniface, who tries to make a 'proper white lady' of her, renaming her 'Julie' and treating her like an animal without feelings or reason. Liana, understandably, is miserable in her new home, the future stretching ahead of her endlessly, meaninglessly. She is not allowed to have her family visit; when she goes to see them, her little sisters call her a princess, and the word itself is 'lovely and strange, from a faraway place'.[39] But she has become so used to luxury, and internalised, perhaps, the prejudices of her new milieu, that she can't bear spending time with them, 'the odour of their bodies and their beds, their food, the creeping smell that came in from the latrine which was too near to the house, and the sharp, rotten smell of the garbage dump [. . .] the smell had seeped into the ground'.[40]

In time, she belongs nowhere. 'She wore her elegance like a varnish all over her,' Gellhorn writes of Liana's early transformation into Marc's ideal wife, as if the 'real' Liana were there all the time, ready to be varnished white or varnished black.[41] But who, exactly, sees her this way? Who is this narrative voice who observes Liana, with the 'finicking voice to go with the neat and tidy French she now spoke', whose table manners are better than Marc's? Marc wouldn't admit such a thing, and Liana – from what we learn of her – doesn't have that level of self-awareness. It must be Gellhorn the social observer, involving her journalist's perspective in the intimate lives of the people she invents.

Eventually, love comes Liana's way, in the form of Pierre,

the recently arrived schoolmaster who has fled the war in France not out of cowardice but because, he says, if he saw a German he would certainly shoot him, and that would only be revisited on the French population. Marc hires Pierre to teach Liana to read, with predictable consequences. When Marc discovers their affair, he tells her to leave his house. Meanwhile Pierre can no longer bear being away from France in her hour of need, and can't take Liana with him – not only would it be bringing her to a war, but, they agree without saying the words, he couldn't bring a black girl back with him.

Gellhorn threads through the novel a motif of irrevocability, the impossibility of 'going back' – both in terms of the various characters' actions, which can't be undone, and also to where they started from: France, for the men, and life with her family, for Liana.[42] There is no direction she can take, no backwards, no forwards. No one can help her; no one can save her, and she can't save herself. Into this trap Gellhorn introduces the notion of responsibility, in this case, the blame that Marc and Pierre must assume for taking Liana out of her world – Marc with money and Pierre with love – and making it impossible to return to it. Thanks to them, 'she had no home and no people'.[43] Hearing the men decision-making on her behalf, Liana feels robbed of any agency of her own, and, facing a future without Pierre in a cold house by herself, takes drastic action. First she burns all of her fancy things leaving her 'as poor as when she started'.[44] Then she opens up a vein, and dies on the bathroom floor, her face 'tired and grey against the white tile of the bathroom floor'.[45]

The novel is critical of the inbuilt, unquestioned mistrust of whites for blacks Gellhorn witnessed in the US and abroad, and takes aim at those who rule without consent; in its study of the impact of war on a little Caribbean island so very far away from any of the fronts, there is an implicit critique of Empire, of powerful nations meddling and instituting Eurocentric hierarchies and value systems everywhere they can sail to. Yet Gellhorn makes some questionable pronouncements, and her representation of Liana's family suggests Gellhorn was not entirely aware of her own biases. She herself writes Liana, to some extent, as an unknowable mystery. Even Liana's suicide is pitiful, as she tries to staunch the flow of blood after she's done it, trying to undo it. She immediately tries to take it back, and dies regretful. We are encouraged to see Liana as a victim, not only of the men in her life, and her mother's ambition, and the colonialist world she is born into, but of herself. This final act of self-harm turns the violence of the culture she lives in on her own body, which is no longer neatly stuffed into white women's clothes but spills messily all over her perfect bedroom and bathroom.

In the end, as Pierre speeds off back to France, the sea-spray rising up against the side of the boat a sad echo of Liana's vividly spurting blood in the previous chapter, Pierre repeats his idea of the homeland like a mantra, pledging his life in defence of France and all it stands for, the *dignité et les droits de l'homme*.[46] *Et la femme?* Gellhorn implies. *Et les noirs?* And all those who are beat down by systems they have no say in, even in the name of France? This global consciousness is the book's strong point, written at a time when 'all the uprooted people were struggling to have a home and live in it, to be part of a human world, to have identity and place and safety'.[47] But how the war would end, and who would have a say in how that world was built, was yet to be determined, as the novel went to print in 1944.

+

Gellhorn had finally left for Europe in September 1943, spending time in New York before catching a boat to Britain. She pleaded with Hemingway in this December 1943 letter, trying to help him to understand why she has to travel. 'I believe in what I am doing too and regret fiercely having missed seeing and understanding so much of it in these years, and I would be no use to you in the end if I came back before I was through . . . You wouldn't really want me if I built a fine big stone wall around the *finca* and sat inside it . . . I'll never see enough as long as I live.'[48] It seems she was very persuasive: soon Hemingway, who had claimed to want to sit out the war in Cuba submarine-hunting, decided to get himself over to Europe to see the D-Day invasions. He went as *Collier's* lead correspondent. She never forgave him. They split up in 1945, the year the war ended, and *Liana* was published. For the rest of her days she would unceremoniously dismiss anyone careless or nosy enough to mention his name.

Was it the institute of marriage that she found so imprisoning, or marriage to Hemingway? I'm inclined to think the latter. It wasn't, in the end, about literary competition; she had enough bravado to stand up to him. Rather, it was about the right to roam. 'Place names were the most powerful magic I knew,' Gellhorn writes in her memoir *Travels With Myself and Another*. In her book-length essay *Things I Don't Want to Know* (2013), a response to George Orwell's 1946 *Why I Write*, Deborah Levy writes of a moment of crisis in her life, when 'life was hard and I was at war with my lot and simply couldn't see where there was to get to', and so she took off for Majorca, where by the end of the narrative she has realised that 'where she had to get to' was simply a socket to plug in her portable typewriter. 'Even more useful to a writer than a room of her own,' Levy concludes, 'is an extension lead and a variety of adaptors for Europe, Asia, and Africa.'[49] How can any sort of long-term relationship, running over the same familiar territory, compete with the endlessly renewable *frisson* of encountering a new place? Gellhorn's most sustaining relationship was with her work, but work undertaken away from home, where something might be about to happen. 'I settle in temporary furnished quarters in foreign places where I know nobody and enter into a symbiotic relationship with a typewriter.' This is a hard-won right.

Gellhorn spent the last few decades of her life living in London; one has to imagine that after all those attempts at homemaking, it wasn't that London was finally right, but, rather, it was finally enough. And it was an ideal place from which to take off again: all flight plans lead to Heathrow, or many do at any rate. She died in 1998, the year before I went to Paris for the first time. She was eighty-nine years old, but it wasn't natural causes. Mostly blind, and very ill with several forms of cancer, she took her own life. She decided when and how she would 'leave'. As if death were just another place to go.

home

NEW YORK

RETURN

But what good are roots if you can't take them with you?
— Gertrude Stein

A young girl, in a hotel room, her first night in a new city – in *the* city, that is to say, in New York City – is wrapped in blankets in a room that is air-conditioned to the point of resembling a cave in a glacier. She has a bad cough and is running a fever, but she is too nervous to call the front desk and ask for someone to turn off the air. How much would she have to tip whomever they sent? Better to freeze than to stiff a bellhop, or worse, to overtip, and look naive. Recalling that first night in New York in an essay years later, Joan Didion asks, 'Was anyone ever so young?'

Eight years later, the girl has become a woman, and the bloom is off the Big Apple. She returns west to California, where she would no longer be hemmed in by the narrowing possibilities of disappearing youth. Her elegy to New York, 'Goodbye to All That', appeared in her collection *Slouching Towards Bethlehem* (1968), at the end of a section called 'Seven Places of the Mind'. By placing the essay after pieces on Sacramento, Hawaii and Newport, Didion suggests not only that New York, like most places, is of the mind, but also that it is a place most often looked at through the lens of other places.

People move to New York from all over the world, drawn to what it stands for: work, success, freedom, acceptance, glamour: give me your tired, your poor, your ambitious, your determined. To approach the city from somewhere else amplifies its power. There are so many viewpoints on the city that 'New York' – the idea – is filtered in the imagination through millions of tiny windowpanes.

And yet for me, it's hard to come to terms with my relationship to New York, especially now that I've left. As hard as it is to see, to really *see*, your mother's face. It is too familiar; you have never not known it, and you cannot be said to have looked at it in any objective way.

+

In Amor Towles's novel *Rules of Civility*, the heroine, born and bred in Brighton Beach but trying to make her way in the upper echelons of Manhattan society, pretends not to know someone from her past when he recognises her at a newsstand. Observing their exchange, the newsvendor pronounces: 'That's the problem with being born in New York [. . .] You've got no New York to run away to.'

+

Didion describes her early crush on the city, having moved there from northern California: standing on a street corner eating a peach, catching a whiff of expensive perfume, she recalls thinking that in New York 'Nothing was irrevocable; everything was within reach'. That is not how it feels to a native New Yorker. Either you've got nothing left to reach for, or the reaching looks like a betrayal of where you started.

Once New York had been the very definition of a city to me, offering freedom to roam, create, become, befriend, fuck, but in adulthood it made me anxious, claustrophobic. The long, long avenues, the tall buildings leaning in, like supervising giants; how can you wander on a grid? The avenues go up and down and the streets go left and right. Once you know it, you know it. My middle-class New York life was just as neatly mapped out: college, career, marriage, house, baby. Repeat cycle with next generation. My live-in boyfriend, a real-estate developer, bought a car. That was the beginning of the end for us. He wanted to speed into the future at 60 m.p.h.; I wanted to walk there.

Has anyone ever been so young? Didion wonders at her twenty-three-year-old self, unable to call and ask for the air conditioning to be turned down. I was twenty-five, and I thought, with the moral resolution (or perhaps the affected maturity) of the very young, that because we lived together I had to stay. My choices narrowed to the width of the passenger seat in his car, and finally I couldn't take it any more. I moved to Paris like I was letting myself out, out into the night air.

+

Nearly a decade after I moved to Paris, I had absolutely no idea where I would be the next year, or the year after, or in five years. A number of events coincided to make me wonder whether I had a future in France. I had seen my request for citizenship turned down; my engagement had collapsed; my right to work was revoked at the end of my student visa, so my employer couldn't keep me on, and I'd learned this too late to apply for another teaching job. I made an appointment at the

French Consulate in New York, and hoped they would be able to help me sort something out.

Travelling to Paris from London two weeks before my appointment, I was stopped by a French customs agent in St Pancras.

'Why do you want to come to our country?' he demanded.

'I live there,' I answered. 'Your country is my country. Sort of.'

'Where's your visa?'

'It expired two weeks ago. I have an appointment to re—'

'You can't come in if you don't have a visa.'

'I guess I'm coming in on a tourist visa.'

'But if you live in France you're not a tourist.'

'Well –'

'So you live in France illegally.'

'No. I have never lived in France illegally.'

'Come with me please.'

He ushered me into a back office where he went through my luggage and looked through the files on my computer. Fearing – what? that he'd refuse to let me into France? what was the worst that could happen? – I showed him my last visa, my airplane ticket to New York, the email confirming my appointment to renew my visa at the consulate. (These are the papers the wanderer has to have on her at all times. *Look, I am moving within legal limits. Look, I am doing nothing wrong.*) I said I had a French doctorate and had taught in the French universities. I told him how my naturalisation request had been turned down because I didn't make enough money, although I had done well in my citizenship interview. (*Most people we get in here don't even speak French*, the woman had confided, with a look that I could tell was meant to reassure me I was the 'good' kind of immigrant.) Eventually someone on the phone told him to let me get on the train, and he indicated I could pack up my suitcase. Fighting tears, I asked him why he had put me through all that.

He shrugged. 'Well, you know,' he said. 'It's hard for us to come to your country too.'

After that, New York seemed like a haven. I wanted to be around my family, around old friends, I wanted to be in a place where instead of being growled at, interrogated and humiliated, I would be welcomed. Maybe this was it, I thought. Maybe it was time to move back home.

+

A few months later, exhausted, doubtful and jobless, I went to New York for six weeks to take stock of the situation only to find that my own city had become unrecognisable to me. Manhattan was crawling with bankers and their toddlers; Brooklyn was overrun with yuppies and *their* toddlers, and the twentysomethings you see on the HBO series *Girls*. It was as if there were two speeds of life in New York: married or very, very young. I didn't know where to insert myself. Watching *Girls*, I didn't know how to understand its aesthetic, its values, its uptalk; is it earnest, is it ironic? A little of both? *How can it be both?* In my day – and *Girls* is the kind of show that prompts you to say things like *in my day* – we didn't have dinner parties for our friends (as dysfunctional as Hannah's seem to be); like Carrie Bradshaw we kept our shoes in our ovens, and met our friends in public. It felt as if the New York I had known had disappeared, like at the end of the film *The NeverEnding Story*, in which Fantasia has been consumed by The Nothing (or in this case, by real-estate developers), reduced to a grain of sand (or in this case, to Brooklyn).

Brooklyn was terra incognita to me – when I lived in the city, I could still afford to live in Manhattan. One Friday night in December, I agreed to meet some friends at a restaurant in Brooklyn Heights. Without an American phone plan, I had no

Google Maps to rely on, so before I left the house I sketched a
rudimentary map of the area in a notebook. I arrived early,
thinking I'd walk around a bit before I met my friends. When
I got off at York Street, the sky already dark at 5.30 p.m.,
Brooklyn looked nothing like its reputation. Where were the
cobblestoned streets, the shops selling vintage clothing, and the
free-trade coffee with baristas drawing flowers in the foam? I
saw only an immense parking garage, chain-link fences, and
towering apartment blocks. I made a few turns and found
myself down some badly lit street. The buildings looked new,
but boxy, a bit raw. A man walked towards me, wearing a
woollen cap. Friend or foe? The cold Decemberish air turned
tense, the way it does for two strangers in a deserted street.

Finally I reached Hudson Avenue, which had the cobblestones, as well as a few shopfronts and a mix of older brick
buildings and newer houses with aluminium siding. Inside the
restaurant, it was warm, with flattering light and brick walls,
the kind of place you could find in Paris or London or New
York and think: this is so Paris, so London, so New York. So
urban, that is, the kind of place where you know exactly what
the food will be like and what kind of evening you'll have
there. It's familiarity was disorienting, as if I had woken up in a
comfortable bed, but didn't yet know whose. I climbed up
onto a bar stool to wait for my friends, ordered a glass of New
Zealand Chardonnay, and cracked open Rebecca Solnit's *A
Field Guide to Getting Lost*.

The word 'lost', Solnit writes, 'comes from the Old Norse
los, meaning the disbanding of an army, and this origin suggests
soldiers falling out of formation to go home, a truce with the
wide world'. 'Never to get lost,' she says, 'is not to live, not to
know how to get lost brings you to destruction.' And yet when
I'm lost, all I want is to slip back into the flow of people who
know where they are and where they're going. If you desert

the army, even if the war is over, you never stop doubting yourself, and wondering if they'd have you back.

+

And so after years of getting lost in strange European cities, here I was, lost in my own. One night in the East Village some friends and I got very, very drunk with a visiting British friend and we went walking north; I think we were going to try to take the train to Brooklyn. 'Where are we going?' I slurred. 'To the L train,' someone said. 'Does the L stop over here?' I asked. I only knew the L as a quick way to get from the West Side to Union Square. My British friend scoffed at me. 'I thought you were a New Yorker.' Looking at the subway map, I see how it looks like one long train line across the East River – a thin, blue stripe marking off Manhattan from Brooklyn like puzzle pieces about to be joined together, making the ride from First Avenue to Bedford Avenue look as uneventful as the ride from Broadway to Sixth Avenue. But in my mind, the East River was a major barrier and the trains that went beyond it did not extend in casual straight lines, but moved unpredictably into a terrain that could not be neatly organised into up and down, left and right. I ended up bailing on Brooklyn and taking the train back out to Long Island, feeling shamefully bridge-and-tunnel. What good were all my years as a New Yorker? While I'd been away, 'New York' had entirely reconfigured itself, without a single change to the map.

+

I have relatives who ask me every time I see them *So when are you coming home?* As if I were some errant member of the family flock, not one of Solnit's Old Norse soldiers who's fallen out of formation to return home to his family, but to take off somewhere else altogether. A deserter. They are first- and second-generation Americans, people who came or whose parents came to the US from Italy as early as the 1930s, or as recently as the 1960s. The intimation is that I don't belong in France, but at home, where I started. Why don't they belong in Italy, then? Or do they feel they do? I've never asked.

It took a few years for my father to stop asking me the same question, and for my sister to stop saying things like *I get it, you can't come back because it would feel like some kind of personal failure, right? But no one would think that.* My mother, on the other hand, sighs and says *As long as you're happy.* She's the only one who doesn't make it about belonging, but being.

+

I could make my own choices in Paris, and make a life for myself in a context that was mine alone. In the circle of friends I formed in Paris, we all had that in common: at a given moment, we had all chosen to leave home and move to Paris. We were all high on the same feelings of possibility.

I met people from all over the world – Russia, Iran, India, Germany, Brazil – feeling an independence I'd never imagined possible. There was a whole world out there and I didn't have to live in America simply because I was born there. I could live anywhere I liked. And I liked living in France.

This was an epiphany. One rainy night over a pasta dinner with my flatmate, we contemplated the enormity of it. We can go anywhere. We can do anything, we told each other.

+

But it wasn't true. Americans can go anywhere, it turns out, as long as we have the cash, but we can't stay. Not without a visa.

This was another reason I hated that security guard. *OK, you can't go to America*, I wanted to say to him, *but you can go to Spain, Greece, Italy, the UK, take your pick.* The project of the European Union was to promote the free circulation of people and goods, a lesson learned from a century of world wars: that borders may serve some administrative purpose but in the pursuit of capitalism and the common good they must be easier to cross. And yet today Europe is experiencing the worst refugee crisis since the Second World War; as I write there are people, mostly from Syria, or Afghanistan, or Iraq, pressing on the border to Germany, trapped in train stations in Hungary, stuffed into camps in Calais, risking their lives to get to the UK, capsizing en route to Greece. Will they get through? If they do, will they be allowed to stay? If so they'll be the Europe of tomorrow, and there are many people who don't want to see that happen, who defend a white, Christian Europe, even if this is largely their own fiction. The far-right don't just think they will be weakened by contact with the Other. They think they'll be the ones drowning.

+

Does an American belong more in America than elsewhere when most of us came from elsewhere? How to account for the violence of founding a country on someone else's land? How can any model of American belonging function unproblematically on top of such a heritage? But then wasn't every country in the world formed out of conflict over who owned the land? All of human history is a story of migrations and conquests. All of us are exiles, but some of us are more aware of it than others.

The real question here is whether any national identity is truly tenable. The post-colonial theorist Homi Bhabha has written that minoritarian identities can be powerful, but not if they concretise into solid formations, battlements defended from behind. They must remain fluid. Americans describe themselves through fractions of other places, suturing their origins to the country whose name alone is not enough to define us, or contain us. What you place before the hyphen – Mexican-American, Italian-American – defines you more than what comes after. My sister and I, with our mixed Jewish–Italian–Irish background, were less ethnically 'pure', so to speak, than a lot of the kids where we grew up, who were only Jewish-American, or only Italian-American, or only Irish-American. We lacked a term for our hybridity. Because we had a surplus of cultural identities, it was as if we had none.

Isn't it the moment when these supplementary identities break down that we truly become 'American'? I don't think so. The way to reconcile these varied histories is not through a proclamation of essence: 'I am this' or 'I am that'. For me, it happens through writing; the attempt to understand, through articulating these strange configurations of identity and belonging, is the only way I can keep from being swallowed up by feelings of rebellion or regret. Which turn to make, which line to pursue, to go down one street is not to go down another, to write about one thing is to ignore a host of others, which you have to exclude, for the sake of legibility. Every sentence a crossroads.

+

As I got older I grew more and more interested in my father's Judaism, and thought seriously of converting, but gave it up; surely in our enlightened times it shouldn't matter which parent is Jewish; they shall know me by the mezuzah on the doorpost of my house.

Passages have to be marked. It is at the borders that 'something begins its presencing', writes Bhabha; it begins to be visible, to signify in a different way. Something happens when we push at boundaries, and cross over them; some ambiguity is sustained, that cannot be absorbed into some kind of homogeneous identity. In my experience those who defend this homogeneity don't much care for border-crossers, those who don't or can't respect boundaries, or, rather, respect them in a different way, by brushing back and forth against them.

It has been a privilege to be able to give form to my wanderlust, to range from the US to Europe to Asia and back again, encountering only the mildest of resistance. But I have learned that it is an act of empathy to be able to un-root yourself, to recognise that none of us are protected by place.

Beware roots. Beware purity. Beware fixity. Beware the creeping feeling that you belong. Embrace flow, impurity, fusion. 'To be unhomed is not to be homeless,' writes this wonderful critic named *Homi*.[1]

+

In August 2015, I got an email from my lawyer telling me my request for French citizenship had been approved. After eleven years of jumping from visa to visa, and two refusals, they finally said yes. You can stay.

Now that it's actually happened, I wonder, what does it mean to me? I prod the idea to see if it releases any secret juices, or heady odours. All I can think is: how will I define myself if I'm no longer tenuously poised at the edge of my everyday life?

And then what does it mean, anyway, to become 'French'? I've made and lost friends here, I've loved here, been heartbroken here, got married here, got pregnant here, lost pregnancies here, been examined and operated on, assessed and ranked, won jobs, lost jobs, taken care of myself and my dog, bought a flat and published books, and I did it all in French.

It doesn't mean anything, this new passport, it does not make me more French or less American; it is a recognition of this commitment to place. It means I can stay. An authorisation I don't take lightly.

Didion's essay, in the end, is about letting go of New York. More precisely, it's about letting go of a fantasy of New York. The girl in the hotel has not truly inhabited, does not know a place from the inside.

I'll spend the rest of my life trying to know Paris from within. So much of it is unknown to me, especially beyond the periphery, but which will soon be integrated into Greater Paris, as the city bursts the boundaries it has kept for the past 150 years.

And then even the places I once knew intimately, I'll walk over them again and know them in a different way. Never the same cobblestone twice, isn't that what they say? Because one day you're walking with the fear that any moment they might make you leave, and the next day you're French.

+

When I fly out of Kennedy, as the plane sits on the tarmac waiting for take-off, I stare out the window trying not to feel too much. My parents just got on the Van Wyck, I imagine. My mother's still crying though she's trying not to. My father's wondering why I don't just come home. And I'm sitting on the tarmac, wondering the same thing.

The airfield at night, in the dark, is so beautiful, suggesting that New York is still the kind of haunted place I'd need it to be in order to stay. Layers of yellow, red, blue lights so the horizon looks rimmed with fire, and the blue-lighted Cross Bay Bridge beyond. The planes hang in the sky as they approach, flashing their lights to signal their descent. A subway train runs alongside us, miles away, a string of lights on a track, the A train on its way to the Rockaways. And then we're forty-five degrees from the earth, and the yellow lights of home arrange themselves geometrically, and become a grid, until they disappear behind the fog and clouds.

But on the other side is Paris.

The poet Marilyn Hacker understands this; she also lives in a New York/Paris dialectic. I once heard her say that when her plane takes off from Paris she cries and cries. Her poetry is deeply sensual, witty and sharp, but I think what I love most about it is her instinctive juxtaposition of New York and Paris. In her collection *Squares and Courtyards*, a pair of poems about the Long Island Rail Road face a poem about the Place du Marché Sainte-Catherine. And in a poem from *Desesperanto*, she writes: 'Paris, elegant grey/godmother, consolation/heart-broken lullaby/smell of the métro station/you won't abandon me.' But it inevitably does. Living between cities, we are abandoned by them as much as they are by us, because if they gave us all we needed, we wouldn't have to leave.

Since I left New York, guilt is more a part of my life than it ever was when I lived there – and I've inherited the instinctive guilt native to both Jews *and* Catholics. Living abroad, I miss weddings, funerals, hurricanes and everyday life, maintaining a lifeline to my parents, sister, friends through Skype, Facebook, WhatsApp. I see New York, now, through the open windows of my computer screen. I see it, like the rest of the world, from someplace else.

When I visit, I feel astonished by how strong the tie is. Heading down the East River Drive, towards my sister's place in Battery Park, under the three bridges as my mom recites the song of the city – *Williamsburg, Manhattan, Brooklyn* – is enough to make me want to throw in the towel and stay. I'm overcome by their rusty solidity, the way they span across the sky, sublimely industrial as they plunge into the soft side of the island. My great-grandfathers built those bridges. In fact, my grandparents met because their fathers were building those bridges together. I come from a long line of engineers, on both sides, building the city brick by brick, tunnelling into the East River silt. You forget, when you've flown off somewhere to live your own life, that the minute you near the place where you began, the force of gravity reasserts its hold, and claims you to the ground.

My city isn't mine any more. And yet it always will be, more than any other. We get to know our cities on foot, and when we leave, the topography shifts. We're no longer as sure-footed. But maybe that's a good thing. It's just a question of looking, and of not hoping to see something else when we do. Maybe it's good to keep some distance from the things we know well, to always be slightly out of sync with them, not to pretend mastery. Beneath the cities we don't recognise are stacked all the cities we do.

Having left New York helps me see it anew. En route to the city, on board the Long Island Rail Road, I think of how it used to be such a boring trip, something to be endured, not enjoyed. But since I moved away, I've been learning to love the industrial palette of the mix of suburbs and city it passes through. The back ends of superstores. Trucks loaded with slabs of wood. Trees, two-storey brick estates, coffee cups littering the carpet of fallen red leaves. *Farmingdale*. A balcony done up for Christmas. A plastic bag tangled in branches. Neo-colonial two-storey buildings with columns and fake clapboard siding. Pine trees manicured to look like Tuscany. (If you can't live in Italy, plant your own.) All Island

Truck Supply LLC. Checker cab station. Pools closed for the winter. No Trespassing. Backyards. Some fenced, some not. Susan's Pub: Home of the 75¢ Beer. *Bethpage*. How to isolate and disentangle barbed wires from energy lines, the asphalt from the concrete from the bricks? Form follows function in a jumbled anti-aesthetic of small suburban industry. *Hicksville. Mineola. Jamaica.* The pseudo-countryside becomes the city. Red sheds top buildings defended with coiled barbed wire. Piles of garbage. Boundary Wholesale Fences. Terraced houses with tiny backyards. Satellite dishes point at the sky, ready to receive communications from other solar systems, or at least from a faraway home. Tunnels. Ten-storey buildings. Fire escapes: the architecture of the tenement. Tudor facades. (If you can't live in Tudor England, pretend you do.) Twenty-storey buildings. Cars parked on roofs. Thirty-storey buildings. Build everywhere. Build anything. Is it cheap? It will do. Put it in brick. Deck the balconies with plastic Santas. A low-flying plane. Semi-detached pastel-coloured houses. Far off a building with Thai accents on the corners of a brilliantly tiled roof. (If you had to leave Thailand, rebuild your own.) Woodside car wash. Back of a billboard. Crayola-box graffiti. Brick landscape. Milestone Kitchen & Bath Corp. Men in orange and yellow safety vests. 'Is it nothing to you, all you who pass by?' (Lamentations 1:12). Steel grey, concrete blue, rusted iron, beneath the preppy thrust of red-and-white-striped smoke stacks. Spokes of the bridges my grandfathers built. Majestic steel skyline. Art deco sharp. Southern anchors gone. *Next stop Penn Station.* This is me. This is me out there.

EPILOGUE

FLÂNEUSERIE

One of the most famous images of a woman walking presents a scene the meaning of which no one can agree on.

A young woman walks down a street in Florence, clutching her scarf to her chest. On the street surrounding her are fourteen men. At least eight are looking at her. One man blocks her path, hands in his pockets. A man to her right has a contorted face, and appears to be grabbing his crotch. Mid-step, she wears a look on her face that suggests something resembling concern, apprehension. The energy of the composition – the curve of the road, her weight as it shifts forward, her skirt as it lifts out behind her – suggests movement forward, and it seems as if she's already gearing up to go around the man standing stock-still in front of her.

Surely it's too easy. It's a moment of mid-century street harassment. Look at what women have to deal with when they walk in public!

But this is not what the girl in the photograph says was happening. Interviewed by NBC's *Today Show* in 2011, on the sixtieth anniversary of the photograph, she said: 'It's not a symbol of harassment. It's a symbol of a woman having an absolutely wonderful time!'[1] For it turns out the woman – whose real name is Ninalee Craig, but who called herself 'Jinx Allen' back in those days and went on to marry a Venetian count – was American, twenty-three years old, and travelling abroad in France, Spain and Italy by herself. The photographer, Ruth Orkin, was also an American woman in her twenties, travelling around on her own, living hand to mouth but loving every minute of it. The photo was taken during a day of 'horsing around' the city with a camera, with Orkin taking pictures of Jinx taking in the sights, asking questions, haggling over prices and flirting in cafes. The scarf was a bright orange Mexican rebozo. The dress was a tribute to Christian Dior's New Look. The handbag was a horse's feed bag. For Craig and Orkin, the thing to take away from the photo is to do with independence and inspiration, about playing with codes, with clothing, with the ways a woman was expected to be or behave.

The woman in the street is an unstable figure, to be sure, like the well-known drawing of the duck-rabbit that proves the ambiguities inherent in perception. Is she a carefree *flâneuse*, or the object of the male gaze, a rabbit or a duck? The more interesting reading is somewhere in between, in that area of tension and friction where our defiance pushes against people's expectations. That the photograph has become such a cult image – adorning walls from college dorm rooms to pizzerias – suggests something about the richness of the energy generated there. That horsing around, silliness and fun that Craig and Orkin claim show us that space is ours for the remaking.

Space is not neutral. Space is a feminist issue. The space we occupy – here, in the city, we city dwellers – is constantly remade and unmade, constructed and wondered at. 'Space is a doubt,' wrote Georges Perec; 'I have constantly to mark it, to designate it. It's never mine, never given to me, I have to conquer it.'

From Teheran to New York, from Melbourne to Mumbai, a woman still can't walk in the city the way a man can.

Cities are made up of invisible boundaries, intangible customs gates that demarcate who goes where: certain neighbourhoods, bars and restaurants, parks, all manner of apparently public spaces are reserved for different kinds of people. We become so accustomed to this that we hardly notice the values underlying these divisions. They may be invisible, but they determine how we circulate within the city.

They exist in between buildings. On either sides of walls. Around fences and railings, down steps and past stoplights and road signs and bollards.

They take shape in underground railways and overground trolleys, skating over and through the earth, tracked to the ground, harnessed to power cables. They live in the negative space of alleyways and dead ends and side streets and courtyards.

They take up space. Spaces within spaces, species of spaces, spaces with the force of social convention as concretely embedded as a stop sign:

Private park. Don't go in unless you have a key. Definitely don't jump the fence. Trespassing.

Public park. Don't go into the park at night. Park's closed after dusk.

Open park. Populated by homeless people who would be very surprised if you sat down beside them on their bench beds. Unless you are a homeless person too. In which case you'd be sitting on your own bench bed.

City plaza. *Place. Piazza. Platz.* How you use it depends on who you are, as the ethnographer Nadja Monnet found when she undertook a study of the Plaça de Catalunya in Barcelona. Although the *plaça* is one of the most famous sights in the city, the locals avoid it, preferring to meet in the nearby bars. Monnet spoke with a (female) tourist who felt uneasy sitting in the *plaça* – an uneasiness Monnet herself shared. 'It's really not a good place to meet up with anyone. You don't know where to put yourself. If you wait in the middle, you feel stupid. You feel exposed.' Monnet quickly realised that even among the locals, fewer women than men used the space, 'although there were peaks in female attendance at the times when school let out or at the end of the work day'. Women alone rarely sit on the benches, 'and when they do, they don't stay long'.

Virginia Woolf's 1927 essay 'Street Haunting' is an attempt to claim an ungendered place in the city by walking through it. Out in the street, we become observing entities, 'part of that vast republican army of anonymous trampers'. Whether or not we want to be androgynous eyes taking in the city, or bodies inviting desire, or any of the myriad ways of being in between, Woolf is telling us that we can integrate ourselves into the world of the city by becoming attentive to the shifts in the affective landscape. It is only in becoming aware of the invisible boundaries of the city that we can challenge them. A female *flânerie* – a *flâneuserie* – not only changes the way we move through space, but intervenes in the organisation of space itself. We claim our right to disturb the peace, to observe (or not observe), to occupy (or not occupy) and to organise (or disorganise) space on our own terms.

ACKNOWLEDGEMENTS

In memory of Jane Marcus
'*And in me too the wave rises*'

That this book exists at all is in large part due to Rebecca
Carter and Parisa Ebrahimi, who believed in it and saw what it
could become: thank you both for your support, patience,
championing – for everything really. Thank you as well to
everyone at Janklow & Nesbit and at Chatto & Windus, for
their hard work and enthusiasm. I'd also like to thank Sarah
Chalfant, Alba Ziegler-Bailey, Kristina Moore and everyone at
the Wylie Agency, as well as Ileene Smith and Jonathan Galassi
at Farrar, Straus and Giroux.

A number of people helped this book in a thousand different
ways, through conversations or suggestions or stray comments.
They include Katherine Angel, Susan Barbour, Lexi Bloom,
Fay Brauer, Zoe Brauer, Amanda Dennis, Allison Devers, Jean
Hannah Edelstein, Mel Flashman, Deborah Friedell, Geoff
Gilbert, Jane Goldman, Heather Hartley, Elissa Jacobson,
Christina Johnsson, Julie Kleinman, Emily Kopley, Sara Kramer,
Pam Krasner, Deborah Levy, Sharmaine Lovegrove, Harriet
Alida Lye, Anne Marsella, Daniel Medin, James Polchin, Simon
Prosser, Rosa Rankin-Gee, Tatiana de Rosnay, Rebecca Solnit,
Stelios Sardelas, Rob Sheldon, Russell Williams.

Parts of this book originally appeared as pieces for Writers
at Liberty, *Granta*, and the essay collection *Goodbye to All That:*

Writers on Loving and Leaving New York (Seal Press, 2013) – thank you to the editors of those projects for allowing me the space to think through some of these issues.

Thanks to the staff of the British Library, the Bibliothèque Nationale de France and the New York Public Library, as well as to Laurence Labedan in Saint-Dyé-sur-Loire, and Pina and Raffaele Caprara at Palazzo Rinaldi.

To my teachers: Mary Cregan, Mary Ann Caws, Catherine Bernard and Jane Marcus.

To Elisabeth Fourmont and Joanna Walsh, best friends and best readers, for making my insights sharper and my jokes funnier.

To my mother-in-law, Carole Wingett – I am always happy when a journey leads to Upland Road.

To my family – Patricia and Peter Elkin, Caroline, Imri and Ainsley Eisner – for giving me a place to start from, and to return to.

To the little bunny too.

And finally, to my partner in that great *dérive* of life, Seb Emina. To quote the late great Kate McGarrigle:

Walking beside you / I'll never get those walking blues.

LIST OF ILLUSTRATIONS

BIBLIOGRAPHY

Angier, Carole, *Jean Rhys: Life and Work*, Boston: Little, Brown, 1990.

Arons, Rachel, 'Chronicling Poverty With Compassion and Rage', *New Yorker*, 17 January 2013.

Athill, Diana, *Stet: A Memoir*, New York: Grove Press, 2002.

Auster, Paul, *Leviathan*, London: Faber, 1993.

Balzac, Honoré de, *Les Petits Bourgeois* (1843), *La comédie humaine*, 7 vols, Paris: Editions du Seuil, 1965–66.

Barthes, Roland, *Empire of Signs* (1970), trans. Richard Howard, New York: Hill and Wang, 1982.

—, *A Lover's Discourse* (1977), trans. Richard Howard, London: Vintage, 2002.

—, *Camera Lucida* (1980), trans. Richard Howard, New York: Hill and Wang, 1981.

Bashkirtseff, Marie, *The Journals of Marie Bashkirtseff*, 2 vols, trans. Phyllis Howard Kernberger and Katherine Kernberger, New York: Fonthill Press, 2012.

Baudelaire, Charles, 'Le Cygne', *Les Fleurs du Mal*, Alençon: Auguste Poulet-Malassis, 1857.

—, *The Painter of Modern Life* (1863), trans. Jonathan Mayne, New York: Phaidon, 1995.

Benjamin, Walter, *The Arcades Project*, ed. Rolf Tiedemann, trans. Howard Eiland and Kevin McLaughlin, New York: Belknap Press, 2002.

Berman, Marshall, 'Falling', *Restless Cities*, ed. Matthew Beaumont, Gregory Dart, Michael Sheringham and Iain Sinclair, London: Verso, 2010.

Bhabha, Homi, *The Location of Culture*, London: Routledge, 1994.

Bilger, Philippe, 'Philippe Bilger: pourquoi je ne participe pas à <<la marche républicaine>>', *Le Figaro*, 11 January 2015.

Blair, Sara, 'Bloomsbury and the Places of the Literary', *ELH* 71.3 (2004), pp. 813–38.

Bowen, Elizabeth, *The House in Paris* (1935), Harmondsworth: Penguin, 1976.

Bowen, Stella, *Drawn From Life: A Memoir*, Sydney: Picador, 1999.

Bowlby, Rachel, *Still Crazy After All These Years: Women, Writing and Psychoanalysis*, New York: Routledge, 1992.

Brennan, Maeve, *The Long-Winded Lady: Notes from the New Yorker*, Berkeley, CA: Counterpoint, 1997.

Burke, Thomas, *Living in Bloomsbury*, London: G. Allen & Unwin Ltd, 1939.

Burns, John F., 'To Sarajevo, Writer Brings Good Will and "Godot"', *New York Times*, 19 August 1993.

Calle, Sophie, *Suite Vénitienne*, trans. Dany Barash and Danny Hatfield, Seattle: Bay Press, 1988.

—, *M'as-tu Vue*, ed. Christine Macel, Paris, Centre Pompidou: Xavier Barral, 2003.

Coffey, Laura T., *The Today Show*, 18 August 2011.

Coppola, Sofia, dir. *Lost in Translation*, Universal Studios, 2003.

Davidoff, Leonora, *The Best Circles: Society, Etiquette, and The Season*, London: Croom Helm, 1973.

de Musset, Alfred, *Confession of a Child of the Century* (1836), trans. David Coward, London: Penguin Classics, 2012.

Debord, Guy, 'Introduction to a Critique of Urban Geography', in Ken Knabb, ed., *Situationist International Anthology*, Berkeley: Bureau of Public Secrets, 1981.

—, 'Theory of the Dérive', trans. Ken Knabb, *Situationist International Anthology*, Berkeley: Bureau of Public Secrets, 1981.

—, *Panegyric, Volumes 1 & 2*, trans. James Brook and John McHale, London: Verso, 2004.

Derrida, Jacques, *The Post Card: From Socrates to Freud and Beyond*, trans. Alan Bass, Chicago: University of Chicago Press, 1987.

Dickens, Charles, *Hard Times. The Shorter Novels of Charles Dickens*, Hertfordshire: Wordsworth Editions, 2004.

D'Souza, Aruna, and Tom McDonough, *The Invisible Flâneuse?: Gender, Public Space and Visual Culture in Nineteenth-Century Paris*, Manchester: Manchester University Press, 2006.

Duany, Andres, Elizabeth Plater-Zyberk and Jeff Speck, *Suburban Nation: The Rise of Sprawl and the Decline of the American Dream*, New York: North Point Press, 2000.

Duras, Marguerite, *Practicalities*, trans. Barbara Bray, New York: Grove Press, 1987.

Ferguson, Patricia Parkhurst, *Paris As Revolution: Writing the Nineteenth-Century City*, Berkeley: University of California Press, 1994.

Flaubert, Gustave, *Sentimental Education*, trans. Robert Baldick, Baltimore: Penguin Books, 1964.

Ford, Ford Madox, Preface, Jean Rhys, *The Left Bank & Other Stories*, London: Jonathan Cape, 1927.

Fox, Lorna Scott, 'No Intention of Retreating', *London Review of Books*, 26:17, 2 September 2004, pp. 26–8.

Frickey, Pierrette M., *Critical Perspectives on Jean Rhys*, Washington DC: Three Continents Press, 1990.

Gallagher, Leigh, *The End of the Suburbs: Where the American Dream Is Moving*, New York: Portfolio/Penguin, 2013.

Gallant, Mavis, *Paris Notebooks: Essays & Reviews*, New York: Random House, 1988.

Garrioch, David, *The Making of Revolutionary Paris*, Berkeley: University of California Press, 2002.

Gellhorn, Martha, *The Face of War*, London: Virago, 1986.

—, *Liana* (1944), London: Picador, 1993.

—, *Point of No Return* (1948), Lincoln, NE: Bison Books, 1995.

—, *Selected Letters of Martha Gellhorn*, ed. Caroline Moorehead, New York: Henry Holt, 2006.

Gray, Francine du Plessix, *Rage & Fire: A Life of Louise Colet*, New York: Simon & Schuster, 1994.

Green, Barbara, *Spectacular Confessions: Autobiography, Performative Activism and the Sites of Suffrage, 1905–38*, Basingstoke: Macmillan, 1997.

Greenberg, Michael, 'In Zuccotti Park', *New York Review of Books*, 10 November 2011.

Groskop, Viv, 'Sex and the City', *Guardian*, 19 September 2008.

Harlan, Elizabeth, *George Sand*, New Haven: Yale University Press, 2005.

Hare, Augustus J.C., *Walks in London*, London: Daldy, Isbister & Co., 1878, 2nd edn, 1879.

Hazan, Eric, *La Barricade: histoire d'un objet révolutionnaire*, Paris: Editions Autrement, 2013.

Hemingway, Ernest, *A Moveable Feast*, New York: Charles Scribner's Sons, 1964.

Huart, Louis, *Physiologie du flâneur*, Paris: Aubert, 1841.

Jack, Belinda, *George Sand: A Woman's Life Writ Large*, New York: Vintage, 1999.

Joyce, James, and Philip F. Herring, *Joyce's Ulysses notesheets in the British Museum, Issue 3*, published for the Bibliographical Society of the University of Virginia by the University Press of Virginia, 1972.

Kurlansky, Mark, *1968: The Year That Rocked the World*, New York: Ballantine, 2004.

Lavallée, Théophile, and George Sand, *Le Diable à Paris: Paris et les Parisiens, Mœurs et coutumes, caractères et portraits des habitants de Paris*, Paris: J. Hetzel, 1845.

Leaska, Mitchell, ed., *A Passionate Apprentice: Virginia Woolf, The Early Journals, 1897–1909*, New York: Harcourt Brace Jovanovich, 1990.

Lefebvre, Henri, *Production of Space* (1974), trans. Donald Nicholson-Smith, Oxford: Blackwell, 1991.

Leland, Jacob Michael, 'Yes, that is a roll of bills in my pocket: the economy of masculinity in *The Sun Also Rises*', *Hemingway Review*, 22 March 2004.

Leronde, Jacques, *Revue des Deux Mondes*, 1 June 1832.

Levy, Amy, 'Women and Club Life', published in *Women's World*, a magazine edited by Oscar Wilde, 1888.

Levy, Deborah, *Things I Don't Want to Know*, London: Notting Hill Editions, 2013.

Litchfield, John, 'The Stones of Paris', *Independent*, 22 September 2007.

Macfarlane, Robert, 'A Road of One's Own: Past and Present Artists of the Randomly Motivated Walk', *Times Literary Supplement*, 7 October 2005.

Magid, Jill, Interview with Sophie Calle, *Tokion*, Fall 2008, pp. 46–53.

Marcus, Jane, 'Storming the Toolshed', *Art & Anger: Reading Like a Woman*, Columbus: Ohio University Press, 1988.

McEwan, Ian, 'How could we have forgotten that this was always going to happen?', *Guardian*, 8 July 2005.

McRobie, Heather, 'Martha Without Ernest', *Times Literary Supplement*, 16 January 2013.

Miyazaki, Hayao, *Ponyo*, Studio Ghibli, 2008.

Monnet, Nadja, 'Qu'implique flâner au féminin en ce début de vingt et unième siècle? Réflexions d'une ethnographe à l'œuvre sur la place de Catalogne à Barcelone', *Wagadu*, Vol. 7, Fall 2009.

Moorehead, Caroline, *Martha Gellhorn: A Life*, New York: Random House, 2011.

Mumford, Lewis, *The City in History: Its Origins, Its Transformations, and Its Prospects*, New York: Harcourt, Brace & World, 1961.

Munson, Elizabeth, 'Walking on the Periphery: Gender and the Discourse of Modernization', *Journal of Social History* 36.1 (2002): 63–75.

Nicholson, Geoff, *The Lost Art of Walking: The History, Science, Philosophy, and Literature of Pedestrianism*, New York: Riverhead Books, 2008.

Niépovié, Gaetan, *Etudes physiologiques sur les grans métropoles de l'Europe occidentale*, Paris: Ch. Gosselin, 1840.

Nora, Pierre, *Realms of Memory: Rethinking the French Past*, Vol. 1, trans. Arthur Goldhammer, ed. Lawrence D. Kritzman, New York: Columbia University Press, 1996.

Parsons, Deborah, *Streetwalking the Metropolis: Women, the City, and Modernity*, Oxford: OUP, 2000.

Perec, Georges, *Species of Spaces*, ed. and trans. John Sturrock, London: Penguin, 2008.

Pollock, Griselda, *Vision and Difference*, London: Routledge, 1988.

Powrie, Phil, 'Heterotopic Spaces and Nomadic Gazes in Varda: From *Cléo de 5 à 7* to *Les Glaneurs et la glaneuse*', *L'Esprit Créateur*, Vol. 51, No. 1 (2011), pp. 68–82.

Quattrocchi, Antonio, and Tom Nairn, *The Beginning of the End*, Panther Books, 1968 (repr. London: Verso, 1998).

Rose, Gillian, *Feminism and Geography: The Limits of Geographical Knowledge*, Minneapolis: University of Minnesota Press, 1993.

Rosen, Lucille, *Commack: A Look Into the Past*, New York: Commack Public School Print Shop, 1970.

Rowbotham, Sheila, *Women, Resistance and Revolution*, London: Allen Lane, 1973.

Rhys, Jean, *Complete Novels*, New York: W.W. Norton, 1985.

—, *Smile Please: An Unfinished Autobiography*, Harmondsworth: Penguin, 1979.

—, *Collected Short Stories*, New York: W.W. Norton, 1992.

—, Francis Wyndham and Diana Melly, *The Letters of Jean Rhys*, New York: Viking, 1984.

Sand, George, *Correspondance*, 26 vols, ed. Georges Lubin, Paris: Classiques Garnier, 2013.

—, *Story of My Life*, ed. Thelma Jurgrau, group trans., Albany: SUNY Press, 1991.

—, *Gabriel* (1839), *Oeuvres Complètes*, Paris: Perrotin, 1843.

—, *Indiana* (1832), Paris: Calmann-Lévy, 1852.

—, *Histoire de ma vie*, 4 vols., Paris: Michel Levy, 1856.

—, *Journal d'un voyageur pendant la guerre*, Paris: Michel Levy, 1871.

—, *Indiana* (1832), trans. G. Burnham Ives, Chicago: Academy Chicago Publishers, 2000.

Sante, Luc, *The Other Paris*, New York: FSG, 2015.

Saunders, Max, *Ford Madox Ford: a dual life*, 2 vols, Oxford: OUP, 1996.

Self, Will, *Psychogeography*, London: Bloomsbury, 2007.

Shikibu, Murasaki, *Tale of Genji*, trans. Royall Tyler, Harmondsworth: Penguin Classics, 2002.

Smith, Alison, *Agnès Varda*, Manchester: Manchester University Press, 1998.

Snaith, Anna, *Virginia Woolf: Public and Private Negotiations*, Basingstoke: Palgrave, 2000.

Solnit, Rebecca, *Wanderlust: A History of Walking*, New York: Penguin Books, 2001.

—, *A Field Guide to Getting Lost*, New York: Viking, 2005.

Sontag, Susan, *Regarding the Pain of Others*, New York: FSG, 2003.

Sparks, Elisa Kay, 'Leonard and Virginia's London Library: Mapping London's Tides, Streams and Statues', in Gina Potts and Lisa Shahiri, *Virginia Woolf's Bloomsbury, Vol I: Aesthetic Theory and Literary Practice*, Basingstoke: Palgrave Macmillan, 2010.

Speck, Jeff, *Walkable City: How Downtown Can Save America, One Step at a Time*, New York: Macmillan, 2012.

Squier, Susan, *Virginia Woolf and London: The Sexual Politics of the City*, Chapel Hill, NC: University of North Carolina Press, 1985.

Sturrock, John, 'Give Me Calf's Tears', *London Review of Books* (21:22), 11 November 1999, pp. 28–9.

Sutherland, John, 'Clarissa's Invisible Taxi', *Can Jane Eyre Ever be Happy?*, Oxford: OUP, 1997.

Tiller, Bernard, '"De la balade à la manif": La représentation picturale de la foule dans les rues de Paris après 1871', Sociétés et représentations, 17:1 (2004), pp. 87–98.

Tompkins, Calvin, *Duchamp: A Biography*, New York: Henry Holt, 1998.

Tuan, Yi-Fu, *Space and Place: The Perspectives of Experience*, Minneapolis: University of Minnesota Press, 1977.

Van Slyke, Gretchen, 'Women at War: Skirting the Issue in the French Revolution', *L'esprit créateur*, 37:1 (Spring 1997), pp. 33–43.

Varda, Agnès, *La Pointe Courte*, Ciné-Tamaris, 1955.

—, *Cléo de 5 à 7*, Ciné-Tamaris, 1961.

—, Interview with Jean Michaud and Raymond Bellour, *Cinéma 61*, No. 60, October 1961, pp. 4–20.

—, *Varda par Agnès*, Paris: Editions du Cahier du cinéma, 1994.

—, *Les glaneurs et la glaneuse*, Ciné-Tamaris, 2000.

—, *Les plages d'Agnès*, Ciné-Tamaris, 2008.

Vicinus, Martha, *Independent Women: Work and Community for Single Women 1850–1920*, London: Virago, 1985.

Warner, Marina, *Monuments and Maidens: The Allegory of the Female Form*, Weidenfeld & Nicolson, 1985.

Whelan, Richard, *Robert Capa: A Biography*, Lincoln: University of Nebraska Press, 1994.

Whitman, Walt, 'Starting Newspapers', *Specimen Days in America*, London: Folio Society, 1979.

Wilson, Elizabeth, *The Sphinx in the City: Urban Life, the Control of Disorder, and Women*, Berkeley: University of California Press, 1992.

—, *The Contradictions of Culture: Cities, Culture, Women*, London: Sage, 2001.

Wolff, Janet, 'The Invisible Flâneuse: Women and the Literature of Modernity', *Theory, Culture, and Society* 3 (1985), pp. 37–46.

Woolf, Virginia, 'London Revisited', *Times Literary Supplement*, 9

November 1916, in *Collected Essays, Volume 2*, London: Hogarth Press, 1966.

—, *Mrs Dalloway* (1925), London: Penguin, 2000.

—, 'Street Haunting' (1927), in *The Essays of Virginia Woolf, Volume 4*, ed. Andrew McNeillie and Stuart N. Clarke, New York: Harcourt Brace Jovanovich, 1986.

—, *A Room of One's Own* (1929), New York: Harcourt, 1989.

—, *The Waves*, New York: Harcourt Brace Jovanovich, 1931.

—, *The Years*. New York: Harcourt Brace & Co., 1937.

—, 'Moments of Being', in *Moments of Being*, ed. Jeanne Schulkind, New York: Harcourt Brace Jovanovich, 1976.

—, *The Waves: two holograph drafts*, ed. John Whichello Graham, London: Hogarth Press, 1976.

—, *The Pargiters: The Novel-Essay Portion of the Years*, ed. Mitchell A. Leaska, New York: New York Public Library, 1977.

—, *The Letters of Virginia Woolf*, 6 vols, ed. Nigel Nicolson and Joanne Trautmann, New York: Mariner Books, 1975–82.

—, *The Diary of Virginia Woolf*, 5 vols, ed. Anne O. Bell and Andrew McNeillie, New York: Harcourt Brace Jovanovich, 1978–85.

—, 'Mr Bennett and Mrs Brown', *The Virginia Woolf Reader*, ed. Mitchell Leaska, New York: Harcourt Brace Jovanovich, 1984.

—, *The Complete Shorter Fiction of Virginia Woolf*, ed. Susan Dick, New York: Harcourt Brace Jovanovich, 1985.

Wood, Gaby, 'Agnès Varda interview: The whole world was sexist!', *Telegraph*, 22 May 2015.

NOTES

FLÂNEUSE-ING

1   Janet Wolff, 'The Invisible Flâneuse: Women and the Literature of
    Modernity', *Theory, Culture, and Society* 3 (1985), pp. 37–46, 45.
2   Griselda Pollock, *Vision and Difference*, London: Routledge, 1988, p. 71.
3   Deborah Parsons, *Streetwalking the Metropolis: Women, the City, and
    Modernity*, Oxford: OUP, 2000, p. 4.
4   Rebecca Solnit, *Wanderlust: A History of Walking*, New York: Penguin
    Books, 2001, p. 233.
5   All translations from French mine unless otherwise indicated.
6   Patricia Parkhurst Ferguson, *Paris As Revolution: Writing the Nineteenth-
    Century City*, Berkeley: University of California Press, 1994, p. 81.
7   According to the historian Elizabeth Wilson, the *flâneur* is a 'mythological
    or allegorical' figure who represents a certain anxiety about the city, its
    attack on individuality, its threatening abyss, its commodification of
    daily life and its possibilities for total self-reinvention. 'The Invisible
    Flâneur', *New Left Review* no. 191 (Jan–Feb 1992), p. 99.
8   Amy Levy, 'Women and Club Life', published in *Women's World*, a
    magazine edited by Oscar Wilde, 1888. See her poetry collection *A
    London Plane-Tree* (1889). Levy committed suicide not long after its
    publication.
9   Pollock, p. 96.
10 Marie Bashkirtseff, *The Journals of Marie Bashkirtseff*, 2 vols, trans. Phyllis
    Howard Kernberger and Katherine Kernberger, New York: Fonthill
    Press, 2012, 2 January 1879.
11 Luc Sante, *The Other Paris*, New York: FSG, 2015.
12 David Garrioch, *The Making of Revolutionary Paris*, Berkeley: University
    of California Press, 2002, p. 39.
13 *The Golden Guide to London* (1975). Quoted in Elizabeth Wilson, *The

Contradictions of Culture: Cities, Culture, Women, London: Sage, 2001, p. 81.

14 Leonora Davidoff, *The Best Circles: Society, Etiquette, and The Season*, London: Croom Helm, 1973. Quoted in Parsons, p. 111.

15 In modernising Madrid, the Arco de Santa María and the Calle de los Urosas (named for the Urosas sisters who owned the land were renamed after Augusto Figueroa and Luis Vélez de Guevara. Only one street was named for an accomplished woman, Maria de Zayas, the seventeenth-century writer. In her article on this subject Elizabeth Munson cites the *Almanaque y Guia matritensepara* of 1905, and the *Guida practica de Madrid* from 1907, which demonstrated 'an extensive account of name changes' starting in 1875 in the ten districts of Madrid, finding a total of twenty-six female names deleted, though Munson does not specify how many male names were dropped, p. 65. Revolutionary Paris saw a similar purging of the city, where anything suggestive of saints or aristocrats was renamed. For a while, the rue Saint-Anne became the rue Helvétius, in homage to a (male) eighteenth-century philosopher. The city, its layout, the names of its monuments, its buildings, its streets, reflects the values of its time; a secular state can only be a more democratic one. Elizabeth Munson, 'Walking on the Periphery: Gender and the Discourse of Modernization', *Journal of Social History* 36.1 (2002): 63–75, p. 72, n. 12.

16 Ibid., p. 66. The Pantheon was originally intended to be a church dedicated to St Genevieve, the patron saint of Paris. But after the Revolution, it became a mausoleum honouring great Frenchmen. *Aux Grands Hommes la Patrie Reconnaissante* – To Great Men, a Grateful Country – is written across its pediment. It's only in 1995 that Marie Curie, who lived nearby, was allowed to be interred there. That is, interred because of her public achievements – another woman, Sophie Berthelot, was the first woman to be buried there, alongside her husband Marcellin. In 2008 they hung portraits of nine women on the front of the building – Olympe de Gouges, Simone de Beauvoir, George Sand, Colette, Marie Curie, a few others. But there are still – still! – only two women buried inside, out of seventy-one people in all.

17 Francine du Plessix Gray claims Colet; Marina Warner and others say Drouet.

18 Francine du Plessix Gray, *Rage & Fire: A Life of Louise Colet*, New York: Simon & Schuster, 1994; Warner, Marina, *Monuments and Maidens: The Allegory of the Female Form*, London: Weidenfeld & Nicolson, 1985. Warner writes that 'during the period after 1871, when Alsace – and Strasbourg – were occupied by the Prussians, the statue became a political altar, the focal point of pilgrimage, and patriotic manifestations there on Bastille Day led to the establishment of the national feast of 14 July in 1880' (pp. 32–3).

19 Virginia Woolf, 'London Revisited', *Times Literary Supplement*, 9 Nov 1916. *Collected Essays*, Vol. 2, p. 51.

20 She is there to commemorate William Lamb's having distributed 120 pails to poor women so they could fetch water from the pump he built, which drew from the nearby River Fleet.

21 Guy Debord, 'Theory of the Dérive', trans. Ken Knabb, *Situationist International Anthology*, Berkeley: Bureau of Public Secrets, 1981, p. 50.

22 Robert Macfarlane, 'A Road of One's Own: Past and Present Artists of the Randomly Motivated Walk', *Times Literary Supplement*, 7 October: 3–4, 2005.

23 He explicitly writes, 'A digression: do I believe that men are corralled in this field due to certain natural and/or nurtured characteristics that lead us to believe we have – or actually do inculcate us with – superior visual-spatial skills to women, and an inordinate fondness for all aspects of orientation, its pursuit, minutiae and – worst of all – accessories? Absolutely. And so, while not altogether abandoning the fantasy of encountering a psychogeographic muse who will make these jaunts still more pleasurable, poignant and emotionally revelatory than they already are, in my continent heart I understand that I am fated to wander alone, or at best with one other, occasional . . . male companion.' (Will Self, *Psychogeography*, London: Bloomsbury, 2007, p. 12.)

24 Louis Huart, *Physiologie du flâneur*, Paris: Aubert, 1841, p. 53.

25 Nicholson writes, 'In London you had Dickens, De Quincey, Iain Sinclair; in New York you had Walt Whitman, Alfred Kazin, Paul Auster'; writing on walking artists he can name only one woman: 'Richard Long, Hamish Fulton, Eva Hesse, Vito Acconci, Joseph Beuys.' In recent years, critics and writers have told the stories of walkers from communities which seem 'marginal' beside Baudelaire or Thomas de Quincey: Langston Hughes, Henry Darger, Joseph Cornell, David Wojnarowicz, breaking out of the rich white model of the *flâneur* but reinscribing his gender as male. In Nicholson's defence, he does reference Margarita Nelken, a Spanish feminist explored in Munson's essay, Ada Anderson and Exilda La Chapelle, nineteenth-century competitive walkers, or 'pedestriennes' (apparently female walking was a 'serious sport and a series business' for a while in America), and Dorothy Wordsworth, who 'walked with [her brother William] and wrote about it in her diary: "March 30, 1798. Walked I know not where. March 31, 1798. Walked. April 1, 1798. Walked by moonlight."' He cites Marcus Poetzsch's essay 'Walks Alone and "I know not where": Dorothy Wordsworth's Deviant Pedestrianism' and goes on to write about a bunch of male Romantic poets. Geoff Nicholson, *The Lost Art of Walking: The History, Science, Philosophy, and Literature of Pedestrianism*, New York: Riverhead Books, 2008.

26   30 Jan 1939, Virginia Woolf, Anne Olivier Bell and Andrew McNeillie, *The Diary of Virginia Woolf, Volume 5*, London: Penguin Books, 1985, p. 203.

27   I counter Guy Debord with his ex-wife, Michèle Bernstein. I counter Iain Sinclair with Rachel Lichtenstein, Will Self with Laura Oldfield Ford, Nick Papadimitriou with Rebecca Solnit, Teju Cole with Joanna Kavenna, but also with Patti Smith, Adrian Piper, Lisa Robertson, Faïza Guène, Janet Cardiff, Yoko Ono, Laurie Anderson, Vivian Gornick, Lavinia Greenlaw, Amina Cain, Chloe Aridjis, Atiya Fayzee, Heather Hartley, Wendy MacNaughton, Danielle Dutton, Germaine Krull, Valeria Luiselli, Alexandra Horowitz, Jessie Fauset, Virginie Despentes, Kate Zambreno, Joanna Walsh, Eliza Gregory, Annie Ernaux, Annett Groeschner, Sandra Cisneros, Halide Adivar, Oriane Zérah, Cécile Wajsbrot, Helen Scalway, Ilse Bing, Fran Lebowitz, Rachel Whiteread, Banu Qudsia, Zadie Smith, Colette, Emily Hahn, Marianne Breslauer, Gwendolyn Brooks, Berenice Abbott, Laure Albin-Guillot, Zora Neale Hurston, Vivian Maier, Lola Ridge, Nella Larsen, Flora Tristan, and on, and on, and on.

28   Self has undertaken this kind of 'research' into places like New York and Los Angeles, but it remains a very British practice, deeply linked to the particularities of London.

29   Yi-Fu Tuan, *Space and Place: The Perspectives of Experience*, Minneapolis: University of Minnesota Press, 1977, p. 6. 'If we think of space as that which allows movement, then place is pause; each pause in movement makes it possible for location to be transformed into place.'

30   For a very good scholarly approach to the *flâneuse*, primarily from a nineteenth-century art-historical perspective, see Aruna D'Souza and Tom McDonough's *The invisible flâneuse? Gender, public space, and visual culture in nineteenth-century Paris*, Manchester: Manchester University Press, 2006.

LONG ISLAND, NEW YORK

1   *Wanderlust*, p. 250.

2   The problem has spread to many American cities as well, as Jeff Speck notes in his book *Walkable City*: 'since midcentury, whether intentionally or by accident, most American cities have effectively become no-walking zones'. City engineers 'have turned our downtowns into places that are easy to get to but not worth arriving at'. Jeff Speck, *Walkable City: How Downtown Can Save America, One Step at a Time*, New York: Macmillan, 2012, p. 4.

3   According to Lewis Mumford, the car is all that remains of the suburbs' claim to 'autonomy and initiative' (p. 493). He worried that 'clever

engineers already threaten to remove the individual control by a system of automation' (p. 494). It's a good thing he didn't live to see the car itself become autonomous in the form of the self-driving car. They say they make driving even safer, once the car is in control ... In *The Society of the Spectacle*, Guy Debord quoted Mumford's contention that 'sprawling isolation has proved an . . . effective method of keeping a society under control'. *The City in History: Its Origins, Its Transformations, and Its Prospects*, New York: Harcourt, Brace & World, 1961.

4   Marshall Berman, 'Falling', *Restless Cities*, ed. Matthew Beaumont, Gregory Dart, Michael Sheringham and Iain Sinclair, London: Verso, 2010.

5   According to Leigh Gallagher the suburbs won't last much longer; they have changed irrevocably as Americans no longer want to live in them. Leigh Gallagher, *The End of the Suburbs: Where the American Dream Is Moving*, New York: Portfolio/Penguin, 2013.

6   *The City in History*, p. 494.

7   We never go to Kings Park Station to get into the city; it takes an hour and a half and you have to transfer at Jamaica, in Queens. We drive fifteen minutes south-west to Deer Park Station, which is on the Ronkonkoma branch of the original Main Line ('Rahng-kahng-kah-mah line, this is the Rahng-kahng-kah-mah line, express to Hicksville, stopping at Bethpage, Fawmingdale, Wyandanch, Deeh Pawk, Brentwood, Central Islip and Rahng-kahng-kah-mah') founded in 1834.

8   Marguerite Duras, *Practicalities*, trans. Barbara Bray, New York: Grove Press, 1987, p. 42.

9   In 1960, the university proposed to build a gym in Morningside Park that would have one entrance for its (predominantly white) students and one (a 'poor door') for residents of Harlem. The controversy over the gym was one of the factors that led to the student protests at the university in 1968.

PARIS, CAFES WHERE THEY

1   Jean Rhys, *Complete Novels*, New York: W.W. Norton, 1985, p. 462.

2   Jean Rhys, *Smile Please: An Unfinished Autobiography*, Harmondsworth: Penguin, 1979, p. 121.

3   Jean Rhys, *Good Morning, Midnight*, in *Complete Novels*, New York: Harcourt, 1985, p. 397.

4   *Quartet*, in *Complete Novels*, p. 14.

5   Diana Athill, *Stet: A Memoir*, New York: Grove Press, 2002, pp. 157–8.

6   Jean Rhys, Francis Wyndham and Diana Melly, *The Letters of Jean Rhys*, New York: Viking, 1984, p. 280.

7   Carole Angier, *Jean Rhys: Life and Work*, Boston: Little, Brown, 1990, p. 136.

8   *Letters*, p. 284.
9   Stella Bowen, *Drawn From Life: A Memoir*, Sydney: Picador, 1999, pp. 195–6.
10 Jacob Michael Leland, 'Yes, that is a roll of bills in my pocket: the economy of masculinity in *The Sun Also Rises*', *Hemingway Review*, 22 March 2004, p. 37.
11 Ernest Hemingway, *A Moveable Feast*, New York: Charles Scribner's Sons, 1964, pp. 4–5.
12 ('Mrs Dalloway said she would buy the flowers herself.')
13 Angier, pp. 174–5.
14 'Outside the Machine', Jean Rhys, *Collected Short Stories*, New York: W.W. Norton, 1992, pp. 87–8. She would sign books, to people she thought were comrades, *To so-and-so from Jean Rhys – Outside the machine.* 'Because you're outside the machine, too,' Jan van Houts recalls being told. Quoted in Pierrette M. Frickey, *Critical Perspectives on Jean Rhys*, Washington DC: Three Continents Press, 1990, p. 30.
15 'I Spy a Stranger', *Collected Short Stories*, p. 247.
16 *Complete Novels*, p. 188.
17 Ibid., p. 18.
18 *Voyage in the Dark* (1934), New York: Norton, 1982, p. 74.
19 See Max Saunders, *Ford Madox Ford: a dual life*, Vol. 1, Oxford: OUP, 1996, p. 191.
20 It sounds like he's been reading Baudelaire: The crowd is his 'element,' Baudelaire writes in *The Painter of Modern Life*; 'For the perfect *flâneur*, for the passionate spectator, it is an immense joy to set up house in the heart of the multitude ... To be at home and yet to feel oneself everywhere at home ... He is an "I" with an insatiable appetite for the "non-I".' Charles Baudelaire, *The Painter of Modern Life*, trans. Jonathan Mayne, New York: Phaidon, 1995, p. 9.
21 Ford Madox Ford, Preface, Jean Rhys, *The Left Bank & Other Stories*, London: Jonathan Cape, 1927, p. 27.
22 Jean Rhys, *Quartet* (1928), in *Complete Novels*, p. 132.
23 Ibid., p. 157.
24 Ibid., pp. 136–7.
25 Ibid., p. 145.
26 *Complete Novels*, p. 371.
27 Ibid., p. 121.
28 Ibid.
29 'The Blue Bird', *Collected Short Stories*, p. 131.
30 *Complete Novels*, p. 242.
31 Ibid.
32 Ibid.

LONDON, BLOOMSBURY

1 Virginia Woolf, 'Moments of Being', in *Moments of Being*, ed. Jeanne Schulkind, New York: Harcourt Brace Jovanovich, 1976, pp. 198–9.

2 'I made up The Lighthouse in one afternoon in the square here.' Virginia Woolf, Anne O. Bell and Andrew McNeillie, *The Diary of Virginia Woolf: Volume 3, 1925–1930*, Harmondsworth: Penguin, 1982, pp. 131–2, 14 March 1927.

3 Virginia Woolf, Quentin Bell and Anne O. Bell, *The Diary of Virginia Woolf: Volume 1, 1915–19*, Harmondsworth: Penguin Books, 1983, p. 9, January 1915.

4 *Diary: Volume 3*, p. 298, 28 March 1930.

5 'London Revisited', *Times Literary Supplement*, 9 November 1916, in Virginia Woolf, *Collected Essays, Volume 2*, London: Hogarth Press, 1966, p. 50.

6 *Diary: Volume 3*, p. 11.

7 *Diary: Volume 5*, p. 331. Tavistock Square today is thought of as a 'peace garden', with a cherry tree dedicated to the victims of the bombing of Hiroshima and Nagasaki, a statue of Mahatma Gandhi and a rock monument to conscientious objectors to the Second World War. It's something of a feminist square as well, boasting not only the bust of Woolf but also one of Dame Louisa Aldrich-Blake, a surgeon and the Dean of the London School of Medicine for Women.

8 Letter to Ethel Smyth, 12 January 1941, Virginia Woolf, *The Letters of Virginia Woolf, Volume Six, 1936–1941*, ed. Nigel Nicolson and Joanne Trautmann, New York: Mariner Books, 1982, p. 460; 25 September 1940, *Letters, Volume 6*, pp. 432–3.

9 Ibid., pp. 428–34.

10 *Diary, Volume 5*, pp. 356–7.

11 I don't mean to suggest that because the walking fed the writing, and because not being able to walk deprived the writing, that all of this was somehow a cause for suicide. Had she lived she would surely have walked again, and written again. But she could not live. She could not bear another war, another breakdown.

12 McEwan, Ian, 'How could we have forgotten that this was always going to happen?', *Guardian*, 8 July 2005.

13 In the time since this was written, Paris was attacked again. More soldiers, more guns, I can be walking blithely around a corner and nearly collide with a man in fatigues carrying an Uzi.

14 *Moments of Being*, p. 196.

15 In her copy of Hare, Woolf apparently copied out a quote from Samuel Johnson into the dedication page: 'I think the full tide of existence is at

Charing Cross.' Cf. Elisa Kay Sparks, 'Leonard and Virginia's London Library: Mapping London's Tides, Streams and Statues', in Gina Potts and Lisa Shahiri, *Virginia Woolf's Bloomsbury, Vol I: Aesthetic Theory and Literary Practice*, Basingstoke: Palgrave Macmillan, 2010, p. 65.

16 Augustus J.C. Hare, *Walks in London*, 1879, pp. 164–5.

17 *Moments of Being*, p. 182.

18 Ibid., p. 184.

19 Ibid., p. 185.

20 Anna Snaith notes that Woolf's 'fictional representations of Bloomsbury focus . . . on the area as a site of suffrage politics. In *The Years*, Rose, an active suffragette, takes Sara to a suffrage meeting in Bloomsbury (p. 134). In the third essay of *The Pargiters*, Nora Graham invites Delia to 'join a queer little society that met in the Gray's Inn Road'. Anna Snaith, *Virginia Woolf: Public and Private Negotiations*, Basingstoke: Palgrave, 2000, p.27.

21 Angier, p. 97. It was walking in Torrington Square that she met her future husband, Jean Lenglet.

22 Martha Vicinus, *Independent Women: Work and Community for Single Women 1850–1920*. London: Virago, 1985, pp. 295–6. See also Sara Blair, 'Bloomsbury and the Places of the Literary', *ELH* 71.3 (2004), pp. 813–38, who reads Bloomsbury as a 'local world' rather than an idea or a coterie, 'at once a habitat and the forms of belonging to it', p. 816.

23 Thomas Burke, *Living in Bloomsbury*, London: G. Allen & Unwin Ltd, 1939, p. 12, quoted in Blair. By which he is referring not to sex workers in a bordello, but to women who worked for a living.

24 Barbara Green, *Spectacular Confessions: Autobiography, Performative Activism and the Sites of Suffrage, 1905–38*, Basingstoke: Macmillan, 1997, p. 194.

25 *Letters, Volume 1, 1888–1912*, p. 120.

26 Virginia Woolf, *The Complete Shorter Fiction of Virginia Woolf*, ed. Susan Dick, San Diego: Harcourt Brace Jovanovich, 1985, p. 24.

27 Ibid.

28 Mitchell Leaska, ed., *A Passionate Apprentice: Virginia Woolf, The Early Journals, 1897–1909*, New York: Harcourt Brace Jovanovich, 1990, p. 223.

29 John Sutherland, 'Clarissa's Invisible Taxi', *Can Jane Eyre Ever be Happy?*, Oxford: OUP, 1997.

30 *Diary, Volume 3*, p. 186; p. 302, 26 May 1924; *Diary, Volume 1*, p. 214, 4 November 1918.

31 'I stop in London sometimes, and hear feet shuffling. That's the language, I think, that's the phrase I should like to catch.' *The Waves: two holograph drafts*, ed. John Whichello Graham, London: Hogarth Press, 1976, p. 658.

32 *The Waves*, p. 183.

33 Virginia Woolf, *A Room of One's Own* (1929), New York: Harcourt, 1989, p. 93. See Susan Squier, *Virginia Woolf and London: The Sexual Politics of the City*, Chapel Hill, NC: University of North Carolina Press, 1985.

34 Virginia Woolf, 'Mr Bennett and Mrs Brown', *The Virginia Woolf Reader*, ed. Mitchell Leaska, New York: Harcourt, 1984, p. 199.

35 *A Room of One's Own*, p. 94.

36 *Diary, Volume 1*, p. 9, 6 January 1915.

37 *A Passionate Apprentice*, p. 228.

38 Ibid., p. 246.

39 Ibid., p. 232.

40 Ibid., p. 271.

41 Virginia Woolf, Elaine Showalter and Stella McNichol, *Mrs Dalloway*, London: Penguin, 2000, p. 4.

42 *Diary, Volume 3*, p. 186, 31 May 1928.

43 *Mrs Dalloway*, p. 88.

44 *A Passionate Apprentice*, p. 220.

45 *Diary, Volume 2*, pp. 47–8.

46 'Street Haunting', Virginia Woolf, Andrew McNeillie and Stuart N. Clarke, *The Essays of Virginia Woolf, Volume 4*, San Diego: Harcourt Brace Jovanovich, 1986, p. 481.

47 *A Room of One's Own*, p. 44.

48 Charles Dickens, *Hard Times. The Shorter Novels of Charles Dickens*, Hertfordshire: Wordsworth Editions, 2004, p. 424.

49 Virginia Woolf, *The Years*, New York: Harcourt Brace & Co., 1937, p. 361.

50 *The Pargiters*, p. 81.

51 Ibid., p. 37. In another passage of *The Pargiters*, Woolf writes that Eleanor 'half meant to walk home through the Park. She would go to the Marble Arch, she thought, and walk a part of the way back under the trees. But suddenly as she glanced down a back street, fear came over her. She saw the men in the bowler hats winking at the waitress. She was afraid – even now, even I, she thought … afraid. Afraid to walk through the Park alone, she thought; she despised herself. It was the bodies [*sic*] fear, not the minds, but it settled the matter. She would keep to the main streets, where there were lights and policemen.' As they grow older, says Rose (who has grown older), they become less visible, and they can walk wherever they like at any time of day (*The Years*, p. 173).

52 *The Years*, p. 112.

53 Ibid., p. 27.

54 *The Years*, p. 29; *The Pargiters*, pp. 41–3.

55 *The Years*, p. 434.

PARIS, CHILDREN OF THE REVOLUTION

1 Elizabeth Bowen, *The House in Paris* (1935), Harmondsworth: Penguin, 1976, p. 152.

2   Charles Baudelaire, 'Le Cygne', *Les Fleurs du Mal* (1857). Translation mine.

3   Honoré de Balzac, *Les Petits Bourgeois* (1843), *La comédie humaine*, 7 volumes, Paris: Editions du Seuil, 1965–6, Volume 5, p. 294.

4   Guy Debord, *Panegyric, Volumes 1 & 2*, trans. James Brook and John McHale, London: Verso, 2004, p. 39.

5   James Joyce and Philip F. Herring, *Joyce's Ulysses notesheets in the British Museum, Issue 3*, published for the Bibliographical Society of the University of Virginia by the University Press of Virginia, 1972, p. 119.

6   Théophile Lavallée and George Sand, *Le Diable à Paris: Paris et les Parisiens, Mœurs et coutumes, caractères et portraits des habitants de Paris*, Paris: J. Hetzel, 1845, p. 9.

7   For more on this fascinating element of Parisian history, see Graham Robb, *Parisians*, New York: W.W. Norton, 2010, and Andrew Miller, *Pure*, Sceptre, 2011.

8   John Litchfield, 'The Stones of Paris', *Independent*, 22 September 2007.

9   Haussmann was not the first to start razing the Old Paris to make way for the New Old Paris; the first wide roads (including the Champs-Elysées) were built by Rambuteau under the July Monarchy.

10   George Sand, *Indiana*, trans. G. Burnham Ives, Chicago: Academy Chicago Publishers, 2000, p. 46.

11   Sturrock, John, 'Give Me Calf's Tears', *London Review of Books* (21:22), 11 November 1999, pp. 28–9.

12   Jack notes that Balzac is praised for his productivity while Sand was mocked: 'There was an implication that such a stream of works was unfeminine in its proportions.' *George Sand: A Woman's Life Writ Large*, New York: Vintage, 1999, p. 3.

13   Alfred de Musset, *Confession of a Child of the Century*, (1836), trans. David Coward, London: Penguin Classics, 2012.

14   Letter to Jules Boucoiran, 31 July 1830, *Correspondance: Tome I*, pp. 676–7.

15   Letter to Charles Meure, 15 August 1830, ibid., p. 690.

16   George Sand, *Story of My Life*, ed. Thelma Jurgrau, group trans., Albany: SUNY Press, 1991, p. 905. The *redingote-guérite* was all the rage that year, a long overcoat that nearly reached to the floor.

17   Ibid., p. 892.

18   Ibid., p. 893.

19   George Sand, *Histoire de ma vie*, Vol. 4, Paris: Michel Levy, 1856, p. 255.

20   George Sand, *Gabriel* (1839), *Oeuvres Complètes*, Paris: Perrotin, 1843, p. 200.

21   Men in skirts were subject to no such regulation. Why this dissymmetry? Why was it so much more threatening to have a woman in trousers than a man in skirts? Especially given that in our own time, the reverse is true.

Why were the lawmakers of 1800 so fixated on controlling cross-dressing women? In an essay for *L'Esprit Créateur*, the historian (and translator of Sand's *The Countess of Rudolstadt*) Gretchen Van Slyke suggests the law was derived from a need to firmly designate women as 'men's Other, as irresponsible tongues and debilitated minds dominated by the dangerous and irresistible drives of ovaries and uterus, as moral and political inferiors in imperative need of masculine tutelage'. This 'is one of the troubling legacies of the French Revolution', p. 34.

22 *Histoire de ma vie*, Vol. 7, Paris: J. Hetzel et Cie, 1864, p. 255.

23 Jacques Leronde, *Revue des Deux Mondes*, 1 June 1832. Cited in Belinda Jack.

24 George Sand, *Indiana*, Paris: Calmann-Lévy, 1852, p. 1.

25 *Histoire de ma vie*, Vol. 1, p. 23.

26 These are the events you might remember from *Les Misérables*; Sand and Hugo as well as Balzac, Dumas and Heine would all write on the failed revolution of 1832.

27 Quoted in Eric Hazan, *La Barricade: histoire d'un objet révolutionnaire*, Paris: Editions Autrement, 2013, p. 89. One eyewitness describes a barricade: 'At the entrance to a narrow street, an omnibus lies with its four wheels in the air. A pile of crates, which had served perhaps to hold oranges, rises to the right and to the left, and behind them, between the rims of the wheels and the openings, small fires are blazing, continually emitting small blue clouds of smoke' (Gaetan Niépovié, *Etudes physiologiques sur les grans métropoles de l'Europe occidentale*, 1840, quoted in Benjamin, p. 141).

28 *Histoire de ma vie*, Vol. 7, pp. 259–64.

29 Sand citing Louis Blanc, *The History of Ten Years, 1830–1840*.

VENICE, OBEDIENCE

1 Paul Auster, *Leviathan*, London: Faber, 1993, pp. 60–1.

2 The photograph, we learn, is meant to mock a 1989 photograph of Brigitte Bardot, who 'in recent years has taken her preference for the cause of animals over that of humans to the point of caricature'.

3 We went there one night not long ago, to celebrate the contracts for my book coming in. Seventeen euros for a *champagne à la menthe* but it was a special occasion, so it was almost justifiable, though publishers don't pay what they used to. To my left sat a heavyset blonde girl with a miniature orange Louis Vuitton bag. To my right a man with a long oily ponytail and a raggedy-looking Yorkie in a Louis Vuitton dog carrier, just like the one I have for my dog, but mine was forty euros at the pet shop while his had leather interlocking Ls and Vs printed on it. When I got home I looked up the price: nearly $2,800. On the Louis Vuitton

website there was a video playing called 'L'invitation au voyage:Venise', in which a model lands in a hot-air balloon on the Piazza San Marco and goes to a masked ball where David Bowie is playing 'I'd Rather Be High' on the harpsichord.

4 Sophie Calle, 'Filatures parisiennes', *M'as-tu Vue*, ed. Christine Macel, Paris, Centre Pompidou: Xavier Barral, 2003, p. 66.

5 The two published versions of *Suite Vénitienne* I've seen, in French and in English, give the dates as February 1980, so I am following suit with my citations, but other accounts of the story give 1979 as the year she followed Henri B. to Venice, and I tend to think they are more accurate. Calle has explicitly said she went to Venice before she did *The Sleepers*, in which she invited random people to sleep in her bed, and that project definitely took place in April 1979. What's more, she had to go back to Venice to retake many of the photographs, so this may have been undertaken in 1980, and perhaps she changed the date in the published version of the project as a result.

6 Ibid., p. 8.

7 Sophie Calle, *Suite Vénitienne*, trans. Dany Barash and Danny Hatfield, Seattle: Bay Press, 1988, pp. 6–7.

8 Ibid., p. 20.

9 Also, that's no way to learn a foreign language.

10 *Suite Vénitienne*, p. 26.

11 Ibid., p. 30.

12 Ibid., p. 38.

13 Ibid.

14 And one of the projects that followed this one would in fact be set in a hotel: while following Henri B., she began to dream about sleeping in his hotel bed. So in 1981, in the project that would become *The Hotel*, she got a job as a chambermaid at his hotel, the Casa de Stefani, and while she was cleaning each room, she took pictures of its occupants' belongings, cataloguing them, guessing what kind of people they were.

15 *Suite Vénitienne*, p. 34.

16 Not long ago a friend told me about a Twitter account possibly belonging to Calle. Maybe it's hers, maybe it isn't, but whoever runs it has only posted once: 'Sophie Calle is ready to follow you.'

17 *Suite Vénitienne*, p. 10.

18 Ibid., p. 50.

19 Jill Magid interviews Sophie Calle, *Tokion*, Fall 2008, pp. 46–53.

TOKYO, INSIDE

1 Coincidentally, Paris's Little Japan is on the rue Sainte-Anne near the Louvre. Perhaps Anne is the patron saint of Japanese people in Paris.

2   That is, the kind of collage poem Tristan Tzara probably can't be said to have invented; likely he just codified it. His instructions:

> Take a newspaper.
> Take some scissors.
> Choose from this paper an article the length you want to make your poem.
> Cut out the article.
> Next carefully cut out each of the words that make up this article and put them all in a bag.
> Shake gently.
> Next take out each cutting one after the other.
> Copy conscientiously in the order in which they left the bag.
> The poem will resemble you.
> And there you are – an infinitely original author of charming sensibility, even though unappreciated by the vulgar herd.

    –Tristan Tzara, 'How to make a Dadaist Poem', 1920.

3   Roland Barthes, *Empire of Signs*, trans. Richard Howard, New York: Hill and Wang, 1982, p. 36.

4   Only occasionally does *kawaii* get turned back against itself. I recently saw a picture of Yuko Yamaguchi, who designs for Hello Kitty, her hair dyed a strange orange and in two high buns on either side of her head, painted-on freckles and red circles of rouge on her cheeks, wearing some kind of pinafore and giving the *kawaii* sign with two fingers. Cute, on her, looks grotesque, subversive.

5   The katakana seem to be more angular versions of hiragana, and while hiragana are used to spell out Japanese words that lack kanji, katakana transliterate foreign words into Japanese.

6   Virginia Woolf, notes for 'Professions for Women', *The Pargiters*, p. 164.

7   Ponyo ponyo, a little fish child / she comes from the ocean blue.

8   Apparently a Japanese onomatopoeia for 'kiss and hug!'

9   So many films about cities are shorts. As if the form were more appropriate to the rhythm of the city. Missed connections. Anecdotes on the subway. City mythologies are built out of fragments.

10 *M'as-tu Vue*, p. 364.

11 Roland Barthes, *A Lover's Discourse* (1977), trans. Richard Howard, London: Vintage, 2002.

PARIS, PROTEST

1   In Gustave Flaubert's 1869 novel *Sentimental Education*, Frédéric Moreau encounters the revolution on his way to visit his mistress, and we are treated to a bit of what it felt like to be surrounded by, though

not actually part of, the action. There are men with muskets and swords. Drums beating. People singing the Marseillaise. Fighting on the Right Bank. People running every which way, with great purpose. 'Everybody was in high spirits; people were strolling about, and the fairy-lights on every floor made it as bright as day. The soldiers were slowly returning to their barracks, looking harassed and unhappy. [...] A vague mass of people was swarming about below; here and there in its midst bayonets gleamed white against the dark background. A great din arose. The crowd was too thick for them to make their way straight back; and they were turning into the Rue Caumartin when, all of a sudden, there was a crackling noise behind them like the sound of a huge piece of silk being ripped in two. It was the fusillade on the Boulevard des Capucines. "Ah! They're killing off a few bourgeois," said Frédéric calmly.' Trans. Robert Baldick, Baltimore: Penguin Books, 1964, pp. 281, 282–3.

2   To Augustine Brault, 5 March 1848, *Correspondance*, Vol. 8, p. 319. Guizot had been education minister and then prime minister under Louis Philippe; Lamartine was a great French poet and statesman. She had surrounded herself with men so prominent métro stops and streets and boulevards have been named for them. Quoted in Harlan, Elizabeth, *George Sand*, New Heaven: Yale University Press, 2005.

3   *Correspondance*, 20 May 1848.

4   Walter Benjamin, *The Arcades Project*, ed. Rolf Tiedemann, trans. Howard Eiland and Kevin McLaughlin, New York: Belknap Press, 2002, p. 243.

5   *Bulletins de la République* (Paris, 1848), pp. 23–4. Quoted in Jack.

6   Tocqueville, *Souvenirs* (Paris, 1893), pp. 209–11. Quoted in Jack.

7   *Théorie des Quatre Mouvements* (1808), *Oeuvres Complètes*, 1841–5, p. 43. Quoted in Rowbotham.

8   *Sentimental Education*, p. 298.

9   Ibid., p. 292.

10 'I detest politics in the conventional sense,' she wrote to Hortense Allart; 'I find it to be a school of rigidity, ingratitude, suspicion and falseness [...] Let us leave politics and therefore men to deal with one another as best they can.'

11 To Armand Barbès, in the Vincennes prison, 10 June 1848, from Nohant, *Correspondance*, Vol. 8, p. 437.

12 Bertrand Tilier, '"De la balade à la manif": La représentation picturale de la foule dans les rues de Paris après 1871', *Sociétés et représentations*, 17:1 (2004), pp. 87–98.

13 Letter to Flaubert, 15 January 1867, *Correspondance*, Vol. 20, p. 297.

14 The minister retorted something along the lines of: 'Well, with your face, you probably don't have to worry about things like that.'

15 Antonio Quattrocchi and Tom Nairn, *The Beginning of the End*, Panther Books, 1968 (rpr. London: Verso, 1998), p. 8.

16 Ibid., p. 46.

17 Mavis Gallant, *Paris Notebooks: Essays & Reviews*, New York: Random House, 1988, p. 41.

18 Ibid.

19 But where are the young women? The accounts of the time are always male, and our fantasies of it are male as well. Olivier Assayas's *Après mai* (2012), Philippe Garrel's *Les amants réguliers* (2005) – there's Louis Garrel again. Bertolucci has gorgeous Eva Green chaining herself to the gates of the Cinémathèque in *The Dreamers* (2003), cigarette dangling from red lips, chest heaving. But the film is solidly from Michael Pitt's perspective; Eva's there as temptation, as problem. What about the girls? What were they doing, thinking, hoping? The only female account I can find – besides Gallant's – is Jill Neville's *The Love Germ*.

20 *Paris Notebooks*, p. 12.

21 *Sentimental Education*, p. 293.

22 *Sentimental Education*, p. 300.

23 *Paris Notebooks*, p. 22.

24 Ibid., p. 42.

25 Walter Benjamin, *The Arcades Project*, p. 12.

26 Jane Marcus, 'Storming the Toolshed', *Art & Anger: Reading Like a Woman*, Columbus: Ohio State University, 1988, p. 183.

27 As I write this, on a chilly October morning, thousands of French high school students are protesting in the streets over the deportation of two immigrant students from France. Leonarda, fifteen, was pulled off her school bus and sent back to Kosovo along with her family, and Khatchik, nineteen, was sent back to Armenia to do his military service. Yesterday, about twenty schools in Paris were occupied by students who built barricades and refused to let anyone inside. 'Education: no borders,' they scrawled on sheets, and they shouted 'Solidarité!' as they marched from Bastille to Nation. Some wore Guy Fawkes masks.

28 *Paris Notebooks*, p. 33.

29 Philippe Bilger, 'Philippe Bilger: pourquoi je ne participe pas à «la marche républicaine»', *Le Figaro*, 11 January 2015.

PARIS, NEIGHBOURHOOD

1 *Cléo de 5 à 7*: the title carries with it a whiff of the louche, with its reference to the hour of the racy *rendez-vous*, the *cinq à sept*, after work and before dinner. It's a slice of the day when one can slip off and do

something just for oneself. Something naughty in a hotel with someone to whom one isn't married. The film was called, at first, *La Petite Fille*. But the actress playing Cléo, Corinne Marchand, saw something else in her, and directed Varda towards *les grandes horizontales* like Liane de Pougy or Cléo de Mérode. 'The hour of the *"rendez-vous galants"* imposed itself,' Varda recalls. (*Varda par Agnès*, Paris: Editions du Cahier du cinéma, 1994, p. 31.)

2   The film makes us complicit with these people in the cafes, the people in the street, everyone who watches Cléo; just as she's a pop star to them, she's the star of a film to us. As she walks out of the fortune-teller's building and down the rue de Rivoli, we watch her from above. The street is full of suits on racks, as it still is today, in certain parts; men approach her trying to sell her a dress. Another says *so, shall we walk together?*

3   'Introduction to a Critique of Urban Geography', in Ken Knabb, ed., *Situationist International Anthology*, Berkeley: Bureau of Public Secrets, 1981, p. 5.

4   *Species of Spaces*, ed. and trans. John Sturrock, London: Penguin, 2008, pp. 58–9.

5   And if the hospitals can't cure you, well, the 14th isn't a bad place to end up for eternity. In my walks, I discovered the wonderful Montparnasse cemetery, very close to the rue Daguerre, where you can find the graves of Jean-Paul Sartre, Simone de Beauvoir (who used to live nearby in the avenue Victor Schœlcher), Jean Baudrillard, Robert Desnos, Marguerite Duras, Emile Durkheim, Léon-Paul Fargue, Joris-Karl Huysmans, Henri Langlois, Pierre Louÿs and Guy de Maupassant, not to mention Albert Dreyfus, Philippe Noiret, Eric Rohmer, Jean Seberg, Louis Vierne, Susan Sontag and Tristan Tzara. (You can keep your Père Lachaise, I thought. This is where I want to live when I'm dead. On that shelf, with those people.) Demy is buried there too. And one day, Varda says, so will she be, 'ten flaps of a crow's wings between our house and our final resting place'.

6   The song, 'Sans Toi', homophonically prefigures Varda's 1985 film *Sans toit ni loi*, literally 'Without Roof or Law', but shown in English under the title *Vagabond*. Varda's synopsis of that film: 'Dirty, grumpy girl goes for a long, furious walk and dies in a ditch' (Gaby Wood, 'Agnès Varda interview: The whole world was sexist!' *Telegraph*, 22 May 2015).

7   Dorothée manages to break Cléo of a little of her superstition: at one point she drops her purse down the stairs and everything falls out. Her mirror breaks. Cléo freaks out about the bad luck to come. Dorothée says, 'You mustn't worry about such things, breaking a mirror is like breaking a plate.'

8   Madonna wanted to do a remake of *Cléo*, maybe set in downtown New

York, with the central character worried she has Aids, the soldier off to fight in Iraq. Varda writes: 'I imagine showing Madonna how to walk down a stairway, when she walks down one in every show she does! That would be funny.' (*Varda par Agnès*, p. 60).

9   Jacques Derrida, *The Post Card: From Socrates to Freud and Beyond*, trans. Alan Bass, Chicago: University of Chicago Press, 1987, p. 23.

10 Roland Barthes, Roland, *Camera Lucida*, trans. Richard Howard, New York: Hill and Wang, 1981, p. 96.

11 '. . . je crois que le décor nous habite, nous dirige.' Interview with Jean Michaud and Raymond Bellour, *Cinéma 61*, no. 60, October, pp. 4–20. Cited in Alison Smith, *Agnès Varda*, Manchester: Manchester University Press, 1998, p. 60.

12 Quoted in Calvin Tompkins, *Duchamp: A Biography*, New York: Henry Holt, 1998, p. 247.

13 Phil Powrie, 'Heterotopic Spaces and Nomadic Gazes in Varda: From *Cléo de 5 à 7* to *Les Glaneurs et la glaneuse*', *L'Esprit Créateur*, Vol. 51, No. 1 (2011), pp. 68–82, 69.

EVERYWHERE, THE VIEW FROM THE GROUND

1   Susan Sontag, *Regarding the Pain of Others*, New York: FSG, 2003, p. 22.

2   Caroline Moorehead, *Martha Gellhorn: A Life*, New York: Random House, 2011, p. 19.

3   Letter to Campbell Beckett, 29 April 1934, Martha Gellhorn, p. 23.

4   Letter to Stanley Pennell, 19 May 1931, *Letters*, p. 12.

5   Cited in Moorehead, p. 3.

6   To Victoria Glendinning, 30 September 1987, *Letters,* p. 468.

7   Martha Gellhorn, *The Face of War*, London: Virago, 1986, p. 89.

8   Lorna Scott Fox, 'No Intention of Retreating', *London Review of Books*, 26:17, 2 September 2004, pp. 26–8.

9   *The Face of War*, p. xiii.

10 Letter to Betty Barnes, 30 January 1937, *Letters*, p. 47.

11 *The Face of War*, pp. 20–1.

12 Ibid., p. 21.

13 'High Explosive for Everyone', *The Face of War*, p. 23.

14 *The Face of War*, pp. 35–6.

15 Ibid., p. 24.

16 Ibid., p. 25.

17 Ibid.

18 Ibid., pp. 26–7.

19 *Letters*, p. 74.

20 Ibid.

21 For example, the first line of her essay 'Messing About in Boats': 'During

that terrible year, 1942, I lived in the sun, safe and comfortable and hating it.' *Travels With Myself and Another*, n.p.

22 *Martha Gellhorn: A Life*, p. 125.

23 'The Besieged City', *The Face of War*, p. 40.

24 Quoted in Whelan, Richard, *Robert Capa: A Biography*, Lincoln: University of Nebraska Press, 1994, p. 275.

25 *The Face of War*, p. 34.

26 Ibid., p. 33.

27 *Letters*, p. 158.

28 Ibid.

29 'Chronicling Poverty With Compassion and Rage', *New Yorker*, 17 January 2013.

30 'Justice at Night', *Spectator*, 20 August 1936, repr. *The View From the Ground*, New York: Atlantic Monthly Press, 1988, pp. 8, 9.

31 *Martha Gellhorn: A Life*, p. 112.

32 *The Face of War*, p. 21. Even as a traveller, she described herself as 'amateur' rather than 'heroic'. 'We can't all be [. . .] Freya Stark,' she wrote in her preface to her 1978 collection of travel writings, *Travels With Myself and Another*.

33 'Martha Without Ernest', *Times Literary Supplement*, 16 January 2013. Gellhorn's editor, Max Perkins, thought the title was too bleak, Gellhorn lost her nerve, and the novel was published under the title *Wine of Astonishment*. In the intervening years, the technical term 'point of no return' passed into everyday language, yet for Gellhorn, 'the words stand as they did when I first heard them; an instruction to men at war, a statement of finality'. In the 1988 reissue, she reclaimed her original title.

34 *Point of No Return*, Lincoln, NE: Bison Books, 1995, Afterword, p. 327.

35 Ibid., p. 330.

36 Ibid.

37 Ibid., p. 292.

38 *Martha Gellhorn: A Life*, p. 221.

39 Martha Gellhorn, *Liana* (1944), London: Picador, 1993, p. 91.

40 Ibid., p. 90.

41 Ibid., p. 22.

42 When, at one point in the novel, Liana runs away from Marc and is then taken back by him, he warns her that if she runs away again she can't come back. Ibid., p. 101.

43 Ibid., p. 207.

44 Ibid., p. 238.

45 Ibid., p. 249.

46 Ibid., p. 252.

47 Ibid., p. 209.

48 *Letters*, p. 159.

49 Deborah Levy, *Things I Don't Want to Know*, London: Notting Hill Editions, 2013, p. 108.

NEW YORK, RETURN

1   Homi Bhabha, *The Location of Culture*, London: Routledge, 1994, pp. 7, 13.

EPILOGUE, FLÂNEUSERIE

1   Laura T. Coffey, *The Today Show*, 18 August 2011.

penguin.co.uk/vintage